THE SUBURBAN GROWER

SUSTAINABLE DIY RAISED BED GARDENING THAT
PRODUCES THRIVING FRUIT AND VEGETABLES FROM
THE FIRST HARVEST

MARISSA CLEMONT

CONTENTS

A SPECIAL GIFT TO MY READERS

Included with your purchase of this book is your free copy
of the *Gardening Planner*

Follow the link below to receive your free copy:
www.marissaclemont.com
Or by accessing the QR code:

You can also join our Facebook community **Homegrown
Sustainable Gardening**, or contact me directly via
marissa@marissaclemont.com.

"If you've never experienced the joy of accomplishing more than you can imagine, plant a garden."

— *ROBERT BRAULT*

INTRODUCTION

If you have enough sun, some wood or building material, and some soil in your backyard, you can turn your space into a green spot with an ambience that soothes your five senses. That calming feeling is why raised bed gardens are picking up in popularity in suburban settings. The obvious advantages of preserving soil integrity, warming up quickly for consistent plant growth, being a pest-free environment, and providing a place to pursue gardening as a leisure activity make it the perfect setup.

Yet, raised beds are not a new concept in the gardening world. The history of raised bed gardening has its roots in ancient Babylon, which had gardens at great heights and secured in unimaginable stone structures, the like of which are nowhere to be seen in the present day. The Hanging Gardens at the palace of King Nebuchadnezzar II was quite different from the way it looks now, and is considered one of the Seven Wonders of the Ancient World.[1] When it was first built, the structure separated the royal family from nature, as the first part of the mighty palace was made only with the sternness of stone. The king's wife, Amytis, began missing her home, the ancient kingdom of Media with its captivating greenery.

The king ordered that the palace turn green: his men built creative gardens at great heights, and found ways to transport water to those heights to maintain the gardens. They used boxes made from stones to contain the soil, and used apparatus such as the one proposed by Greek mathematician, Archimedes, to raise the water to the high gardens.[1] In this way, the Hanging Gardens and the rich collection of creatively placed gardens across the palace served as a means of food security, and became a source of fresh produce for the royal family and all inhabitants of the palace.

Fast forward a few centuries, and the practice came to be widely adopted during the period 10,000 BC and 7000 BC.[2] Vegetable gardening was found in several places in the provinces of South America, China, Asia, India and Africa during this same period. The people of Greece came to be known as skilled at growing olives, figs, sesame, barley, apples, asparagus, onions and cabbage. Gradually, the ancient gardeners began experimenting with different aspects of vegetable gardening, such as growing larger fruits, opting for early harvest, and aiming for longer shelf life.

In Central America, people began to grow corn, and developed several varieties. They also grew peppers, tomatoes and beans, and exported them to Europe when explorers set out on their expeditions around the world.[2] The Peruvians of South America cultivated potatoes, a staple crop that soon spread across the globe in its numerous varieties, colors and shapes. In the region which is now the United States, corn, beans and squash were primarily cultivated by the First Nations People, as they could be stored efficiently. Slavery is a prominent part of US history, and slaves were employed in farming and gardening for tasks such as preparing the ground, irrigation, maintenance and harvesting.

Vegetable gardening received a setback after the advent of commercial agriculture, as people began to prefer greater efficiency in their farming pursuits. World War II was a turning point in the history of vegetable gardening.[2] People living in America and England invested time and money in growing their food to support the war. In doing so, people started to associate vegetable gardening with fortitude, self-reliance and patriotism. Food rationing and relevant advertising motivated people to grow carrots on their own.

Towards the end of the war, chemical factories whose main activity was to produce nitrogen for bombs started investing in nitrogen as a fertilizer, which became an integral part of vegetable gardening for many subsequent years. The obvious harm to the environment through the use of chemical fertilizers was soon acknowledged, however, and people started switching to organic farming and organic vegetable makes it a big plus for your raised bed garden.[9] On the downside, it takes a bit of effort to work with stone, as it is quite heavy. Furthermore, you may have to use concrete and put in extra effort and cost if you decide to build a raised bed garden that is high. Since it warms quite quickly, it may not be the best choice for people living in hot climates. Finally, cinder blocks, which fall under the category of stone, may become a health hazard, as they may contain heavy metals or fly ash.

Bricks: Bricks cost less than most other alternatives. They are strong but far less durable. You may want to choose bricks to construct your raised bed, but be aware that you may need to invest in skilled labor for the construction. Another option is to learn how to DIY so that you can build the bed yourself. Regardless of what method of building you use, the best choice of bricks for your raised beds is engineering bricks due to their weather resistance. Engineering bricks impart a more robust structure, and give better performance than ordinary bricks since they have low water absorption capacity and high compressive strength. They provide a great deal of protection against water and frost. Their uniform size and shape make it convenient to quickly construct your raised garden bed.[12] If you want a cheaper option, domestic bricks cost less; however, they're not as durable as they are quite porous.

Paving Slabs: Paving slabs are a good ready-to-use choice for constructing raised beds. To construct raised beds using paving slabs, about six inches of the slab may be buried in the ground. This leaves about 18 inches of the slab above the

In Central America, people began to grow corn, and developed several varieties. They also grew peppers, tomatoes and beans, and exported them to Europe when explorers set out on their expeditions around the world.[2] The Peruvians of South America cultivated potatoes, a staple crop that soon spread across the globe in its numerous varieties, colors and shapes. In the region which is now the United States, corn, beans and squash were primarily cultivated by the First Nations People, as they could be stored efficiently. Slavery is a prominent part of US history, and slaves were employed in farming and gardening for tasks such as preparing the ground, irrigation, maintenance and harvesting.

Vegetable gardening received a setback after the advent of commercial agriculture, as people began to prefer greater efficiency in their farming pursuits. World War II was a turning point in the history of vegetable gardening.[2] People living in America and England invested time and money in growing their food to support the war. In doing so, people started to associate vegetable gardening with fortitude, self-reliance and patriotism. Food rationing and relevant advertising motivated people to grow carrots on their own.

Towards the end of the war, chemical factories whose main activity was to produce nitrogen for bombs started investing in nitrogen as a fertilizer, which became an integral part of vegetable gardening for many subsequent years. The obvious harm to the environment through the use of chemical fertilizers was soon acknowledged, however, and people started switching to organic farming and organic vegetable gardening.[2] Organic farming provides a way to grow healthy, sustainable and organic food.

People who were involved in raised bed gardening for growing their own vegetables soon realized that there are costs associated with the initial setup, but that those costs are worth the initial investment in the long run.[3] Over time, people began to optimize several aspects of raised bed gardening, such as measuring the yield per square foot, planting and weeding techniques, solving the problems associated with water logging, and selecting the right quality of soil for sustainable farming.

The Suburban Grower explores the different techniques used in vegetable gardening in the present suburban environment. It builds on the history of vegetable gardening and discusses the pros and cons, and what you can do to make a beautiful and thriving vegetable garden. This book not only guides you to set up your garden, but it also provides several insights into the minute details surrounding vegetable gardening, such as understanding the direction of sunlight, selecting the right soil, measuring the setup of raised beds, and many more aspects to make your garden sustainable and a source of fresh produce.

1

BENEFITS OF RAISED BED GARDENING

What Is Raised Bed Gardening?

A raised bed refers to a garden bed that is built up rather than down. This approach tackles all sorts of gardening issues. There are simple ways to create raised beds, such as using boxes to contain garden soil, or simply making a heap of soil. Garden boxes work well as raised beds, as they are designed to serve as a "retaining wall" that is essential for successful raised bed gardening.

Raised bed gardening is an incredible technique for growing a wide range of plants, including vegetables and fruits. It allows you the freedom to work with a number of soil types and promote efficient drainage. The different plants that you can cultivate using raised beds include herbaceous perennials, shrubs, rhododendrons, heathers, currants, strawberries, blackberries, raspberries, alpines, small trees, and vegetables. Regardless of what you want to plant and grow, a raised bed will help you achieve your gardening goals due to the high success rate of growing crops in a raised bed.

Advantages of Raised Beds

The major advantages of raised beds are their ability to provide an efficient drainage system, provide a raised temperature for soil, make a medium for easy watering, provide an appropriate soil base for plants, improve the root health of plants, and manage all of this easily and in a timely manner.

When using raised beds, the soil bed is raised above ground level. Although this feature serves as an advantage most of the time, it may prove to be a disadvantage when a drought occurs, making it necessary for the plants to be watered more frequently, which is a challenge when water is scarce.

That being said, raised beds provide several ways to optimize the use of soil to make a garden with plants flourish with health. Firstly, the soil in raised beds stays much warmer in spring, as the drainage built into raised beds helps get rid of excess water much faster. To achieve the best results, the raised beds must be filled with fertilizer-enriched topsoil to provide optimal nutrition to the plant roots. Adding organic matter to the soil gives even better results. It is possible to grow plants in a soil type that is different from what is naturally available. In other words, it is possible to grow plants that thrive in acidic soil, even when the soil that is naturally available is alkaline.

The Basics of Gardening With Raised Beds

Here's a quick list of things to consider when beginning with your raised bed:

1. The time to set up raised beds depends on soil conditions. Plant roots absorb nutrients below the ground level, and double-digging the soil (24 inches approximately) before setting-up the raised bed is

recommended in order to have a flourishing raised bed garden. Digging up at this point allows you an opportunity to remove debris and rocks so the growing roots are not obstructed, and you can also take off and restrict the growth of roots from nearby trees. You can add amendments to the soil by double-digging it. For example, adding peat to clay-like soil helps it to drain well and improves aeration. It is a good idea to lighten the soil by adding peat moss. Lime can also be added to improve the soil pH. [100] Late summer is a good time to start if there is a water logging problem in winter. Alternatively, raised beds may be created in the winter months, provided that the soil is not frozen or has become too wet.

2. Planning a raised bed is quite simple. To begin, all you need to do is decide on its size and location. The recommended size for your raised bed is 1.5 meters or less, as this will allow you to tend to your plants without accidentally stepping on them.

3. When leaving space for pathways between beds, make sure they are wide enough to accommodate your needs, such as wheelchairs or wheelbarrows. The recommended minimum width of pathways is 1 foot for walking, and 18 inches for wheelbarrows. This, however, is completely up to you. There are no real rules here: you can let your creativity shine.

4. To get started with your raised bed project, either buy a ready-to-use kit or buy the material you wish to use, such as timber, timber lookalikes, masonry, or

sleepers. Different materials have their own pros and cons. When using masonry, it is possible to obtain a long-lasting raised bed, although it costs more. Conversely, timber doesn't last as long, but it can be quite cheap. Sleepers may also be used to construct your raised bed as they are long-lasting, but they are difficult to use and quite bulky. One good alternative is a timber look-alike that gives good performance at a relatively fair price.

5. Another important consideration is the council regulations that may restrict the choice of materials used to construct your raised bed. This is particularly applicable to a conservation area. If you plan to construct your raised bed along the roadside or a boundary, there may be certain restrictions on the height of the raised bed. Your local planning authority is in the best position to sort out what will work best for your project.

Choice of Materials for Raised Beds

There are several materials that may be used to construct raised beds, such as timber, stone, or paving slabs.[13]

Timber: Timber is a prudent choice of material due to its versatile nature. Several types of untreated wood are suitable for raised bed gardening. Black locust or redwood is long-lasting and quite resistant to rot. These types of wood will, however, cost you three or four times more than the other types of wood. Black locust is durable and has a long lifespan: it lasts twice as long as concrete and even longer than stone. It is a dense wood, and high in antioxidants, which makes it resistant to rot and insect attacks.[15] Another type of wood that is resistant to rot is cedarwood, which lasts almost fifteen years. Cedarwood also has a unique luxurious look, but costs a lot more than others. Cedarwood is also resistant to rot and insects, and is durable and moisture-resistant. It requires minimal maintenance, and does not split or warp easily. Cedar is also an environment-friendly option.[16] Douglas Fir is another good choice: it is not only affordable, but also lasts quite a long time – up to seven years.[6] Douglas Fir has moderate durability, with varying colors and straight or wavy grain; however, this wood may cause skin irritation, nausea, and a runny nose. Infections from splinters are also quite common.[7]

If you're looking for a simpler alternative for a brief period, then you may want to choose untreated wood and coat it with a preservative. Wood preservatives generally have the tendency to leech into the soil, which may be avoided by lining the wood with a black plastic sheet. Wood from red cedar or oak lasts a long time, even when it has not been treated.

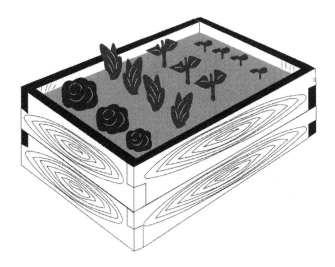

Stone: Stone is one of the most expensive materials available for construction, and using it may mean you require skilled labor to set up your raised bed. There is a wide range of choices when selecting stone for your raised bed, including stone meant for wall construction and natural stone.

There are several advantages to using stone as a material for your raised bed garden. Firstly, it is a very durable material, and does not suffer any form of damage from wind, water or insects. If you don't have the budget for stone, there are a few options, such as sourcing it from your backyard, a neighbor, or even a construction site. Even home improvement stores like Home Depot carry materials like bricks and pavers to build your raised bed garden. Stone also warms up quickly, allowing the soil to warm up, which makes it a big plus for your raised bed garden.[9] On the downside, it takes a bit of effort to work with stone, as it is quite heavy. Furthermore, you may have to use concrete and put in extra effort and cost if you decide to build a raised bed garden that is high. Since it warms quite quickly, it may not be the best choice for people living in hot climates. Finally, cinder blocks, which fall under the category of stone, may become a health hazard, as they may contain heavy metals or fly ash.

Bricks: Bricks cost less than most other alternatives. They are strong but far less durable. You may want to choose bricks to construct your raised bed, but be aware that you may need to invest in skilled labor for the construction. Another option is to learn how to DIY so that you can build the bed yourself. Regardless of what method of building you use, the best choice of bricks for your raised beds is engineering bricks due to their weather resistance. Engineering bricks impart a more robust structure, and give better performance than ordinary bricks since they have low water absorption capacity and high compressive strength. They provide a great deal of protection against water and frost. Their uniform size and shape make it convenient to quickly construct your raised garden bed.[12] If you want a cheaper option, domestic bricks cost less; however, they're not as durable as they are quite porous.

Paving Slabs: Paving slabs are a good ready-to-use choice for constructing raised beds. To construct raised beds using paving slabs, about six inches of the slab may be buried in the ground. This leaves about 18 inches of the slab above the soil. To prevent the slabs from moving over time, it is a good idea to use concrete haunching that is about a foot in depth to make the construction more stable. The slabs can be secured using metal plates at their joints. The overall cost is far less than most other alternatives.

Why Raised Beds Are Perfect for You

A number of good reasons exist for using raised beds for gardening, but the most important is the aim to create nutrient-rich soil over which people don't casually stroll. Also, using raised beds in your home for gardening provides an aesthetic value and a unique ambience, and adds to the beauty of your home. Raised bed gardening is perfectly suitable for beginners, as it is a simple method to begin cultivating with only a little out-of-pocket investment.

Even inexperienced gardeners are able to accomplish quite a bit in just a year. Simply put, it only requires a box with some fertilizer and soil, which serves as the ideal medium to grow the seeds of your choice. For eager beginners, it also means less work than the traditional way of gardening or farming, which requires tilling the soil, adding fertilizers in calibrated amounts, repeating the tilling process, seeding, weeding, and continuing with weeding throughout the growing season. Here are a few reasons why raised beds could be your best choice for gardening.

A No-Tilling Method to Successful Soil Preservation

Raised beds allow you to set up your soil in an easy and effortless manner, while providing the option to add the nutrients to the top layer of soil.[8] In a raised bed, the top layer of soil holds all of the nutrients, including compost, fertilizer, mulches, and even soil conditioners.

The technique saves you from a lot of physically demanding hard work. Worms can be added to the bed to make up for the tilling that would otherwise need to be done at regular intervals.[8] In the case of raised beds, the worms push through the soil, replacing the tilling activity naturally. Raised beds also eliminate the need to plow the soil, which serves as a big advantage because the soil composition is well-preserved, and it is possible to build the natural characteristics of the soil over time.

A Weed-Free Plantation

Raised beds are often covered with dark plastic, cardboard or mulch in the spring, and this activity kills all weeds that may have grown during the winter.[8] When it's time to begin planting again, rake off the dead weeds before they get an opportunity to invade the plants you're trying to cultivate.

A Low-Physical-Strain Gardening Option

Strained back and knees are common conditions that result from weeding out the unwanted plants that may hurt your lovely garden. Weeding the garden can be one of the most time-consuming activities gardeners face. Hand weeding is quite a daunting task, and even young gardeners are likely to feel exhausted after a hard day's work. You can select a convenient length for your raised beds depending on the plants you wish to grow. This makes it quite convenient to do the planting and weeding, and protects your back and joints from developing chronic skeletal problems.

A Good Barrier Against Slugs and Critters

Slugs and pests are a major concern in traditional gardening. When using raised beds, however, the tall sides of the box containing the garden tend to slow down the slugs and prevent them from reaching the plants.[8]

A number of gardeners agree that slugs find it very difficult to slither over copper blazing, which can be used to line the garden box. Other alternatives to prevent slugs include the use of hardware cloth on the lower part of the box, a barrier against them getting at the root crops. The garden boxes are also built in such a way that they serve as good protection against domestic pets destroying the plants. Your plants can also be easily protected from birds by adding any desired covers, plastic hoops, or cold casings.

A Good Option for Tenants

The temporary nature of the raised bed may make it quite easy for you to convince your landlord to let you have a beautiful garden. Raised beds may be an attractive prospect for landlords: a flawless, clean and appropriately constructed garden box can improve property estimations.[8] In certain cases, when the landlord is not quite convinced by the temporary nature of the raised bed, a removable nursery box may just be the thing that will take care of the gardener in you. All you have to do is fix the removable nursery box to the ground, and place cardboard over the grass that's inside.

Your next step is to fill it with soil. The box serves as a terrific portable garden, and you can take it wherever you go.

A Practical Solution for Wet Areas

In areas that are constantly flooded, or in wet areas such as marshy yards, the best choice for a full growth season may be a raised garden. To get a good raised bed garden in these conditions, you can construct one with a depth of 11 inches. The most mainstream depth for a raised bed is 11 inches, as this provides a good drainage system for the plants. A raised bed can handle a large amount of water during heavy rains, as the drainage system promptly eliminates any excessive water at regular intervals.

Suitability of Raised Beds

Raised bed gardens are extremely flexible for successful planting, and allow you to work with a large selection of plants.

Vegetables

Vegetable growing using raised beds provides several advantages to gardeners. The foremost advantage is the health benefits of home-grown vegetables. Health concerns regarding the rise in the use of fertilizers and pesticides in commercial farming is one reason many gardeners choose to grow their own produce. Avoiding fertilizers not only saves you from the detrimental effects on your body, but it also protects the environment.

To grow vegetables in raised beds, grow them in blocks so that they are able to spread uniformly with minimal competition. This method also helps to keep the weeds out. Vegetables grow better because the beds can be warmed much earlier in spring, and nutrients can be concentrated much better. Additionally, gardeners can do easy rotations by using a large number of narrow raised beds.

Fruits

We don't necessarily need an orchard to grow fruit at home. With the current trend of living in urban and suburban areas, raised bed gardens are the answer when growing your own fruit. It is quite possible to grow a number of fruits using raised beds in small backyards, or even on balconies, including strawberries, raspberries, figs, apples and blackberries.[13]

Alpines

Alpines may sometimes be regarded as tricky for the gardener. Alpines are versatile as they have the ability to survive climatic changes.[13] For this reason, raised beds are commonly preferred by gardeners who have just started out. Alpines also do not require a lot of maintenance, and can be grown easily. They're also attractive, and add aesthetic value to your garden. Some examples of alpine plants include the pretty ink-purple flowers of Armeria, the deep pink flowers of Dianthus Popstar, the star-shaped apricot, and the pink flower-laden little plum, as well as the late spring evergreen, Winifred Bevington.[4]

Small Trees and Shrubs

Small trees and shrubs can be used to add greenery and variety to your garden.[13] Small trees and shrubs do not require a lot of space for growth over time, and are perfectly suitable for growing in raised beds. Some examples of trees for raised beds include Acer griseum or 'Paperbark maple', Amelanchier, Crataegus persimilis 'Prunifolia',Sorbus 'Joseph Rock' with its white spring flowers, and Prunus 'Amanogawa'. In general, trees measuring less than16 feet or 5 meters are most suited for raised bed gardening.[95]

You can also include several shrubs in your garden, such as evergreen conifers, which come in various sizes and shapes, winter-flowering shrubs such as witch hazel, evergreen Mahonia, Sarcococca, and evergreen Viburnum tinus; shrubs with winter berries such as cotoneaster and evergreen pyracantha; and winter-flowering heathers such as ajuga and ivy.[96]

Ericaceous or Lime-Hating Plants

Lime-hating plants are the acid-loving plants.[13] These kinds of plants don't grow well in areas where the pH of the soil is high. Soils with a high pH are known as alkaline soils. Examples of lime-hating plants are Camellia, Azalea, and Japanese maples. These plants can be successfully grown by adding acidic soil in only those raised beds where these plants are grown.

Benefits of Raised Beds

To sum it all up, raised bed gardens are extremely efficient at increasing soil temperature. The soil in a raised bed garden has better drainage, so it heats up pretty fast during the spring.[13] This increase in the temperature of the soil helps the plants to absorb more nutrients and water from the soil to promote the growth of plants. Raised beds can also be used to enhance root health in plants. When we fill the beds with soil that is rich in nutrients and organic matter, it results in extremely good root zone conditions.

They are easy to maintain, and do not require constant attention and hard work. The soil volume in raised beds is much higher than the traditional containers, which helps in managing them with watering. Raised bed gardens also provide mobility to gardeners. Since the soil level is higher, you have to stoop less to weed, water, and do other gardening tasks. Lifting the raised beds 1 to 3 feet high makes planting workable for individuals with restricted mobility.

In addition to their aesthetic appeal, raised beds offer numerous advantages to mature gardeners, as well as those who have just started their gardening pursuits.[14]

Water Management and Waste Prevention

There are a number of options when it comes to watering raised beds, including punctured plastic sprinkler hoses, canvas soaker hoses, and low-volume dribble tubes. These water system techniques function exceptionally well in long beds with a narrow frame.[14] Raised beds not only prevent water wastage, but also help fight infection and disease by guiding water to the soil, and not just watering the surface of leaves.

Increased Productivity

Raised beds can be designed prudently, allowing the planting of vegetables at higher densities so that they are far enough away from each other to not become overcrowded. At the same time, they are situated closely, in such a way that weeds are not allowed to take root.[14] Raised bed gardening helps to produce more fruits and vegetables for every square foot planted. Additionally, you'll have far fewer problems when it comes to nematodes that attack the roots and influence plant yield.

Minimal Soil Compaction

Raised beds are a great way to avoid soil compaction, as there is no risk of someone accidentally walking over the planted bed. The gardening technique is beneficial for the plants as well as for the soil. Raised beds allow you to use the ideal blend of soil for your plants, enriched with organic matter, to provide ample nutrition for the plants enclosed in the raised bed. As an example, soil can be prepared specifically to meet the needs of edible plants grown in raised beds, using the required organic fertilizers and potting mixes and maintain an ideal pH for the plants to grow.[10]

Another important way to minimize compaction is to use "sheltered kits" that serve as a protective mechanism against heavy rains. [11] Sheltered kits are offered by many companies that ship all required structural units, such as anchors, beams and wooden planks. These kits create a stable structure as protection against harsh weather conditions, while providing ventilation and illumination for your plants to breathe, thrive, and grow into healthy crops.

The ability to prevent soil compaction makes raised beds the gardening technique of choice for most garden-lovers.[17] Experts have a similar opinion about the woes of compacted soil. The University of Georgia Cooperative Extension believes that raised beds could be a great upgrade for the garden when there are many pedestrians and active children to consider. A raised box provides assurance that soil compaction will not occur. When the soil is properly aerated, it not only allows the roots to go deeper; it enhances the life of the soil.

Minimal Soil Run-Off

Soil is contained in a confined space, which prevents soil runoff. It is always held inside the planter, and there is minimal chance of the soil going elsewhere – even if there is a heavy downpour. Preserving soil means preserving a diverse microbiome. The only exception is when a base is missing, in which case an overflow drains downward. This arrangement also preserves soil composition and the nutrients and supplements added to it. Heavy rains do not deplete the soil, unlike in traditional gardens.[17]

Choice of Soil

Numerous gardens have shallow soil of low quality, which is not adequate for growing vegetables. High quality soil promotes the development of bigger roots and a better plant yield.[5] A raised bed garden allows you to choose different types of soils according to the plant. Thus, raised bed gardens give us the opportunity to add diversity to our gardens.

Possibility of Early Planting

The soil has far better drainage and warms quicker in raised beds, which makes it possible to accomplish early planting. An important consideration among gardeners is that many plant over winter in a raised bed.[8] The key to successful planting in a raised bed is the untilled and nutrient-rich nature of the soil. Good soil composition guarantees better temperature management.

Bringing Together Your Community

Raised beds are a pleasing sight, and often keep neighbors happy in urban settings. A raised bed vegetable garden serves as the ideal way to attract and build a community: people with similar interests are always looking for enriching conversations. If you're building your garden for yourself and your neighbors, then you will most likely attract a number of people on the lookout for a place to walk or take their dog for a stroll. Your garden-loving neighbors may even want to assist in tending your garden. Above all, a good crop is a treat for you and your neighbors, as everyone gets to have a taste of the freshest vegetables and fruits of the season.[18] Raised beds make it quite simple to maintain pathways and provide a good yield by only occupying minimal space in your backyard or garden.

2

COMMON MISTAKES IN RAISED-BED GARDEN SETUP - AND HOW TO AVOID THEM

Common Mistakes to Watch Out For

As we have discussed, raised bed gardens provide a multitude of benefits, including easy access, an improved drainage system, aesthetic appeal, the ability to select an appropriate soil type, and faster warming of the soil. Raised bed gardens work best for your vegetables and favorite plants, but you want to avoid a few mistakes to make good use of your time and hard-earned money. Before you even get started building your beds, it's helpful to be aware of the common mistakes so that you know that you're setting off on the right track.

Gardening Without Planning a Location and Orientation

Planning a raised bed without giving due consideration to the location could be your biggest mistake when designing your garden. To make sure that this doesn't happen to you, consider the movement of the sun and take into account the arrangement of the raised bed. You need to understand the path of the sun and how much sunlight your plants will receive a few years from now. [19] Trees that have just been planted may grow sooner than you expect and end up shading your garden when you really require a sunny environment for your plants to thrive.

An effective strategy to use when deciding on the location and orientation of your garden is to take into account the way shadows travel throughout the day.[19] To help you, consider looking at websites that show data on the path of the sun, including sunrise, sunset, shadow length, and duration of daylight. Analyzing the data helps to identify the precise conditions for a period of time so you don't stumble across any surprises when you've finished working on the beds, adding the perfect soil, and planting your crops.

Also consider buildings, trees, and other structures surrounding your selected location.[19] Raised beds do well when they are south-facing, so you may want to incorporate this in your plan when designing a raised bed garden. When you have set up your garden after giving due consideration to all these factors, you will definitely be able to realize a picture-perfect array of plants, exactly resembling the arrangement you desire.

When you have calculated appropriately and decided on the orientation of your raised beds, it is time to plan how you will arrange the plants you intend to grow. A commonly followed order of growing plants in raised beds is to have the lower crops at the front, then the mid-height crops, and then the tallest crops at the back of your raised bed.[19] In rare cases, you may want to plant a tall crop in the front portion of the raised bed if you plan to have a vegetable requiring shade at the back.

Using Pressure-Treated Lumber

You are definitely better off avoiding pressure-treated lumber: there are concerns about the chemicals used in treatment, which may not be suitable for edible crops. While you may have heard of several claims about the safety of the product, you want to be extra cautious when it comes to handling your home grown produce.[25] Pressure-treated lumber contains chemicals, and there is a risk of the chemicals leaching into the soil and getting into your planted crop.

Pressure-treated wood is often treated with chromated copper arsenate, which contains inorganic arsenic. Needless to say, arsenic is a poisonous chemical. Arsenic gets readily absorbed into the human system – and stays there. A build-up of arsenic overtime could create chronic sickness. Even though pressure-treated wood was banned by the Environmental Protection Agency (EPA) in 2003, the trend has changed over recent years, with different types of chemically-treated wood available on the market. These different types of woods use different types of copper. They are less risky than the chemicals in use before, but even though these types of copper only harm the human system when large quantities of the chemical are ingested, our bodies still do not absorb them well. Moreover, your plants may die if they absorb the toxic chemical.[19] It is best to make a different choice of material and rule out chemically-treated wood to eliminate the possibility of health hazards.

Although manufacturers may reassure you that it is perfectly safe to utilize pressure-treated lumber for your raised bed garden, chemicals may have an adverse effect on the immune system, and children are quite sensitive. You want to make a good choice right from the start to ensure your family stays healthy.[25] Although pressure-treated lumber is not recommended for gardening, you could definitely use it in other areas, such as for your fence or deck framing to achieve a robust setup.

Building With Concrete

If you're looking at a long-term plan for your raised bed garden, then concrete could be a tempting choice, as it helps to achieve a permanent structure. While this quality makes concrete a good material to prevent any rotting, the downside is that if you want to change the position of the bed, then the concrete structure would have to be broken up using tools like a sledgehammer and a jackhammer.[25]

Concrete is not a recyclable material, and also comes with a few other disadvantages, such as its tendency to leach lime into the ground, creating an unsuitable medium for plants that require acidic soil. Its susceptibility to developing cracks in the winter months when water enters minute crevices, freezes, and expands to make a large-enough and irreparable crack, and its lack of aesthetic appeal when you use it all by itself, also make it a less than desirable material.[25] The materials best suited for building your raised bed garden include cinder, stone and bricks, which are recyclable.

Choosing Wood Without Considering Climatic Conditions

When you're deciding what type of wood to choose to build your raised bed garden, consider the climatic conditions. Most gardeners prefer to go with wood as it is affordable and can be procured quite easily. Wood tends to deteriorate quickly, however, and may not be as durable as other materials.[19] If you are set up in an area which experiences frequent rainfall, your wooden structure is more likely to face damage from weathering, and you may have to change the timber quite frequently. Wood is a more prudent investment in dry areas that do not experience rainfall very often and there is a lower probability of the wooden structure getting soaked by water and breaking apart.

Exposing End Grain and Not Capping It

Using posts at the corner of raised beds is a common practice among gardeners. Posts measuring 2x2, 4x4, or 2x4 feet are generally used in raised bed gardens. The posts are used in the corners of raised beds, and their corners are tied to keep the sides of the beds secure. This method adds strength to the raised bed garden. The primary disadvantage with this construction, however, is that it allows water to get absorbed into the exposed end of the post when it rains or when the raised beds are irrigated.[25] Water-soaked posts soon start to decay and rot, making them the ideal medium to sustain insects and pests. This is not a desirable outcome for your beautiful garden.

To use posts the right way to make a good raised construction, it is a good idea to use caps for the posts. The caps may be derived from the same wood as the post itself, or you could invest in decorative iron caps. Another alternative is to use solar lights for the post caps. Solar-powered caps illuminate your garden for night-time gardening.

If you are still not satisfied with any of these alternatives, you may want to choose metal brackets to reinforce the raised beds from the corners. [25] In this way, you can do away with the posts and still achieve a sound infrastructure for your raised bed garden.

Making the Beds Too Wide

Choose an appropriate size for your raised bed so that you don't need to step into the soil to reach for the plants. A width of 4 feet is ideal for a raised bed that can be reached from both sides. If you have a bed against a fence, then you want to stick to a smaller width, about 2-3 feet, so that it is easy to reach the plants conveniently.[25] Having a manageable width for your raised bed keeps you from stepping on the soil, which may cause soil compaction and drainage problems.

Failing to Plan Pathways

When you design with the raised beds too close together, it gets difficult to kneel down between the beds and do your gardening. It is also quite difficult to work with any sort of equipment if you have only narrow gaps between the beds. [19] Before beginning to construct your raised bed garden, decide what you will carry along the pathways if you want to do your gardening efficiently. Think about different options that will assist you in tending to your plants. If you plan to use a wheelbarrow, weed trimmer, or lawn mower to tend to your garden, then you may need wider pathways. Moreover, if you plan on using a garden tractor, then it may require a lot more space, and you will want to set up your pathways accordingly. In effect, it makes sense to visualize how you are going to use the pathways and who is going to be gardening in order to set up the right width for your circumstances.

If you have more plants and require more space to plant them all, then make sure you have pathways in between the beds. Pathways are essential, as you want to go around your array of raised beds, weeding out unnecessary plants and parasites. You may also want to plant additional seeds or harvest the crop when it is time to do so.[25] You could choose the size of the pathway depending on whether you want to use a wheelbarrow to traverse the pathway. Gardeners typically go with 3 feet for the pathway as the typical width, but even a width of 2 feet will suffice if there is just one person tending to the garden.

You will want to consider other factors that may influence the size of the raised bed. You want to choose different dimensions if you have short arms or if your kids are willing to assist you in your raised bed gardening endeavors. You, your family members, or any friends who want to help may have mobility issues, and if so, you'll want to design the bed so that the middle portion is reachable from a wheelchair.[19] There is no hard and fast rule about the ideal width of the raised bed: you just need to choose a size that is appropriate for your requirements. Similar to determining the width of the bed, it is also important to determine a flexible size for the length so that it is convenient when you want to walk to the other side of the bed.

Finally, get your team to understand how and where you plan to build the raised bed.[19] Brainstorm and arrive at solutions that will work for you and your fellow gardeners. Sometimes, gardeners prefer to have the bed on stilts so it comes to their ideal height and they can stand and tend to the plants rather than kneeling down, which can prove to be uncomfortable for some people.

Failing to Plan Irrigation

Another big mistake is forgetting about watering systems. Before you set up your garden, think of the best way to set up a watering system.[19] If you want to hand-water, then plan how you will set up the hose, and make arrangements for the equipment you will need to water your garden. Even if it is as simple as getting a hose, measure your garden pathways, and get the appropriate length to water your garden conveniently. You may want to set up a more complex irrigation system such as a sprinkler system to water your garden at regular intervals, in which case the best time to set up the irrigation is before the start of your raised bed gardening project.

Using the Wrong Soil

Picking the right kind of soil for your raised bed is an important step to achieving a sustainable garden. Soil that has too much sand may end up turning into concrete when mulch is not used to protect it. One method to improve the soil quality is to use cover crops.[25] Choice of manure or compost is also an important consideration. Sometimes, the herbicides used on hay fields to get rid of weeds are not broken down after horses consume the hay. The manure you get from these horses may still contain active herbicide, which is not be ideal for your raised bed garden. Active herbicides in the manure may stunt plant growth or even kill the plants. In such cases, the only choice you may have is to change the soil in the raised bed garden.

Do not automatically choose the native soil in your garden to plant your raised beds. Although you may be able to successfully cut down on the costs, it may not be the best soil for your selection of plants. You want to test your soil to check if it works well for your crops. If it doesn't come back perfect, you want to blend it with different varieties of soil to get the right mix that suits the needs of your plants.[19] When selecting the soil mix that suits what you plan to grow, you want to consider its ability to retain water, and get an expert opinion on how to make it nutrient-rich. You also want to consider whether the soil is properly drained to prevent a water-logging problem later on. In effect, you want to stay away from soil that has nutrients depleted or a quality of soil that has a problem with water drainage. Soil also needs to be replenished by adding nutrients to it after each crop rotation, and at the close of the growing season. These simple precautions will lead you to getting the best possible soil for your raised bed garden.

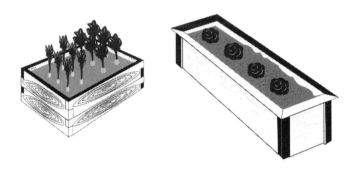

Failing to Plan for Weed Control Between Beds

Weeding out the unnecessary parasites on your pathways is as important as maintaining your vegetable garden. This is an often-neglected area, and many gardeners pay a high cost if they don't pay attention to the weeds infesting the pathways.[19] The weeds, when left unchecked, eventually find their way into the raised beds.

One of the most popular approaches to controlling weeds around raised beds is mulching.[19] Many gardeners cover their pathways with a protective layer of straw, grass clippings, bark chips, or stones to prevent the weeds from growing. Mulching has a number of benefits, including preservation of the moisture in the soil and enhancing its health and fertility. Mulching also adds an appealing look to your vegetable garden, as well as cutting down on the growth of weeds around pathways.

Things to Consider Before Preparing Raised Beds

Most experienced gardeners recommend constructing raised beds with untreated wood, where the plants are able receive sunlight for about six to eight hours daily. The size of the raised bed really doesn't matter, and a number of safe materials can be chosen when wood is not available. Materials that may prove toxic to the soil and plants should be avoided. These considerations are discussed in the previous section.

This section covers important considerations if you are to be successful in planting a sustainable raised bed garden.

Dealing With the Existing Grass

In addition to getting rid of weeds in your pathways, you should also get rid of grass by covering it up with cardboard, and then with a layer of soil.[22] This technique causes the grass to break down, and you will have a new site for your gardening venture. You can also get rid of the grass in your raised bed by digging a trench around the bed, and then sliding the spade just under the grass. Once you have the spade beneath the grass, lift it up so that the grass comes off as strips or small chunks. Turn over the strips so the grass is smothered and breaks down to provide nutrients to the soil over time.[97]

Installing an Irrigation System

There are several things to be careful about when installing the irrigation system of your choice for your raised bed garden. While setting up a garden hose is quite straightforward, organizing a drip irrigation system requires a bit of planning.[22] The most common way to set up a drip irrigation system is to use ready-to-use gardening irrigation kits available on the market. These kits provide all the components required to install a raised bed garden. A coverage area of about 75 square feet is covered by the drip-system, which is a great way to save water. Drip watering promotes the growth of green and healthy plants with minimal use of water and far fewer weeds. The system can be installed quite easily, and does not require any specific plumbing skills. The equipment is set up to water the roots of plants using a simple insertion and removal system for the fittings. A hose is also included in most kits, and the whole assembly can be completed quite quickly following the instruction manual.

The Quantity and Type of Soil You Will Need

In addition to the soil considerations discussed in the section above, you want to use soil calculators to find out exactly how much you will need to fill your raised bed.[22] Soil calculators give you an estimate of the soil required for your raised bed garden when you provide basic information, including the style of your garden, its shape, and its precise measurements. A simple figure in terms of cubic yards of soil is provided along with the quantity of fertilizer required for your raised bed garden. Using a calculator allows you to determine the right quantity of soil to fill your raised bed with a quality that is superior to the native soil.

As an example, if you plan on a 3x6 bed, you will require about 15 cubic feet of soil. The blend may be made up of 9 cubic feet of topsoil, 4.5 cubic feet of compost, 1.5 cubic feet of potting mix, and 1.5 cups of organic fertilizer.[20] Nutrient rich soil with organic matter allows plants to grow well, and they also have access to the right quantity of much-needed water and nutrients.

Consider Whether You Should Stake the Sides

Raised beds tend to shift over time. To overcome this problem, it is a good idea to install midpoint stakes. If you're unsure of how to organize the placement of your raised beds, it's a good idea to follow one of the premade layout plans.[22] One of the preferred techniques in vegetable gardening is suggested by Mel Bartholomew, who proposes the square foot gardening method, which is based on dividing the space using 1 square foot blocks to form a grid for your vegetable garden.[23]

The next step is to decide how many seeds must be added to every square of the grid, and what the density of plants per square foot should be. While some gardeners may prefer to have a single vegetable in a square foot area, others may want to have several in the same space. A good way to decide on the density of plants per square foot is to consider the size of the plants you intend to grow.

Once you have decided on the way to divide your area and are ready with the wooden frame, it's time to fix the stakes to the sides of the beds. You can easily do this by fixing 18-inch stakes into the ground and evening them out in line with the top of the bed. You can secure the stakes to the wooden sides of the bed using 2-inch screws.[21] This technique is essential: it makes sure the soil stay in place, as the bed does not move and is properly secured to the ground beneath it.

Plant Spread and Height

One of the most important decisions when starting out with your raised bed garden is to understand the space that your plants will require as they grow. The height required at maturity is the figure you want to estimate. Another important estimate is to do with the depth of the roots. When you have these two figures right, you are able to focus on growing your vegetables and bush-type plants, as they have shallow roots. Some vegetables that will grow well in your raised bed garden include bok choy, onions, lettuce, endive, cabbage, tomatoes, arugula, broccoli and spinach.[24] The roots of these vegetables measure about 12 to 18 inches at their maturity stage. Fruits you could grow in your raised bed garden include blackberries, strawberries, raspberries and blueberries.

One important consideration here is to keep ample space for the roots of your selected plants to thrive throughout the growing season. If you have constructed a raised bed that's not deep enough for the plants you selected, then the roots may travel into the soil underneath the bed and come in contact with toxic chemicals or unsuitable soil.[24] In order to overcome this problem, go for a depth that you're confident will hold the plants you selected.

Building Materials

When you make a choice for your building material, choose something that is durable. A number of building materials have been discussed already; the most suitable material for most gardeners is untreated wood, as it serves as the best option for organic gardening. Some types of wood that do not decay include redwood, cedar, and black locust. Rocks and bricks are other durable materials. If you're concerned about the gaps that stones may have when used to build your raised bed walls, use a liner to contain the soil and prevent it from running off.[24]

Time and Schedule

Time is a significant factor when building your raised bed garden. You need to consider when to start planting the different types of crops so you are not overwhelmed by the produce. Careful scheduling is an important skill in raised bed gardening. Lettuce, spinach, and other greens grow quickly, and you can plant them in spring. During the warm weather, you can clear the area and grow bush beans. Spring greens should be removed in the warm weather, as they may bolt or turn bitter. Finally, when you have harvested your bush beans, you can go ahead and plant a fall crop, such as lettuce or spinach.[98]

3

PREPARING, PLANNING, AND BUILDING RAISED BEDS

C onsidering the Possibility of Ready-Made Raised Beds

Raised bed gardens are an appealing sight, and they require much less work than a traditional garden. You may, however, have several cost concerns regarding the installation and maintenance of raised beds. It is quite possible to build your own raised bed with the tools available on the market.[28] There are, however, also several DIY toolkits if the idea of building from scratch is too daunting. Several companies offer kits containing aluminum corners that you can use with your choice of material, such as galvanized steel, composite wood, cedar, or recycled plastic.[30]

You can use these kits to make your own raised bed garden with a raw material of your choice. The most common type of wood is cedar, as it is not just durable but also resistant to rot. Cedar is also easy to assemble, as it is light and can be handled with ease. One of the most commonly used woods available in kits for raised bed gardening is Vermont white cedar. Other forms of natural cedar beds are also available, and require minimal time to assemble.[28]

You can also buy complete kits, which often use composite lumber built from post-consumer recycled plastic and hardwood fibers. These types of kit are suitable for growing organic crops, are long-lasting, and are easy to assemble. Since they use wood composite, you don't have to worry about maintenance or warping. When you're short on time, composite raised garden beds work best, as the only thing you have to do is slide the timber in the joint and use the zinc plates to screw the pieces of wood together.[28] Kits like this also come with stakes,, which allow the raised bed to be fixed securely in the ground.

Another material commonly used in raised bed garden kits is recycled plastic. These kits are made from high-density polyethylene, and come in a variety of colors. Using plastic is a good choice if you find lifting the heavy timber a challenge, and the plastic beds are far easier to assemble.

When to Buy a Raised Bed Kit

Sometimes, you may not have all the resources or enough time to set up everything from scratch. This is when you're better off investing in a ready-to-assemble kit. The availability of different materials means you can select a material that is suitable for you to work with and also looks elegant in your garden or backyard.[28] Most raised bed garden kits also come with a warranty from the manufacturer. Some materials are biodegradable, and if you have environmental concerns, you get the best of both worlds in terms of not just saving time building the beds, but also achieving a set up that does not harm the environment. An additional advantage is that choosing a durable kit such as plastic means you can set up your beds once at low cost, and relax for a couple of years as your garden flourishes.

If any of the following apply to you, a raised bed kit could be the right solution for your garden.

You Need a Quick Solution

Any gardening venture requires time, and you have a long checklist to complete when setting up your raised bed garden. This includes everything from selecting the right soil and fertilizer, to selecting the right crops and planting them when the time is most suitable. You need to make comprehensive plans about what crops will do well in your climatic conditions, and when to plant and harvest them. To make the task simpler, you can invest in an affordable raised bed kit that is ready to set up to save a lot of time and effort.

You Don't Have the Tools or Space to Build

Raised bed kits also work well when you have space constraints or few tools to build a raised bed from scratch. In this scenario, you may as well buy the whole kit rather than buy the tools, as it will cost much less. When space is a concern, and you have to set your beds up on a paved area or some location other than your garden or backyard, a ready-to-setup kit will work much better than building raised beds the traditional way, as a kit is a more compact option.

You Need a Solution That's Easy to Clean and Move

Raised beds made from pre-made kits are easy to move, and if you're planning on a mobile option that allows you to plant your preferred crops in a compact space, then ready-to-build raised beds work best. Besides, the portability, durability and compactness of off-the-shelf raised bed kits make it very simple to clean up your space after moving them from one place to another.

Building Your Own From Scratch

While buying a DIY kit can be a great quick fix, building your own from scratch can be more economical, and can be tailored better to your requirements. When you have selected the right type of wood and its size, stain the wood to preserve its natural color and lustre overtime. Sometimes, gardeners prefer that the wood ages naturally, which means you will see the color fading and the material bio-degrading over time.[28] If you want to slow down the degradation process for wood, it's a good idea to use non-toxic materials (borax (for preserving against borers), glues and adhesives, limewash, chalk and cement paint, sodium carbonate, or tung oil) to treat the wood as this option will prevent the chemicals from leaching into the soil and harming your plants.[99]

When you have your material ready, it's time to put the corners together with joints and screws. Most metal screws tend to rust and stain the wood when they come in contact with moisture. Therefore, it's always better to use stainless steel screws or coated deck screws. Use anchor joints for the corners, and drill holes in advance to make sure you can screw into the wood without it splitting. Another alternative for your corners is stacking brackets.

An important consideration to prevent wooden beds from bending from the weight of the soil is to use cross beams to support the length and width of your raised bed.[28] Cross beams generally help when the size of your raised bed is larger than 8 inches.

Raised Bed Design Ideas

Raised bed gardens offer the most flexibility to planters, who can choose to create almost anything, from simple permanent beds for plants that flourish all through the year, to something really creative and elaborate that soothes your senses every time you visit your garden.[33] To qualify as a raised bed, all that your garden requires is to have its soil above the ground level in an enclosure made from either wood, stones, or recycled material. Here are a few ideas you can work with when you want to construct your raised bed.

Built-in Raised Beds

Built-in raised beds are quite easy and convenient to construct. When you're building this type of raised bed, you don't go underground, but build the bed above the ground in the place you consider suitable for the growth of your selected plants.[33] This type of construction serves as an effective way to prevent tunneling pests from destroying your crops. As with all other designs of raised bed, you have complete control over the type and quality of soil you want to include in your garden, as well as the irrigation and water drainage system you want to install for the sustainability of your chosen plants. Built-in raised beds can also be constructed so that their walls are wide enough to accommodate people to sit and enjoy a relaxing evening with friends, or get absorbed in a book with the soothing smells of your plants creating ambience.

Sheet Metal Raised Beds

Raised beds constructed from sheet metal provide a lot of flexibility to construct the shape of raised beds that you prefer. Like most other raised beds, sheet metal beds are also above the frost line. This causes the soil to warm up much faster in the spring.[33] Warm soil gives you the opportunity to start planting seeds faster. The metal is a good conductor of heat, and is able to retain "ambient heat" in the soil, which is great for thriving plants.

Square Foot Raised Beds

Square foot raised beds are achieved by dividing up the gardening area into square foot blocks, which is typically one square foot per block. Dividing up the area in this manner allows you to plant an intensive garden with a specific variety of crop in every square foot. As you are able to increase the number and variety of seeds planted, your productivity also increases. Square foot raised beds prevent soil compaction, allow efficient water drainage, and also preserve soil quality. Gardeners usually choose to make raised beds that are 6 to 8 inches above the ground to allow the vegetables to grow well.

Herb Spiral

Herb gardens grown in breath-taking spirals are inviting to most plant-lovers. Herb gardens are made from naturally sourced materials, and mostly follow the permaculture technique to grow the herbs and fruits.[33] Permaculture gardening is another way to say "permanent culture," and involves using the natural elements, including wind, water and sunlight, to grow your plants. When you plant your seeds using this technique, you want to make use of all that is available in your garden, such as the soil and other natural materials to support the growth of your plants and seeds. In doing so, the only thing that you invest in is the plants and the seeds, which makes this gardening technique quite popular.[35]

The other advantages of permaculture gardening are that you do not harm the soil or environment, and minimal labor is required to accomplish the gardening. Designing an herb garden with this approach requires you to plan a design beforehand, and stick to the growth and harvest timing as it occurs naturally. Spiral gardens are a pleasing sight because of the way plants are arranged in a spiral design.

Hoop House Raised Beds

Hoop house raised beds take more time and effort during their initial construction, but you can easily accommodate a large variety of plants across all growing seasons in this form of construction. This type of multi-season vegetable garden provides a lot of flexibility in the type of plants you choose to grow, and also protects them from animals and pests.

Hoop house raised beds can protect your crop from frost, and you are at an obvious advantage during the springtime. [33] This style of bed enables you to stretch a protective material such as plastic over the plants. A simple technique to stretch the waterproof material is to use PVC pipes that can bend at a curve. The PVC pipes can either fit inside the edge of the raised bed, or they can be fixed outside its edge using screws. You want to get the right measurements for the sides of your raised bed before you start. You also will need to use metal brackets wherever required to secure the PVC pipes tightly, using screws to secure the edges to the raised bed.

Raised Bed Border

Raised bed borders work well in most gardens, including those that have steep slopes. Raised beds may be built at the lower sections of the steep slope using a material such as stone, and you can experiment with different layouts, incorporating different layers of flowers, planting the perennials at the back of the raised bed, and creating a border with the shrubs to achieve a wide variety of colors and structures for your garden. [33]

Trough Gardens

Animal feeding troughs are a popular choice for raised bed vegetable growers. They serve as ready-made containers to hold the soil of your choice, and do not need any specific construction or assembling. Prior to setting up your garden in a trough, it is a good idea to make holes at the bottom to make sure they have adequate drainage. [33] Besides conducting heat and warming up the soil to the desired temperature, metal troughs bring a new and different look to your garden. Metal troughs provide a lot of convenience to the gardener, and save time and effort. You will, however, want to make sure you are able to add that extra water to your plants when the weather gets really hot.

Custom Designed Raised Beds

The best thing about raised-bed gardens is that they can be designed with a lot of flexibility and customizability.[33] Raised bed gardens need not be boring. You can create a combination of different styles and heights of raised beds in your garden by building a multi-level raised bed garden. To add that extra ambience to your garden, you could add landscaping, add benches or build an elaborate seating area, or add lampposts between raised beds to create an atmospheric feel. The best thing about creating a green corner like this is that it gets better with time. An example of this is when creating a rustic look for your garden, as your plants grow and the wood acquires a rugged look from weathering. Alternatively, you can opt for a contemporary look, installing a modern raised bed that will be a talking point at dinner parties.

Deciding on the Size of Raised Beds

Making a decision about the right size of the raised bed can be a laborious task. There are several factors that are likely to influence your final calculations. Some of these aspects include space constraints, conditions of your chosen soil mixture, and the aesthetic factors you want to integrate in your final design.[31] However, no matter what you choose, remember that as long as you consider your growing needs, it is perfectly alright to get creative and build curved raised beds or even L-shaped beds.[29] Even random shapes look great for your vegetable garden. The considerations for length, height and width are indicated below.

Length and Width

The primary factor that influences the length and width of your raised bed frame is the space constraints of your garden. When designing the bed size and location in your garden, consider not just their size, but also the space between the beds that you want to use to walk around. The other factor you want to consider when finalizing a size for your raised beds is how much length you need to get to the center of the raised bed comfortably. An accurate calculation in this respect ensures that you will not have to step on the soil and compact it.[31] A common measurement for the width of a raised bed is 4 feet. In certain cases, for instance, if you have a wall on one side and you can only reach your plants from one side of your raised bed, a width of 3 feet will serve the purpose.

Height

In terms of the height of your raised beds, most gardeners select about 6 to 12 inches. It all depends on what you plan to plant. When constructing a raised bed on inferior soil, you would be best building a container with a height that is good enough to accommodate the roots of your growing plants without them traveling into the ground soil that may have contaminants. Deep beds are also suitable when you want to water your plants less frequently, as they have a larger surface area to hold the moisture. Deeper beds mean that a larger area is available for the soil. A larger quantity of soil exerts greater pressure on the sides, and you want to choose an appropriate thickness of the walls to achieve optimal support for the soil.

Here are a few tips to help you decide on the best size for your raised beds according to your choice of vegetables[26]:

- Raised beds with the dimensions 4x4 feet or 4x8 feet are generally manageable, even if you're just starting out.
- A 12x24 foot raised bed is enough to feed a family of four, and will have enough space to contain some zucchini, a lot of squash, and a couple of peppers, as well as tomatoes, beans, okra, eggplant and cucumbers. A raised bed this size could also accommodate herbs such as thyme, marjoram and oregano.

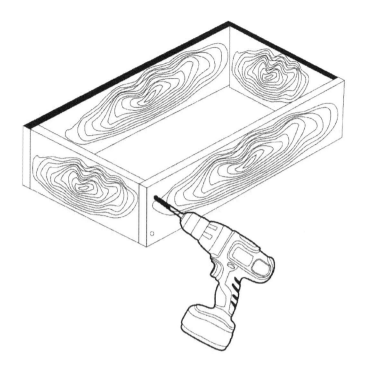

Choosing the Material

There is a large number of materials to choose from when constructing your raised bed garden, and your choices are likely to be influenced by the climate in your region, your budget, your style, and the availability of materials in your area.[27] As well as the traditional materials discussed earlier, gardeners can make use of several creative materials, including galvanized steel tubs, large stones, wine barrels, and other types of unusual container to grow their favorite crops.

Safety and durability are common concerns when choosing a good material for a vegetable garden. Wood is the primary choice of material for raised-bed gardeners, and there are several different categories of lumber used for the purpose. [27] Durable materials are chosen so that they are able to handle continuous exposure to moisture and changing weather conditions. Durability is also related to how much pressure the chosen material can withstand on its walls from the soil in the bed. Concrete and metal beds generally last much longer than wooden beds.

Materials that cost more generally also last longer due to their high quality. It's best to strike a balance between the cost of the material and its strength. If your preferred high-quality material costs a fortune, then you may be better off selecting something with a slightly lower cost: you will still benefit from all the advantages of raised bed gardening, even with this small compromise. [27] Always compare prices before selecting your material.

The following sections describe the different materials used for raised bed gardening to help you choose the right material for your garden.

Traditional Cedar Wood

The best wood for your raised bed garden is either cedar wood or redwood, as they are beautiful and durable, and are able to resist termites, moisture and rot. Costs of the different types of wood vary widely according to the region and type of wood. For example, cedar is cheaper in the eastern region of the United States. [27] However, redwood is far more affordable on the west coast. Wood generally lasts about ten years before the signs of weather damage begin to show. Redwood offers the most resistance to moisture; indeed, water storage tanks were once constructed using this wood. Cedar and redwood contain high levels of tannins that repel termites and rot, even though they are classed as softwood.

Using Wood

Other softwoods include pine, juniper, spruce, and Douglas fir. The average lifespan of softwood is between four and seven years. Hardwood lumber, such as walnut, black locust, teak, oak, beech, maple, hemlock and oak, is denser and more durable.[27] The quality of lumber can be easily assessed by studying the Forest Stewardship Council (FSC) certification, which guarantees that the wood was procured from a forest that was managed well, taking care of social and environmental concerns, and providing economic benefits to the local community.

When constructing the beds, you want to consider how thick you want the sides of your raised beds, and then select the right thickness. Thicker beds last longer than thin ones, as they have greater strength. You may sometimes be advised to seal off the wood to protect it from weathering. Protective sealers protect the wood when the weather is very humid or when there is a high rate of precipitation in the area. If you opt for a sealer, make sure you secure the wood with a natural sealant such as Tung oil.[27] Soft wood is generally suitable for sealers, and it's a good idea to consult the manufacturer's manual to apply a coat of the sealant to secure the wood. In drier areas, wood may not be coated with a sealer, in which case, it fades away to different tones such as pink, amber or gray over time.

Using Metal

Raised beds made from metal are sleek to look at and highly durable. They do not suffer from the adverse effects of moisture that wood does (such as rotting, shrinking or swelling up). Metal beds require minimal maintenance, and keep the soil warm longer than any other material. If you are living in an area with mostly wet climate, then galvanized steel is a great choice for your raised bed.[27] You may never have to worry about the soil getting too hot because even when the metal conducts more heat, the moisture in the soil balances the amount of heat retained. The different options you have when constructing your metal raised bed include using corrugated sides in a wooden frame, using prefabricated metal containers, and using animal feed troughs. Both steel and galvanized metal (coated with zinc) resist corrosion and rust formation, and are suitable for edible crops, but you will need to drill holes to drain water from the bottom of the raised bed. Zinc is also good for your plants as it supports many functions, such as the formation of chlorophyll and the development of roots. A rule of thumb you want to remember is to replace the beds when the interiors show signs of corrosion.

Using Natural Stone

Natural stone is a good choice for your raised beds. Durable without a doubt, stones such as small boulders, cobblestones and flagstone are great stacked up or secured using an adhesive. What I love about using stone, is that you can use your creativity to arrange the stones together to get an interesting look for your vegetable garden. Stones are great at giving your garden an artistic touch, and hold the soil well without suffering any particular impact from the weight or pressure of the soil they're holding.

What to Avoid

An important consideration that dictates your choice material is its safety: for example, the risk of leaching toxic chemicals into the soil, as discussed in the previous chapters. Painted or chemically treated wood is definitely not advisable for edible gardens. Concrete may also contain chemicals that may settle in the soil and get absorbed by plant roots. Heavy metals, arsenic and lead are other toxic contaminants that may harm the soil. Certain materials like old car tires and Styrofoam coolers must also be avoided.[27] Styrofoam coolers contain a material called polystyrene, which is a carcinogen. Old car tires, meanwhile, contain a host of toxic substances, including heavy metals, benzene, and polycyclic aromatic hydrocarbons, and must be avoided as they pose health and environmental hazards.

Choosing the Right Location

Choose a location that offers at least eight hours of sunlight every day. It's okay to select a very sunny spot, as this will allow your plants to thrive in a warm climate. Soggy areas must be avoided at all times, especially places in your garden that are low and wet. You also want to make sure you have easy access to the watering hose to be able to water your garden adequately during your growing season.[30]

Choosing the Soil

When you have chosen the right location, it is relatively easy to get rid of the weeds and fill your raised bed with the soil of your choice, preferably in the combination of 60 percent topsoil, 10 percent potting soil, and 30 percent compost.[30] Soil volume may vary in different areas chosen for the purpose, and it is a good idea to choose an approximate quantity that is a little over your calculated volume. If you don't have access to high quality topsoil, you could select a mix of compost and potting soil as an alternative. Peat moss is also a common addition, and preferred by many gardeners.

If you're interested in a homemade soil blend, then a 50% blend made from your compost with the addition of fish compost, mushroom manure, and animal manure, and combined with 50% screened topsoil consisting of healthy loam is suitable for your raised bed garden. Another option is to use a premium soil blend consisting of one-third vermiculite, one-third peat moss, and one-third compost.

Adding the compost helps to get rid of the weeds, but it needs to be replaced each year.

One popular method of soil building is the lasagna method. [36] This requires you to fill the bottom of your boxes with grass clippings, leaves, organic materials, straw, and wood chips. Next, add a layer of cardboard, and then the soil. Layering the soil in this way causes the mixture to break down and form compost overtime.

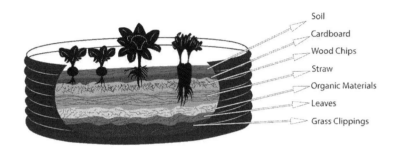

Soil
Cardboard
Wood Chips
Straw
Organic Materials
Leaves
Grass Clippings

Irrigation Options

Measuring Soil Hydration

You don't want to just depend on the rain when it comes to keeping your plants adequately hydrated. One way to find out how much rainfall has occurred is to use a rain gauge. This is not the only measurement that will help you estimate how much more water your crops will require, as soil properties also dictate a lot about the water content.[30] Soils that have more clay tend to hold a lot of water, while sandy soil is not able to hold as much. Loamy soil is a variety of soil that is able to retain moisture and is alsodrain well. A good way to supply adequate water to the plants is to use compost so that the soil holds more water by acting like a sponge.

Another quality of compost is its ability to keep the soil well aerated. Therefore, adding compost is beneficial for clay-based soil, as well as sandy soil. While compost allows sandy soil to hold more water, it keeps the clay-based soil aerated and well-drained. Draining excessive water is essential for plants, as they absorb oxygen through their roots and may struggle to drain when planted in soggy soil. To make sure your bed has the right amount of water, feel the moisture content simply by putting your finger about three inches deep into the soil every week. The finger test is always a good estimate, as wilted leaves may not indicate dehydration, and the plant may employ wilting simply as a strategy to prevent water loss from the surface of its leaves.

The different types of options available to irrigate your raised bed garden include[36]:

- Drip Irrigation: The most popular means of irrigating the raised bed garden is the drip irrigation method, which is built by a network of hoses that have holes for water to trickle and drip into the soil slowly.
- Sprinkler Irrigation: A sprinkler has holes attached to the end of a hose, which are used to spray water.
- Soaker Hose: A soaker hose is a porous hose that can soak out water along its full length. The hose is

placed in such a way that water can percolate to all parts of the raised bed.

- Wicking: Wicking is the method of filling up a porous reservoir under the soil. The reservoir is set up to wick out water into the soil at a slow pace. A special type of primitive olla pot or special garden bed is used for the purpose.
- Hand Watering: The traditional method of irrigation is hand watering, which is accomplished by watering the bed with a sprayer or using a hand-held nozzle.

It is also a good idea to invest in one of several automated irrigation systems, such as a timed sprinkler system,[30] water wands, drip irrigation systems, and soaker hoses.

Preparing the Raised Bed Area

Most of the time, you are unlikely to find the perfect ground to build your raised bed. There will usually be shrubs, weeds or turf growing on the land. This will require you to prepare a decent space for your plants to breathe and thrive in the natural surroundings.[34] Here are a few considerations when looking at planting your garden when it does not look like the perfect space for your plants.

- If your space has lawn, then get rid of the turf using a sod cutter. If you're on a tight budget, then using a shovel will give you the same result.
- When you have taken away all the grass and found a clean space for your garden, you want to consider

keeping the grass, as it will turn into compost for your plants after a few months.

- If the area has weeds, you may not achieve the desired smooth surface by just pulling them out. The best solution for getting rid of weeds is solarizing 2-3 inches below the surface of the soil. You want to allow about two or three weeks to do this so that the weeds and their seeds are destroyed and do not regrow. The best time to embark on solarization is in the summer, as the process uses trapped moisture and heat. To solarize an area, mow it, soak it, and then cover with a plastic sheet. Seal the edges, or bury them into the soil about an inch deep so that no moisture escapes. Check the plastic throughout the summer, and make sure you repair any gaps and holes with duct tape to keep the moisture in. Leave the plastic for about two months, during which time, any weeds as deep as 3 inches in the soil will be killed.

- If the area has shrubs growing, you want to take them off by digging or grinding them. You don't want to worry about the stumps or roots left behind, as you will be using a raised bed to prepare the growth medium for your plants. The parts of the shrubs left over after grinding will eventually break down and add more nutrients to your soil. Tilling is another method you can use to make a level ground for your raised bed. It comes with certain disadvantages, however, such as a loss of soil structure elements.

- Hardscaped locations such as parking lots and sidewalks can also prove useful as raised beds. When you want to use a hardscaped surface, you want to make sure there is enough room for water to drain out easily. Deep beds are your best options, and a cardboard layer may not work well, as it is likely to get soaked and disintegrate. Another material that may impede the water drainage is gravel, which may not allow water to travel well from a denser area to a less dense area.

How to Build a Simple 4x8 Foot Raised Bed

The following step-by-step process will show you how exactly you can go about constructing a 4x8 foot raised bed[32]:

- Mark a rectangle with the dimensions 4x8 where you would like to build the raised bed.
- Level this area by removing unwanted material such as turf, weeds or shrubs.
- Get two 8-foot 2x12 boards, and two 4-foot 2x12 boards. Screw the boards together at the corners using 3 ½ -inch long deck screws. You want to pre-drill the holes so that the wood doesn't split during construction.
- Make sure the frame fixes well onto the chosen area. If there are any irregularities in the ground underneath, then you want to scrape out some of the

soil with a shovel, and make sure your raised bed fits well and is level.

- Fill the frame with a mixture of potting mix and soil. If you're on a tight budget, you can make do with a mixture of 50% compost and 50% native soil, without spending a single extra dollar.
- Wind a 25-foot soaker up and down your raised bed to soak the soil well and water your plants adequately. Use pins to secure the soaker hose in place. You want to use the pins meant for landscape fabric, or make your own pins by bending a 1-foot long bailing wire in half.
- Plant your chosen crops along the hose, and add mulch to the top of the soil to make sure it retains enough moisture.
- Turn on the soaker hose, and water the raised bed. You could also use a sprinkler irrigation system to keep the soil moist.

Quick-Fix Formula for Raised Bed Building: A Quick Recap

Now that you know the quickest way to build a decent raised bed for your vegetables, fruits and herbs, it's time to learn the finer points to make your plan a success.[25]

- You want to make sure you either select wood that isn't pressure-treated, or go for brick, blocks or stone to avoid toxins finding their way into the soil and affecting your plants.

- The standard width recommended for raised beds is 4 feet. You may, however, want to use a smaller size for your raised bed so that you're able to access it from all sides. When you want more room for your plants to grow, you want to build a couple of raised beds with a maximum width of 4 feet.

- Capping the end-grain is an important practice to prevent the water from getting absorbed into the post and rotting and disintegrating it. Use decorative caps to cover the tops of your posts to prevent the water and moisture from seeping in.

- Invest in high-quality soil to avoid problems in the long run. For example, soil that has too much sand in it is likely to turn into concrete overtime. Covering with mulch is also a good way to maintain your soil quality. Too much compost or herbicide also contaminates the soil, which may need replacement, as it tends to hinder the healthy growth of plants otherwise.

Installation Tips and Final Details

It's always a good idea to select a wide range of vegetables such as tomatoes, lettuce, carrots, cucumbers, peppers, potatoes, onions, leeks and herbs. [30].Productivity is a key consideration in raised bed gardening, so you want to plant as many varieties of crop as possible, while giving each of your plants enough space to grow and spread. It's also important to keep in mind that plants grow to different heights in different regions. For example, the vines of a bush watermelon grow to about 3 to 4 feet, while those of Ruby, which is a full-size watermelon, grow to about 15 feet. Furthermore, tomatoes grow to different heights in different locations – while they grow to about 7 feet in Texas, the typical height is just 4 feet in Vermont.

When planting different species side-by-side, it's a good idea to consider their growth pattern – climbing, trailing, or bushy, for instance – so you can estimate how they will affect their neighboring plants. As an example, lettuce and cucumber should not be planted together, but it's a good idea to plant lettuce with carrots. Plants compete for space in a raised bed, and you want to use cages, stakes, or other similar installations to keep the plants apart and prevent them from encroaching on each other's space, making sure the vegetable garden is more manageable.[30]

Another great way to achieve a faster harvest is to start growing with plants rather than planting seeds and waiting for them to germinate. Doing so helps you achieve the harvest almost a month in advance.[30] This way of planting is also good for protecting the plants from frost. When plants have a short growing season, such as about 100 days (as is the case for peppers or tomatoes), there is no way you can get a mature plant before the frost begins if you start from seed. This is when it makes sense to start your project with a baby plant rather than a seed. It also makes sense to start growing with baby plants when you're just planning to have one or two plants of a certain species. The plants that will do well from seed include root vegetables such as beets, carrots, salad greens, corn, squash, cucumbers, peas and beans. Finally, most gardeners prefer to grow potatoes from tubers, while onions may be grown directly from their seeds.

The time you plant your crops is as important as any other consideration in raised bed gardening. You want to consider what type of plants you want in your raised bed garden, since some plants can tolerate cold weather, while others cannot. Broccoli and lettuce are some examples of plants that can be grown in cold weather, while tomatoes and basil cannot survive temperatures below 40 degrees.[30] The dangers of frost are most prominent between March and May, and you want to make sure you avoid planting cold-sensitive plants during this season. Furthermore, gardeners who prefer to plant in warm climates start their projects in the fall as opposed to the spring season, as they are able to avoid the midsummer heat. The other option is to take advantage of two periods for planting –i.e. late winter and early fall.

The ideal soil temperature for plants is 60 to 70 degrees F, which is considered moderate, while certain other plants grow well in cool soil which has a temperature close to about 45 degrees F. Crops such as melons and eggplants will only germinate when soil temperatures reach about 60 degrees F.

Watering the plants on a constant basis is important when you're starting out in order to keep the soil moist and provide an ideal medium for plant growth. This practice also allows seeds the required time to soften their outer coat and germinate over several days by gradually absorbing the water.[30] When you don't water the raised bed adequately, there is a chance that the seed may not germinate as expected, and you may have to reseed. A popular way to keep the soil moist is by covering it with shade netting or some other fabric to prevent the water from evaporating very quickly.

Seedlings should be planted during calmer weather conditions as a windy and sunny environment can cause harm to the seedlings. Protecting the seedlings from excessive heat allows them to grow roots to the right depth, where they are able to absorb the nutrients from the soil.

Intensive planting is a good strategy for keeping weeds at bay. Whenever you spot weeds growing in between your plants, make sure you get rid of them immediately to make sure they're not competing for moisture, space and nutrients. Fertilizers may only be required during the midseason, and a water-soluble fertilizer with fish emulsion, humic acid and seaweed works best for most plants.,[30] [36] A few key points to keep in mind include:

- The best orientation for a raised bed is the longer side facing south, which ensures that all plants receive equal sunlight. When the other side of the bed happens to face south, the taller plants may block some of the light and leave the shorter ones in the shade.
- If you're using a portion of the ground that is not generally used for gardening, then you want to dig about 16 inches and turn over the soil, remove rocks and unwanted material, and then compact the soil at

the center. This leaves an even edge along the sides to set up your raised bed evenly.

- Add compost, lime and peat to your soil, and then spread the soil across your bed. Spray water over the bed evenly, and add more soil to the top of the bed. Rake the bed to get an even layer of soil, and start planting.

- Burrowing pests are a nuisance in most raised-bed gardens. The best option to prevent pests such as moles is to use a galvanized mesh across the bottom of your raised bed so that it continues about 3 inches upward, along the sides of the bed.

- You want to level the bed, as the soil may not be the same after several waterings. You will also need to use a stiff board along the length and width to get the correct level reading and make sure the bed stays the same.

- Avoid stepping on the soil in your raised bed (and train your pets to stay off the bed too), as this may compact the soil and limit aeration, adversely affecting root growth.

- There may be roots growing under your raised beds, and it's a good idea to pull them out prior to planting your garden. Roots from other trees and plants will steal the nutrients you added in measured quantities, leaving your crops undernourished. If there are trees with roots protruding into your space, then you want to install a barrier to keep them from encroaching into your garden.

- As discussed in the previous chapters, leave space for

pathways between beds, and mulch them to prevent weeds from growing. Keep them wide enough for the wheelbarrow or the mower.

- Harvesting can begin as soon as you feel a crop is ready to eat. You want to pluck them out just before their peak ripeness to get the best flavor.
- To maintain the crops, remove diseased or damaged plant material, spent foliage, and pests that may be harming your plants.
- Provide support to plants whenever they need it, and tidy up your garden regularly.
- To ensure healthy and productive plants, fertilize them regularly using an organic and granular fertilizer. The best times for fertilization are at the time of planting the crop and during the midseason.

4

THE WHAT AND WHEN OF
PLANTING: PLANNING, ORDERING,
AND SOWING

P lan Meticulously for a Sustainable Raised Bed Garden

Seed shortages are a common occurrence, and you need to plan well if you want to harvest at the right time of the year. Raised bed gardening is a popular pursuit among many gardeners, and consequently, placing an order for seeds only a season ahead may not really work. You could try to get the seeds you want from gardening stores, but there is no guarantee you'll secure the seeds you desire.

You want to plan at least a year in advance to make sure you have all your supplies in place at the right time.[44] Having a chart of all the activities essential to maintaining your raised bed garden, including soil composition, planting condition, crop rotation, and vegetable selection, helps you keep track of all the important information and carry out your gardening successfully.

Your Family's Preferences

Factor in the likes and dislikes of your family when you plan your garden. You may want to have some extra vegetables to share or trade with your neighbors, and it's a good idea to make space for them in one of your raised beds. Perhaps you want to invest your time and effort in growing something that matures faster, allowing you to gain more time and more crop cycles.[44] Maybe your family doesn't need many tomatoes, and you'll be better off planting just a few plants, rather than having a whole bed full of tomato plants. Whatever your preferences, be guided by these rather than the idea that you must grow a particular amount of any crop – after all, it's your garden.

Growing Conditions

Having a good harvest depends not on the number of plants you're growing, but rather on the quality of plants, the soil, and the growing conditions. The produce from your crops can double when the plants are provided with the right soil enrichment and proper care throughout the season. The most surprising part is that when you have the right conditions for plant growth, you may need only half as many seeds. [44] Finally, spacing the plants out properly will ensure that they get the right quantity of nutrients and can produce a good crop.

Seed Varieties

Purchasing seeds is one important consideration for the eager gardener. You're at an advantage when you buy larger packages of seeds and store them well. If you already have favorites from growing vegetables in your backyard, continue using the varieties you like.[44] Store seeds under ideal temperature conditions, as discussed in the next section.

Observation and Recording

A good garden can be organized by maintaining a folder with all entries pertaining to the time for planting, conditions, and the seeds used. Staying organized is good for the productivity of your garden, observing all aspects of gardening and recording them. Making a note of new and creative ideas for the whole year has the added bonus of making a great journal for you and your children.

Here's another checklist to refer to before starting out, just to be sure you have everything in place.[41] You want to include this comprehensive list of things when planning your vegetable garden for the coming year. This will let you know when to sow seeds, how to rotate crops, and how to make a succession planting schedule.

Sunlight: Look for a site with enough light (eight hours of full sunlight). When you cannot find a spot like this, you are better off with vegetables that can thrive when there's less light, such as green leafy vegetables.

Bed Size: Select a convenient bed size, such as 4x8 feet, to reach all parts of the bed throughout the planting cycle. Leave the right space for pathways between beds, as discussed in previous chapters.

Growing Season: Vegetable gardening can be carried out in the cold, warm or cool seasons. The cool season lasts through fall and spring, and has a temperature between 40 and 70 degree Fahrenheit, with a good amount of moisture. The most suitable vegetables for this season include green leafy vegetables, carrots, broccoli, beets and cabbage. You are all set for an enjoyable gardening experience with few insects and mosquitoes troubling you. Garden pests are few during the cool season.

The warm season lasts between spring and the beginning of the fall frost. Vegetables grown during the warm season cannot tolerate frost, and require warmth to be able to thrive through the season. The best vegetables to grow during this season include cucumber, tomatoes, squash and pepper.

The cold season is long and cold, and your best choice of crops could be winter salad greens, kale, leeks, carrots and scallions. Crops planted in the cold season are transplanted in mid-to-late summer.

Small Spaces: Small spaces can be utilized with small containers, or by growing dwarf plants or space-saving varieties of plants. Some examples of space saving varieties of plants include the 'Patio Baby' eggplant and the 'Patio Snacker' cucumber.

Seed Planting Timing: The dates for starting your garden or transplanting are between spring and fall frost dates, on average. Plant your cool season crops some weeks before the last spring frost, and plant your warm season crops after the last frost date. Indoor plants also depend on frost dates, as you want to calculate when to start based on when your spring frost is expected. On the other hand, cold season vegetables are planted based on first fall frost, and not the spring frost.

Soil Test: Feeding the soil is a must for a sustainable garden. When you do the feeding, you want to test it after a few years, and repeat the cycle to find out what organic nutrients you need to add to the soil to continue to nourish it. Key ingredients to add to your soil are composted seaweed, organic granular fertilizer, and aged manure. Add the nutrients when you start planting, as well as between the crops. Test the soil for pH, as most crops grow well when the pH is between 6.0 and 7.0. Acidic soils generally require lime in the appropriate quantities to obtain an ideal pH for plant growth.

Succession Planting: Plan so that you know what to plant when one of your crops has been harvested. Follow the harvest months of summer, fall and winter before starting out to stay organized with succession planting. Once you have the list of plants for each season, you want to make a plan by the month to stay on schedule.

Crop Rotation: Rotating crops according to a specific schedule helps prevent depletion of nutrients and protects your crops against pests. Having a 3-4 year rotation schedule works best. To rotate the crops effectively, group them by family, and then rotate the family. For example, you want to group kale, cabbage, broccoli, radish, turnip, and the like under the cabbage family. On the other hand, squashes, cucumbers, and melons go under the gourd family.

Pests and Disease: Choose insect-resistance and disease-resistant varieties of seeds, rotate your crops, and use lightweight barriers to protect them from pests. If you have animals invading your garden, then an electric fence may work best. Deer netting also works for small spaces, and an insect barrier fabric protects against insects.

Seed Tips to Keep in Mind

Understanding the different seed varieties and storing them well, as discussed above, is important to maintaining a sustainable raised bed garden. Here are a few other considerations with regard to choosing the right seeds for your garden.

- Diverse Seed Varieties: Further to the season-specific crops, you can even go for unusual global crops, such as amaranth, or those that offer a higher degree of resistance to disease and insects, such as 'mountain magic' or 'defiant' varieties of tomatoes, or 'Amazel' if you want to have basil in your garden.[44]
- Easy Seeds for Beginners: If you're just starting out, you want to pick some easy vegetables, such as radish, beet, pepper, spinach, peas, green beans and kale. It's also a good idea to plant flowering plants such as marigolds to keep the pests away and make sure pollination occurs in time.[45]
- Seed Classification: There are different types of

seeds to choose from, but the most basic classifications are short-lived, medium-lived, and long-lived seeds. Some examples of short-lived seeds include leeks, onion, spinach, parsnip and corn. Pumpkin, peas, carrots, celery, beans, eggplant, squash, and parsley are medium-lived seeds. While short-lived seeds last just a year or two, medium-lived seeds last as for as long as five years.[44] Long-lived seeds such as radish, melon, turnips, lettuce, cabbage, collards, broccoli, cauliflower, and Brussels sprouts easily last more than five years. Your local seed company will have the right selection of seeds that are suitable to grow in your area.

- Storing Seeds: When you have collected all the seeds for your raised bed garden, label them properly with the date and name, and store them in resealable bags in a cool, dry area. The ideal temperature to store seeds is 40 to 50 degrees Fahrenheit, and you will need to add a desiccant if you find there is too much moisture in the air.[44] Finally, maintain a gardening folder to keep track of your planting endeavors so you can easily remember where you are with your yearly progression.

Spacing

The best source of information on the spacing required for your plants is the seed packet, as it will list the width and height of the mature plants, as well as how much spacing the seeds will require. An effective way to plant your vegetables is by intensive gardening, as it allows them to stay close as opposed to spaced equally in rows.[23] This allows you to water your garden less frequently, and also limits the growth of weeds. As the plants grow, they maintain good air circulation, which helps to curb disease.

Experts suggest different spacing for every type of plant. The recommended spacing for asparagus is 12-18 inches, while onions require just 3-4 inches. Turnips require 2-4 inches, but pumpkins can grow to a good size, and require about 24-36 inches between them. The spacing for mustard is 3-4 inches, and for lettuce leaves, it is about 3-6 inches. Brussels sprouts require about 15-18 inches, just like cabbage, which is also 15-18 inches between the plants. The spacing for dill is 6-8 inches, while parsley requires 4-6 inches of space.[42]

You will find the spacing required for both the plants you choose online and those you buy offline in the form of published diagrams from expert gardeners. One such simple illustration, based on the recommendations from K-State Research and Extension of the Johnson County, is depicted below. You want to have a similar plan, preferably hand-drawn or printed, for all the crops you plan for the year in order to avoid a last minute rush.

Another effective method is the square foot gardening method.[23] In this method, you divide the raised bed into 1x1 foot squares. You plant one species of seed per square foot. The number of seeds for each square foot depends on the plant size. If your plant grows longer and wider over the growing season, then you want to have a less dense square-foot bed for the seeds. On the other hand, if your plant won't get that large, you want to increase the density of seeds to maximize your produce.

Just like any other garden, you require an area with enough sunlight, where you can build your raised bed using the material of your choice. You want to put your measures in place to increase the life and durability of your chosen material, and fill it up with the ideal soil combination you figured out for your plants. When you have the bed filled with soil, you should set up the grid with wood or string.[43] Finally, plant your chosen seeds in each square foot, and apply the techniques you learned to water your garden and maintain it. More information on choosing your plants, watering, and harvesting is covered in the chapters that follow.

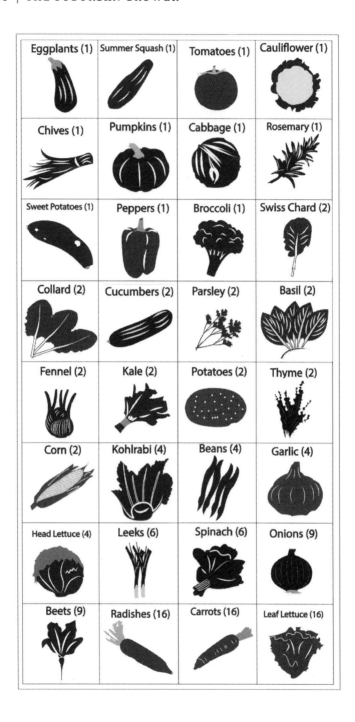

Planting Tips

Planting is the most important activity in setting up your raised bed garden. Here are the key aspects you want to consider when planting your garden.[23] [38] [40] These tips were covered in detail in the previous chapters: they're summarized here to make sure you don't miss out on anything.

- Direction of the Sun's Rays: Look for the direction of the sun to make sure you're not planting the taller crops in front of the shorter ones, and that all plants get enough light to grow well. You can look for the information on plant width and height on the seed packets before you decide exactly where to place the seeds.
- Compact Plant Varieties: A great way to plant is to choose compact plants that sprawl. Many traditional varieties of plants will take up most of the space in your raised bed, but when you choose the compact variety, they will just take up a section of the area.
- Flowers for Pollination: When you have a couple of flowers in your vegetable garden, such as marigold, nasturtium and alyssum, you can relax while they attract pollinators and help you combat pests.
- Succession Planting: Another important characteristic of the vegetable garden is that a single crop is not the end of your planting. Succession planting is made easy by choosing the right crops.

For example, cucumbers and tomatoes grow well in summer heat. When you harvest your peas, your next step is to use the same space for root vegetables such as carrots, and harvest the crop in the fall season. Peas, which mature early, may be followed by eggplant. Basil, broccoli, radish, beet, lettuce, kale, turnip and mustard are some of the most suitable vegetables for succession planting.

- Staggered Planting: A good strategy to increase your yield is staggered planting. Many times, the crop you plant at the beginning of summer may give you a good yield for the first and second time, followed by lesser and lesser yield during the rest of the summer months. You can maximize your yield by planting part of the row when the season starts, and then planting the rest of the seeds after about two or four weeks have passed. This means you will have mature crops ready to harvest every few weeks, and you can replant the area with the same crop or different crops to continue getting fresh produce throughout the season.

- Intercropping: Another great way to add more plants to the raised bed and make it more productive is intercropping. Intercropping refers to pairing plants in your vegetable garden. This means that two or more crops will grow closely in the same space, mostly in the same row. For example, beans, corn and squash are good examples of crops you could choose for intercropping.

- Maturity Rates: Another way to increase the yield of

your crop is to use the maturity of your chosen plants in an informed manner. When you make a choice of the crops you want to plant, look for information on when they mature: early season, mid-season, or late season. This information is usually available on the seed packet. Different varieties of the same plant have different maturity rates. Some of these vegetables include cabbage, corn, tomatoes, carrots, cauliflower, eggplant, peas and Brussels sprouts.

Layout Ideas

Arranging the crops in the right way is an important skill, and goes a long way towards ensuring they get the right amount of sunlight, water and space to grow. Here are a few important guidelines on arranging your crops in your raised-bed garden:

- Plant your crops according to the season: peas, lettuce and broccoli are the cold-season crops; peppers, tomatoes and cucumbers are the warm-season crops. The rationale behind choosing the crops in this way is to ensure that the soil is warmed up to the right degree for each crop, and this happens only when you match your crop to the season.
- Tall crops must be planted on the north side of your garden so that the shorter plants get enough sunlight. If it so happens that a portion of your garden

remains in the shade for most of the day, have the cool-season vegetables take up that space.

- Crops that mature quickly have a short harvest period, and those that take some time to mature have a longer harvest period. For example, bush beans mature very quickly, and have a small harvest period. On the other hand, tomatoes take some time to reach full maturity, and produce during a longer window.

- As mentioned earlier, you want to stagger your crops, planting every few months to ensure a year-long harvest and great produce from your garden.

Here's an example of a proposed arrangement of the vegetables for a 4x8 raised bed garden by Tara Nolan of *Savvy Gardening*.[23]

When to Plant

As you move closer to the big day, there's one last thing you want to be careful about before you begin planting: the ideal time to plant your crops. Here are a few considerations that will go a long way in giving you a productive garden:

- Look at what the vegetable encyclopedia says about the season your chosen vegetables can tolerate well. [39] Also consider your growing zone according to the USDA zone map.[37]

- Use the guidelines on the seed packets to determine the most favorable conditions to plant your seeds.

- Water your bed deeply and thoroughly after planting the seeds, and make sure your soil retains moisture.

More information on watering is covered in the preceding chapters.

- Transplant your seedlings in a cool and calm area. When seedlings are young, they may not fare well in a hot, windy and sunny spot. Cover them with garden fabric if you can't find a suitable spot to transplant them.

5

WHAT TO GROW PART 1:
VEGETABLES

Your choice of crops depends on your tastes and the likes and dislikes of your family members. Experimenting with the easy crops when you start as a new gardener can be a lot of fun. Start with the vegetables and crops that are easy to grow: you will get a sense of success with the choices that you make, even with little effort.

Low Maintenance Crops

The following vegetables often work best for novice gardeners:

<u>Bush Beans</u>: Bush beans are also known as 'common beans'. They grow into small bushes, no more than 2 feet in height. They are native to Latin America, and widely grown in Argentina. Subtropical climate works well for them, as frost impedes their growth. Bush beans must be sown into the soil directly, as opposed to being transplanted.[53] They require a

minimal soil depth of 8 inches, and an optimal temperature of 70-80 degrees Fahrenheit. The best soil type for bush beans is silt loam or clay with slightly acidic or neutral pH (between 6.0 and7.0). Use a soil that drains well and is rich in organic matter.

Sowing is simple, and you want to keep the seeds an inch below the soil and 3 inches apart. Plant the seeds in an area that receives six to eight hours of sunlight, and space out the rows so that there is about 18-24 inches of space for the plants to thrive. After planting the seeds, tap gently to level out the soil. Water with a sprinkler, and wait about 8-10 days for them to germinate. Soil temperature that is less than 60 degrees Fahrenheit causes the seeds to germinate in about two weeks.[53] It's always a good idea to plant when the temperature is warm, as you have a lower risk of the seeds rotting away.

Do not till the soil, and do not add too much nitrogen fertilizer. Instead, use organic compost, sheep manure, or worm castings to add the required nutrients to the soil. Your soil needs enough moisture for germination, but waterlogging must be avoided. To make sure you have a regular supply of pods, continue to harvest every now and then. The time required for the crop to mature is about 45-65 days.

Bush beans are available in many varieties, and you can explore the benefits of each of them in order to select the one that works best for you. Make sure you keep away rabbits and deer by using fences. Insects can be kept at bay with some herb plantations around your crop.[53] Aphids can be sprayed away with water jets, washing off the leaves, and beetles can be simply picked up and disposed of in soapy water. Fungal diseases will require infected plants to be removed to prevent the disease from spreading.

Peas: Fresh peas, rich in fiber, iron and protein, mature fastest in spring. The bush varieties grow to a height of about 16-30 inches, while the tall types may grow even higher than 3 feet. Trellising is a common technique used to contain the bush varieties, while the taller ones need support. Different seeds provide different produce.[51] For example, the heirloom variety gives you 7-foot tall plants with delectable pods in a non-edible shell. The edible shell pods, like the sugar snap, contain tiny peas, and the plants grow 28 inches in height.

To sow the seeds, prepare a well-drained soil bed containing organic matter. The ideal pH for peas is 6.0-7.5. Plant the seeds about 1.0-1.5 inches beneath the soil, and maintain a distance of 12-18 inches between the rows. Irrigate the bed with plenty of water, and add phosphorus to the soil for best results.[51] You will not require a nitrogen supplement, as the plants gather their own nitrogen.

Pull out the weeds when necessary. Use neem oil to treat aphids when they appear, and use an insecticide spray to get rid of mildew. Fresh pods can be eaten immediately. It's also a great idea to leave the pods to dry, and you can use the dry peas to make soups for a whole year.[51] Edible peas can be picked when they are tender.

Cherry Tomato: Cherry tomatoes can keep your family happy right through spring and fall. They are a delightful sight to look at with all the color varieties available, including red, pink, chocolate, yellow, and mahogany. They have a mild, tangy taste, and grow to about 2 inches in diameter.[61] Their maturity rates differ, with some varieties ready for harvesting in just 45 days, while others take 80 days to ripen. The average time window for the harvest is 55-65 days. Their varieties are classified as heirloom, hybrid and heirloom hybrid.

If you are using seeds to start the crop, then you need to plant them six weeks before the last frost date. They may be transplanted outdoors six weeks after the last frost date, when the plants are 12 weeks old. When you have planted the seeds, install the required support to help your plants grow well. Maintain a soil pH of 6.2-6.5, and pick a location that gets at least six hours of sunlight during the day. Adding Epsom salt or lime when planting helps to prevent problems with rot or blossom.[61]

Make sure you pull out "suckers" that grow between the main stalk and branches. Feed the plants twice a week with an 18-1-21 tomato formula, and deep-water them every week. Tomatoes get their ripe color about 10 weeks after pollination, and can be picked every day or every alternate day. Doing so maximizes your produce.

Summer Squash: Your garden never seems quite complete without zucchini and a couple of varieties of summer squash. Squashes come in several different varieties: the scalloped squash grow about 5 inches across, and resemble a spaceship. They come in several colors, from creamy white to bright yellow, ideal for roasting and stews. Other popular varieties are the zucchini, bright yellow squash, and the black beauty.

The ideal soil pH for squash is 6.0-6.5, and you want to space the plants out depending on whether they will grow into bushes or vines. The bush variety goes well with the rest of the vegetables in your raised bed garden.[59] If you plan on using seeds, start the seedlings in summer, about three or four weeks before transplantation. Seeds germinate in 8 days, with a soil temperature of about 70 degrees Fahrenheit. If you plan on growing bushes, sow the seeds about a half inch deep, and space rows closely, with no more than about 2-3 foot gaps between the plants. In the case of vines, seeds must be planted about 2 inches apart, and the vines must be allowed to spread out. Water them well, and observe if the leaves wilt during the day, which is a sign that they need more water. Avoid watering at night, as mold and rot can set in easily. Use slacker hoses if you don't want to water in the hot sun.

Soil with compost or fish emulsion works well with squash. Plant the crops in the same area, and practice crop rotation. It's always better not to use the plots you used for cucumber or melons, as any diseases may affect your squashes quickly. [59] Mold affects all plants, and can be avoided by watering them from the ground, or spacing them apart. Vine borers may cause the stems to break, and the affected pieces must be discarded at the earliest. Rot and blossom can be treated with lime, and the overuse of potash or nitrogen fertilizers should be avoided. It's good to mulch the soil to help it retain moisture and calcium.

Summer squashes can be picked when they are about 4-5 inches long. Slice out the fruit from the vine without pulling at it. Even the squash blossoms are edible, and can be enjoyed fried, but make sure you leave some of the blossoms on the plant as they are required for the production of further fruit.[59]

Cucumber: Crunchy cucumbers are a must-have for your salads, and their anti-inflammatory properties make them chosen popular vegetable in many gardens. Cucumbers fall into two categories: one used for the slicing and the other for pickling. The perfect soil for cucumbers is sandy soil, but any well-drained soil is good enough to grow them.[52]You want to maintain an ideal pH of 5.8-6.5 for your crop.

Cucumbers may spread out or need a trellis to climb. They have deep tap roots that need at least 3-4 feet of space beneath the plant. Seeds should be planted an inch deep, and the germination takes about five to 10 days. Seedlings may be transplanted 2 feet away, leaving 4 feet of space between the rows.[52] You want to use organic mulch for your raised bed, as it retains moisture and stunts the growth of weeds.

Weekly watering is required for a healthy cucumber crop, and drip irrigation is the preferred method. Watering sufficiently produces a good flavor in the fruit. Pull out the weeds promptly as you see them, and apply a nitrogen fertilizer in the quantity of ¼ cup per 10 feet in the row.[52]

Use a jet of water to get rid of the aphids, and treat any beetle invasion using a chemical treatment. Other diseases that may affect your cucumber crop include mildew, virus, or wilt disease.

The typical time to harvest is in 50-70 days, and you are good to go 10 days after the female flowers bloom. Crisp and tender cucumbers taste best, and the large ones often turn bitter. Harvest them regularly to encourage continuous produce.[52]

Garlic: Growing garlic is easier than you might think. Garlic is good for digestion, and has healing properties. Garlic bulbs grow perennially, just like shallots, onions and leeks. Garlic grows to an average height of 18-24 inches, and gives out a strong aroma.[64] Garlic blooms appear in white and pink, attracting pollinators in late spring. Mature bulbs are used for further propagation, and produce larger bulbs. There are two varieties of garlic: the softneck and the hardneck. Softnecks are easier to grow, are more productive, and last longer. Hardneck stalks are rigid, and remain upright.

Garlic can also be grown from seed. It requires fertile and well-drained soil, and loam works well with garlic. Garlic requires well-drained soil, with a pH of 6.0-7.5. For acidic pH soils, it is highly recommended to add lime a couple of weeks before planting. It requires a sunny area, and temperatures of 40-50 degrees Fahrenheit lasting 6-12 weeks during winter. Garlic requires a long period for growth, and spring sowing is not recommended.[64] Plant the bulbs at a depth of 2 inches, with the pointed tip upward, leaving about 4-6 inches between two successive rows. Firm the soil after planting, but do not compact it. Fertilize when growth starts after spring, and every 30 days after that, with an all-purpose fertilizer such as 5-5-5 or 10-10-10 ratio for nitrogen, phosphorus and potassium. Use granular fertilizer for the whole bed. Use a 6-inch mulch to protect against frost, cold and wind, resist weed growth, and retain soil moisture.

It is time to harvest when the lower leaves have yellowed, withered and died. Garlic has a high sulphur content, and can repel pests and fungus. You can get rid of aphids, moths, rabbits, deer, beetles, flies and gnats by having garlic spread all over your garden.[64] The plants that benefit from the properties of garlic include eggplant, spinach, carrots, beets, roses, peppers, thyme, kale and dill, to name just a few.

You want to protect your crop from basal rot by avoiding planting the damaged cloves. Downy mildew is another area of concern, which is the result of too much water or plants being too close together. The way to get around this problem is through good air circulation, drainage, and proper spacing.[64] Fungal infections such as Penicillium decay may be treated by drying cloves thoroughly. White rot is a potential problem, which affects the stem and bulbs, and requires prompt removal of infected plants.

The time to harvest is a few weeks after summer, when bulbs mature and foliage stops growing. September is usually the time in the US to pull out your bulbs. To pull out without damaging the plant, loosen the soil around the bulb. Brush off the soil, and clip the roots to store the bulbs. Garlic leaves and immature bulbs are also edible parts of the plant.[64] Garlic bulbs can be dried by hanging them in a dry area with good circulation of air. The process can take anywhere between four and six weeks, and is known as curing.

The healing properties of garlic are due to its compound allicin, which is activated 10 minutes after crushing it, and is effective against fungi, bacteria and viruses. Garlic must be consumed quickly before the allicin oxidizes. Temperatures above 140 degrees Fahrenheit render it ineffective.[64]

Leaf Lettuce: Leaf lettuce grows easily, and is full of nutrients, particularly, potassium and Vitamin A. Plant lettuces in early spring in loamy, well-drained soil, enriched with organic matter. Maintain a soil pH of 5.8-6.5 for good germination rates for the seeds. Leaf lettuce grows with shallow roots, and must be protected from weeds and water stress. One way to reduce weeds is by preparing the soil a few weeks before planting, allowing weeds to grow, uprooting them, and bringing the seeds to the surface to remove them.[62] Sow seeds in a successive manner; germination begins about 7-10 days after sowing. Lettuce seeds are small, and can be spaced 4-8 inches apart when they are a few inches in height, if required. Sow the next batch after some weeks, and keep them moist. In this way, you will have multiple rows of lettuce after every two weeks all through your growing season.

It's easy to get rid of aphids by spraying jets of water. Planting onions between lettuces also keeps the aphids at bay. Sprinkle finely ground egg shells around the plants to deter slugs and cutworms, and use a fence to keep rabbits and deer away from your crop.[62] Sometimes, the leaves may look scorched at the tips: if this happens, check whether the water content and pH levels are appropriate.

Several varieties of lettuce are available, including "Grand Rapids" and "Lollo Rosso."

Fast-Growing Vegetables

Succession planting for the spring, summer and fall months is a good way to accommodate fast-growing varieties in your vegetable garden, such as leaf lettuce, arugula, turnips and radish. These varieties, when planted one after the other, increase productivity and minimize the growth of weeds.[54] Using this strategy, you may like to plant spinach and peas to be harvested in May and June, followed by planting beets, lettuce, and bush beans.

Baby Kale: Kale has numerous health benefits, and helps to prevent several chronic diseases, such as heart disease, diabetes and cancer. It is a rich source of vitamins and minerals, and has a rich flavor. Start planting kale seeds about 5-7 weeks prior to the frost, in a bed with a minimum depth of 12 inches. Seeds may be planted about half an inch deep in loamy soil with a pH of about 5.6-6.8. Pick an area that has sunlight for at least 8-10 hours per day, and water the plants well. Frost makes the kale sweeter, and hot climate under shade makes it bitter. If you see the leaves rotting, add about 6 inches of mulch and an organic fertilizer to keep cutworms, aphids, flea beetles, and cabbage worms away. Pick the withered leaves, and support the plant with bamboo sticks.[50] Harvesting begins 70-95 days after sowing the seed, and 55-75 days after transplanting. Start harvesting the leaves by cutting the stems at the crown when they are about the size of your palm. Store the leaves you want to consume, and use the rest for compost.

Asian Greens: Asian greens come in different flavors, textures and shapes. Sow the cold-season variety at the end of summer for them to proliferate in autumn and the following months. Sowing after every few weeks gives a steady supply of leaves. Prepare the soil by sprinkling an organic fertilizer and raking it. Sow the seeds about an inch deep, and space the rows about 6-10 inches apart.[63] Water the plants well. Take away the weeds as they appear, and remove the slugs to protect the leaves. Cover with an insect mesh to protect against flea beetles and pigeons. Harvest the greens by cutting at the base of the plant, but leave some leaves in order for the plant to recover.

Arugula: Arugula is a fast-growing plant for the cool season. Its peppery leaves are often added to salads. It is also a medicinal plant, and useful in reducing inflammation of the skin and promoting hair growth. Arugula comes in different varieties, such as wild arugula and rocket arugula. Seeds can be planted as soon as the soil is ready in the spring. They can be planted in sunny areas or in partial shade, about ¼ inch deep, in rows that are set about 10 inches apart. Seeds may also be broadcasted, and germination happens after a few days. To have a continual harvest, sow once again in late summer, after the spring crop has finished. Keep the soil moist, and water frequently.[46] Harvesting is possible only a few weeks after the seeds are sown. Pick leaves in the evening to avoid them wilting. Pick the leaves when the plant begins to flower and bolt. Delaying the picking may cause them to get bitter. Small flowers are also edible, and have a spicy flavor.

Radish: Radishes also grow easily and mature quickly. Successive planting is best in early spring and early fall. Radishes belong to the cruciferous vegetables family, similar to cabbage and arugula. Their "engorged taproot" can grow from as small as an inch to about 24 inches deep. Radishes come in a variety of colors, including pink, yellow and white. [60] Early radishes require cool months (early spring and autumn) and mature in 20-30 days. Midseason radishes can grow in succession between May and August. They mature in 30-40 days. Late radishes are sown in winter and late summer. They mature in 60-70 days. Prepare loose and fertile soil with organic fertilizer, and let the temperature reach 40 degrees Fahrenheit. Apply all-purpose fertilizer (nitrogen, phosphorus and potassium) in the ratio 10-10-10 or 16-16-18, with a cup per 10 feet of the row. Sow seeds a ½ inch deep, about 12-18 inches apart. Maggots and flea beetles can be problematic for your crop, and can be fixed through three-year crop rotation and avoiding planting where cabbages have been planted. Timely harvesting ensures that the roots do not get bitter and woody. Simply pull the roots and brush off the soil.

Bok Choy: Bok choy is a leafy vegetable with green or light purple leaves that are white towards the center. They have a central stalk and bulbous bottoms. The center is juicy and sweet, and generally cooked and eaten or consumed raw. Bok choy is grown in the cold season when the temperature is 55-70 degrees Fahrenheit. It needs moist soil, and can tolerate heat to a certain extent. It is rich in folate and the essential vitamins A, K and C. It is also a rich source of minerals and polyphenols. Seeds must be sown 4-5 weeks before the last frost date. Soil must be well-drained and contain organic matter and compost. The ideal pH is 6.0-7.5, and sun exposure for at least 3-5 hours is required. They may be sown ¼ inch deep, with an inch of spacing between them. Germination takes just 4-8 days, and seedlings may be transplanted when they are about 2 inches high.[49] Avoid watering the leaves to avoid rot. Crop rotation, intercropping, succession planting, and mulching are good practices for bok choy. Celery and thyme repel cabbage worms, onions reduce the occurrence of root maggots, and cilantro and rosemary protect against aphids and flea beetles. Mild winters causes bok choy to go dormant, and in this case, bolting happens during the following season. Plant successively if you want a continuous harvest. To harvest, cut the plant above the level of the soil. This keeps the center leaves in place, and the plant can continue to grow. To save the seeds, allow the plants to bolt, and save the seed pods for the next season.

Spinach: Spinach grows well in several soil types. Seeds must be sown 8 weeks before the last frost. Kale and lettuce are good accompaniments for spinach in your raised bed garden. Spinach comes in many varieties, including the Malabar red stem and the New Zealand spinach. Spinach grows well in shade, and the soil must be watered well. Hot temperatures can cause the plants to bolt (shoot up and resemble a flower). [58] Leaves may be harvested with a little part of the stem when they reach 3-5 inches in length. This allows for a continuous supply of fresh leaves. Leaves that grow to about 6 inches have a different flavor.

Turnips: Turnips have a good nutritional value, and can be stored well. They belong to the mustard family, and come in different colors, sizes and flavors. Sow seeds in well-drained soil, ½ inch deep, and in a place that is sunny or has partial shade. Begin in spring when the soil temperature reaches 40 degrees Fahrenheit. Long and cool seasons allow succession planting and a continuous supply of harvest. Turnips need moist soil until sprouts appear, and when the plants get a few inches tall, plant them about 4-6 inches apart. Plants should not be fertilized: organic matter should be enough for the plants to grow well.[47] Avoid waterlogging, and use mulch. When you see caterpillars, handpick them, and spray away the aphids with soapy water. Place a cardboard ring around the stems to stop cutworms, and use wood ash to prevent maggots from damaging the plant. White flies go away with a spray of garlic oil or soapy water. Crop rotation is a good way to prevent disease such as mildew or whitespot. Harvest the plant when it is 2 inches in diameter by pulling the whole plant out. To harvest only the leaves, pull out the ones outside, and leave the ones growing in the middle to allow them to regrow. Fall crops must be harvested before a hard freeze, as too much freezing and thawing causes roots to crack and develop rot.

High-Yield Crops

If you have a small garden, you can still achieve a great harvest if you invest in high-yield crops. These crops give you more harvest per square foot of your garden. The recommended high-yield vegetables for your raised bed garden are pole beans, which grow 10 feet and higher, peas, which give you a harvest over several weeks from their 5-foot tall vines, zucchini with its massive harvest, speedy salad greens, the heavy tomato crop, and a variety of cucumbers. [55] It makes sense to elaborate on the abundant produce of the pole beans and zucchini due to their several advantages:

Pole Beans: Set up pole beans using a trellis to make the best use of planting space, as they give three times the normal yield. The ideal soil temperature to sow the seeds is 60 degrees Fahrenheit, and this is also the temperature of the ambient air. Pole beans will give you about five harvests during their planting season. Use a soil enriched with organic matter and fertilizer, and add structural supports that allow the plants to grow 5-10 feet high. Seeds are planted about 4-8 inches apart. The distance between rows should be 24-36 inches, and seeds should be sown about an inch deep. Keep watering until about 2-3 inches of the soil is moist. Make sure that the soil is neither soggy nor dry. Start harvesting the beans when the pods are swollen, and pick them every 3-5 days so make sure the beans do not get bitter or woody. The yield from a pole bean plant is several pounds of beans, and harvesting leads to more flowers, and increases the life of the vines. Pole beans come in many different varieties, including the Kentucky Blue and the Kentucky Wonder.

Zucchini: Zucchini requires very little effort, and gives abundant produce in a short window of time – so much so that it may sometimes get exhausting to harvest them over and over again. Zucchini belongs to the same family as pumpkins and cucumbers. Young fruits under 7 inches may be eaten unpeeled, but the mature fruit needs to be peeled and grated. These juicy squashes come in several different varieties, including scallop, vegetable marrow, crookneck and cocozelle.[57] Zucchini also requires rich organic and fertile soil made from the right constituents, and plants require spacing to avoid pests and mold. A pH of 6.0-7.5 is most suitable for growing zucchini. Add a layer of mulch after planting to retain the moisture and nutrients while slowing down the growth of weeds. Use an appropriate amount of water to avoid water logging or over-soaking the leaves. At the time of blooming, apply a balanced liquid fertilizer with 50 percent strength. Start harvesting the squashes when they are about 4-6 inches long. Harvest regularly to maximize your produce.

6

WHAT TO GROW PART 2: SOFT FRUITS

Raised beds provide an ideal set up to grow your berries by protecting against parasitic weeds, as their delicate, shallow roots are prone to damage from weeding tools. When using raised beds to grow these crops, mulching with straw, bark or chopped leaves can serve as an effective technique to keep the weeds and pests away.[66] This also gives you the opportunity to achieve the ideal soil pH for your berries, as you can add the right amount of fertilizer and nutrients to make it an ideal environment for your soft fruits before planting.

To grow berries, you need a soil pH of 4.0-5.5. Add sulphur to the soil at the time of planting your crop, and apply an acidic fertilizer at the time of blooming. Add compost and rotted manure. When you grow strawberries, you may need to protect them from birds and chipmunks using bird netting, and also take care there is no overcrowding.

Blackberries and raspberries grow aggressively, and the plants are quite thorny. Growing them on the ground is never a good idea, as they can spread as far as 10 feet in a short time if left unchecked, and can even take over other plants in the vicinity. Using a raised bed prevents these problems, and you can prune and pick your berries quite conveniently.

The abundant produce you get from growing soft fruits saves you a lot of money. They require little space, and mature quickly, which gives you a good continued harvest sooner rather than later. They just need watering once a week when the weather is dry. A 2-inch layer of organic mulch is beneficial for the plants, and will help them to absorb nutrients.[71]

Strawberries: Strawberries are a good choice for beginners as they come in early, late, and mid-season varieties. If you choose to grow from seed, then the time to sow is early spring. It may take almost a month for them to start germinating. The fruits start coming in only after a year. A good practice with strawberries is to remove all flowers in the first year so you get an extensive harvest with bigger fruit the following year. You can even start strawberries with bare roots, but make sure they look healthy and have the crown intact. Also make sure they are not affected by mold or rot. Soak them in water for an hour before putting them in the soil, with the crown on top of the soil for the leaves to start. Ensure there is enough space for the roots to grow. [70] [71]

The ideal soil pH for strawberries is 6-7. The plants require sunlight for a minimum of 6 hours. The only soil types that may hurt your plant is one with a lot of clay or one that doesn't drain well. Add about 3 inches of compost into the soil to improve nutrient content and draining ability. Also use a nitrogen-phosphorus-potassium fertilizer in the ratio 10-10-10. Pull out weeds as they appear, and do not plant in spaces that have been used to grow peppers, tomatoes, potatoes or eggplants, as your strawberry crop may be affected by verticillium wilt. The harvest window extends for quite some time, allowing you to pick your fruits from spring all the way to autumn. Popular varieties include June bearing, everbearing, with harvest June and early fall, and day-neutral, with harvest from early spring to frost. Strawberries give you fruit in the first summer after they are planted.[70]

Strawberry plants require minimal maintenance: all you have to do is trim the leaves a little after you have harvested the fruit. When flowering begins, make sure you lay a layer of straw under the plants to protect the fruits lying on the ground, as the mud can rot them. The autumn crop or the perpetual variety gives you a fresh supply of fruit even later. Strawberry crops need to be protected from frost using an appropriate row cover. Diseases like the leaf spot, powdery mildew, or leaf scorch may affect your crop, and most of the diseases can be prevented with good circulation of air, proper water drainage, planting a disease-resistant variety, and picking the right location.[70] [71]

Raspberries: Raspberries also provide a high yield with little effort. The two varieties of raspberry you want to experiment with are the summer-fruiting and the autumn-fruiting varieties. Raspberries of the autumn season are easier to grow, as all that you require for them to blossom and fruit is a reasonable structural support.[71]

With the little care they require, you can enjoy a good supply of fruit from late summer, until the first frost occurs. During the first year, you will see green stems shooting from the ground, mainly producing leaves. The woody stems that yield fruit start appearing from the second year. The two main varieties are everbearing and summer bearing. The everbearing variety gives fruit between June and July in the summer season. The summer bearing variety gives fruit in June.[69] [71]

Plant your raspberries in a spot that receives full or partial sunlight. The ideal soil pH is 5.5-6.5. The recommended distance between rows is 24 inches. Keep the different varieties separate. Add organic compost, and make sure the soil drains well to prevent root rot. As with other berries, apply a balanced fertilizer of nitrogen-phosphorus-potassium in the ratio 10-10-10 during early spring. The plants give you a great harvest for as many as 15 years or longer. The best part is the number of hybrid varieties available, such as the tayberry, loganberry, and boysenberry, which are obtained by cross pollinating cane fruits such as raspberry and blackberry. When you have a couple of rows of each of the berries in your raised bed garden, you will enjoy a selection of the tastiest berries in big delicious clusters and bunches.[69] [71]

To prune them, all you have to do is cut off the crop from the base of its stem in late winter, just before the frost comes in, so that new stems grow back in spring time. Unlike the traditional thorny varieties, modern raspberries do not have sharp thorns, and give you sweeter fruits. To maintain the raspberry crop, simply cut the old canes to allow the new ones to grow.[69] [71]Maintain an ideal height of 5-6 feet to ensure a good quantity of fruit. Thinning your crop by leaving out the stronger canes gives larger fruit, and leaving the crop without thinning gives small fruit but a high yield. To encourage more fruit, dig out and replant the suckers and remove the diseased and dead canes (stems). Use trellises for the summer variety, but the everbearing type does not need them, as it grows into short and strong canes. When working with trellises, make sure their height is as good as the mature plant. The major diseases you want to watch out for are spur blight, anthracnose, and cane blight. Thinning and drip irrigation are two best practices to reduce the incidence of disease. Use netting to keep the birds away, and water jets to get rid of the aphids. Just as with strawberries, verticillium wilt is a problem for raspberries. Harvesting is as easy as separating the berry from the receptacle for a delightful sweet treat.

Blackberries: Blackberries are the easiest to grow of all the berries. They require a sunny spot and soil enriched with leaf mold and compost. Well-drained loam, which is slightly acidic, is generally suitable for growing blackberries. Avoid soil with a lot of clay, as it drains poorly. You can get started with blackberries by getting a potted plant from the market, or even bare roots. The time to plant them is early spring. Blackberries that can be grown from seeds must be planted in the fall. Plants should have a space of 5-6 feet between them, and trellis support must be fixed to help the canes grow well and make harvesting easy.[68] Blackberries planted from seeds start giving fruit from the second year. They grow over 3-5 feet in height. Water the blackberry plants about an inch per week, preferably using ground-level irrigation. Use a 10-10-10 proportion of balanced fertilizer in spring, and then again, with compost and manure, in fall.

There are different varieties of blackberries, including erect thornless blackberries (which do not have thorns and require no cane support), trailing thornless blackberries (these have sprawling canes that require support with trellis or wire to hold them above ground level), and erect thorny blackberries (which have sharp spines and require no cane support). The harvesting period for blackberries is June to August.[68] Fruits have tiny globes or drupelets with a white core. Blackberries are initially green, turning to red in the interim, and finally black when they are ready to harvest. Canes that have produced fruit in the second year must be trimmed after the harvest. New canes that haven't produced fruit must be pruned at their tips to 3 feet in the summer. Pruning encourages branching and more fruit production. Canes that have produced fruit must be trimmed to the ground after harvesting. Get rid of the canes that were damaged during winter when it is early spring. Later, thin out the remaining canes, leaving out 4-5 strong canes. You can create more plants from stem cuttings: plant 4-inch pieces from the end of the stem in late spring, providing there has been good rainfall and a mild temperature. Keep the soil wet after planting, and wait for the roots to form in 2-4 weeks.

Blackberries require little maintenance. Remove weeds as they appear, as they may interfere with the shallow roots. Raised beds are a good arrangement for blackberries, as they protect the flower buds from late spring frosts. Use mulch to cover the roots to provide them with enough nutrition and moisture, and protect them from weeds. Temperatures below zero are not favorable for blackberries, and the wet spring soil with sub-zero temperatures may even lead the plants to die. On the other hand, a hot and dry environment isn't favorable either, and may result in stunted fruits full of seeds.[68] Watch out for common diseases such as crown gall, anthracnose, and stem blight, which you can avoid by procuring healthy plants. Insect attacks from crown borers and stink bugs are common but keeping the crop healthy will prevent them. When a viral attack occurs, such as calico virus, and yellow blotches appear on the leaves, it is advisable to remove the affected plants and destroy them.

Red and White Currants: Red, white, pink and black currants require less sunlight, and can even grow in the shade.[71] They provide a great deal of nutrition, especially potassium, phosphorus, iron and Vitamin C, and have minimal fat. You will want to consult with a nursery, however, about possible restrictions on growing them, due to the risk of white pine blister rust. To plant the currants, prepare the soil with good drainage and organic matter, especially if it contains clay or sand. Maintain a soil pH of 5.5-7.0. Choose a spot with a lot of sunlight but partial shade. A temperature over 85 degrees Fahrenheit is unsuitable for currants, and may cause them to drop their leaves. Spacing between the plants should be 4-5 feet. Water them about 2-4 inches, taking care to surround the plants with organic mulch to keep the weeds at bay.

Even a single variety of currant can give you a good yield, as they pollinate their own flowers. Planting two different varieties can give you bigger fruit. Currants just need to be pruned when winter sets in to encourage the growth of many fresh stalks and fruit.[71] Mildew may cause problems, which can be avoided by adding all-purpose fertilizer in the ratio 10-10-10 during early spring, about 12 inches from the trunk of the shrub.

Gooseberries: Almost any type of soil is suitable for self-pollinating gooseberries, but they require a cool season and organically enriched soil with a pH of between 5.5 and 7.0 to grow well. Gooseberries come in different varieties that may be consumed either raw or cooked. Sandy or clay soil requires manure, compost or peat to be added to it. Plants must be kept 4-5 feet apart. They have a distinct taste (sweet to mild-tart) and their flowers naturally attract butterflies and bees. The two main varieties of gooseberries are the European and American varieties. The European variety gives a larger fruit with a stronger taste. The American variety, however, gives better produce, and is resistant to disease. Colors vary from light green to maroon, red, pink, deep purple, and yellow. The average height is 5-6 feet. When planting seeds, soak them for a few hours, and sow them ½ inch deep in spring. Gooseberries need sun exposure for about 6 hours per day, and roots must be covered in mulch to keep them cool. Fertilize with a 10-10-10 proportion of all-purpose fertilizer.[67] [71]

The first year is not the harvest year, and you should take off all the blossoms. Gooseberries start giving a good yield from the second year onwards like most other crops. Ripening happens over 4-6 weeks. Use gloves when harvesting: the ripe berries can simply be collected in a tarp by shaking them off the plant. Pruning and mulching are good practices for the growth of gooseberries, and help to produce fresh stalks and fruits. Gooseberries are not affected by diseases and pests as much as other berries. They also require minimal maintenance. They can be grown on trellises, against a wall, or cut into small shrubs. Trellising is a good way to avoid fungal disease. They do not rot quickly. You will need to protect the plant from roaring winds. Thorny stems can pose inconvenience at the time of harvesting. Trimming the tops to 6-10 inches promotes growth of the plant. Stem cuttings can be used to propagate gooseberries. Cut the cane so that the top cut is an inch above the bud and the bottom cut is below the bud. Bury about a third of the cane. Then cover the rest of the cane with straw so the tip is visible. Another way to propagate is through layering, which is when you bend a low-growing branch and cover it with several inches of soil, securing it with a brick. Clip the branch the following spring, and dig up the plant: you will find a good number of roots and leaves.[67] [71]

Birds are attracted to gooseberries, and you can discourage them by spraying the crop with sugary syrup like Kool-Aid every few weeks. Keep ladybugs away with strong jets of water, and aphids with insecticidal soap water. Pruning is a good practice against currant borers, and fruit worms need to be handpicked to protect your crop. Gooseberry stem girdlers are another nuisance, and you will need to snip off 8 inches of the tips of your plants. Diseases like anthracnose and powdery mildew may affect your crop. The former can be controlled by removing all infected leaves, and the latter can be tackled with a fungicide.[67] [71]

Protecting Berries from Birds

Birds can cause quite an inconvenience to crops, and a number of scare devices such as look-alikes of predators, noise-makers and reflectors prove useful in scaring them away. Another effective way of keeping birds away is bird netting. The ideal time to install bird netting is about 2-3 weeks prior to the maturation of the fruit. Birds can be a menace to your other crops too: paper bags are a good way to protect corn ears as they mature, and garden fabric is useful to protect germinating seeds.[65]

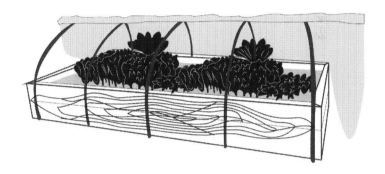

A crop cage is an enclosure for your entire crop made out of sturdy poles and wrapped with netting. You can get in and out of the cage using zippers installed on the sides. Steel poles add strength and stability to the cage, and connectors run across it to keep the netting in place. At about 6 feet, the cage is tall enough to allow you to harvest your fruit comfortably. It is easy to assemble and take apart at the end of your crop cycle.

Another way to protect your crops from the birds is to use super hoops that cover an entire row of your crop. Super hoops can be arranged and covered with an appropriate netting. Ready-made super hoops are available for 3x3 or 3x6 raised beds, and there are high-rise super hoops available for your taller crops. They also differ in width, with the wider hoops available to accommodate the taller crops.

Another option for your smaller crops are bird pop up nets, which fold flat to store them away, and open to form a semicircular net for your small dwarf berries or salad greens. The material used to construct dwarf netting is either steel or polyethylene. The accordion shape allows good protection for the whole plant, keeping birds and insects away as it grows to a decent size for harvesting.

7

WHAT TO GROW PART 3: HERBS

R aised beds can serve as wonderful environments for herbs, as they require minimal maintenance, and you can change the position as you like. This means you can have your herb garden right next to your kitchen and get the freshest, most aromatic herbs anytime.[72] The location you choose must be protected from frost and receive sunshine in the sunny months.

Herbs grow well in compost with a neutral pH, organic matter, and good water drainage. It is not a good idea to add nitrogen to the soil, as it may take away the original flavor of the herbs. The best way to plant a selection of herbs is to go with the taller ones towards the center of the bed, and shorter ones to its sides. This type of arrangement allows all varieties of herbs to receive sunlight, and is convenient for weeding and harvesting.[72] Do not plant your herbs too close together, as they will need space to grow and cover a decent amount of space.

You can grow a number of herbs in your raised bed, including oregano, chives, parsley, thyme, sage, tarragon, rosemary and basil. It's always a good idea to protect the herbs with net tunnels, grow houses, cloches, pop-up meshes, or greenhouses. Maintain them by taking out the weeds, and any dead branches or leaves. Use a general-purpose fertilizer during the growing period. Not all herbs grow in the same way, and while some herbs last only for one season, others grow perpetually. Taking cuttings just above the leaf intersection stimulates growth.[72] Harvesting is as simple as that. Once you cut the herbs, they should be used immediately.

The following herbs are the delight of every kitchen, and a few notes on sowing, growing, and harvesting those herbs goes a long way towards helping you make delightful dishes and flavorful salads.

Basil: Basil is one of the most popular herbs, and a worthy ingredient in many of of your dishes. It also serves medicinal purposes. It is much savored in Mediterranean cuisine, and sweet basil, in particular, is a significant part of the Italian cuisine.[79] It is considered a sacred herb in India, and useful in most herbal teas and as an essential oil.

Basil can be started from seedlings, leaf cuttings below a leaf node, or seeds. To start the plants using seeds, keep the seeds warm and moist in a greenhouse 3-6 weeks prior to the anticipated last frost. When seedlings germinate, water them once or twice daily, and when they mature to about 3-4 inches in height, transfer them into the soil.[79]

Basil requires soil enriched with vermiculite, compost and peat. The soil must not be very acidic and well-drained. The ideal soil temperature is 50-55 degrees Fahrenheit. Warm temperatures give a generous harvest of basil. Therefore, the best season to grow basil is summer, as it requires a minimum of 8 hours of sunlight. Plant basil 4-6 inches apart, allow seeds to sprout, and thin them before transplantation. The plant reaches maturity in 60-69 days, and the harvesting can begin anytime in the 60-90 day window. Replacing plants every year gives the best harvest. Basil can reach a height of 10-18 inches, and the plants can occupy considerable space as they grow.[79] Basil can be planted with bell peppers, potatoes, tomatoes and eggplants. It can be planted close to chamomile, but not in the vicinity of anise or culinary sage.

Basil can repel mosquitoes and flies. Japanese beetles and slugs tend to invade your basil plantation, however, and must be promptly removed by hand. Since basil has delicate leaves, strong jets of spray may damage the leaves. Fungus can attack your crop, and watering the crop well, as well as having a good drainage system, promotes the growth of the crop. Dispose of any leaves that have been affected by fungus.[79]

Harvesting is all about pinching the top tip of the plant, allowing better growth. Continue clipping with clippers whenever you need the basil, and also clip the flowers as they appear.[79]

Chives: Chives are a flavorful herb that grow without a lot of effort. These hardy perennials, which thrive in the late winter season, do not require much maintenance. Bright green leaves with purple, white or lavender flowers attract pollinators, and the plant is known to repel carrot rust flies and Japanese beetles. They do well on the edges or at a single spot in your raised bed garden. Both flowers and leaves add a distinct taste to your salads. Chives grow in clumps and form bulbs. Their clumps can be separated after every 2-4 years. They grow to a height of 12-24 inches, and a width of 12 inches. Chives can be planted along with squash, parsley, potatoes, peppers and tomatoes.[80]

Chives come in many varieties beyond the regular variety, such as Siberian garlic chives, garlic chives, and giant Siberian chives. Chives grow well in a sunny area (at least 6 hours sunlight) when the soil is watered well and rich in organic compost (or a mix of coconut coir, peat and sand). Add organic fertilizer before planting, and space the plants 8-10 inches apart. Water regularly, and add mulch to retain moisture.[80] They are a versatile herb, and do quite well even when they get as little as 4 hours of sunlight. Root rot could be a problem when the soil does not drain well, however. Chive clumps and seeds can be planted to grow chives. Seeds must be started indoors about 8-10 weeks prior to the last spring frost. If the soil is ready, it's never a bad idea to sow the seeds directly.

Plant clumps may be divided every 2-4 years, in early spring or late winter. They can also be divided in early fall. Dividing the plant is as simple as watering it, cutting leaves a few inches above ground, and then gently tapping at the roots to get clumps out for planting elsewhere. Chives take a few weeks to set firmly in the ground after diving, and this is when they are ready to harvest. The harvest is usually worthwhile from the second year onwards. For vigorous growth, cut off the flower buds before they bloom.[80] Harvest leaves in the early morning, and leave a bit of the base to allow the plant to grow back. Deadheading is another good way to encourage the growth of new flowers.

Mint: Mint is used extensively, from flavoring confectionary products to making aromatic teas. Mint is a perennial, and grows quite easily, spreading quickly. There are almost 20 species of mint, and there are hybrid varieties too. It has a refreshing taste and a sweet smell, and mint blooms from mid to late summer. Mint propagates through its stolons or runners above and below the ground, and is widely used to treat respiratory and gastrointestinal problems. Mint seeds are difficult to germinate, as they are tiny, and most gardeners prefer dividing the roots or using stem cuttings to propagate the herb. The root can be divided and placed in a soil with an equal ratio of sand, peat moss or vermiculite, and aged compost. Water regularly, and protect from direct sunlight until the plant sets its roots firmly in the soil.[74]

To grow the herb from stem cuttings, place stems cut from the leaf nodes in a glass of water until the roots start forming in about 10-14 days. The stems can be planted in soil after 3-4 weeks. These small potted plants can be sheltered for 4-6 weeks, making sure the soil is moist throughout, and then transplanted in your raised-bed.[74]

Mint requires a soil of pH of 6.0-7.0, and the soil must be enriched with organic matter. Growing plants need full or partial sun exposure, and the variegated variety needs to be kept in the shade. The plants need to be replenished with all-purpose fertilizer in the 10-10-10 ratio. Spacing between plants should be 12 to 24 inches. A 2-inch layer of mulch is always good to keep weeds under check and retain moisture. These plants do well in frost.[74] They do, however, generally stop growing in winter, and it's best to cut back stems in autumn and cover with a layer of mulch.

Keep spider mites and aphids away with strong jets of water, and remove the diseased plant parts to tackle anthracnose, powdery mildew, and mint rust. The best time to harvest is in the summer when the oils are most aromatic, as plants receive almost 14 hours of sunlight.[74] Harvest before flowering begins on a sunny day by cutting off the tips below the first or second swirl of leaves. Mint can be harvested 3-4 times a year in this way.

Cilantro: Cilantro or coriander leaves are an integral ingredient in Asian and Mexican cooking. The whole or crushed seeds are added to most preparations of Asian cuisine. Cilantro grows to about 12-24 inches. Cilantro flowers have medicinal uses, and the plant has anti-inflammatory and analgesic properties.[73] Coriander grows best in cold weather, with ideal temperatures between 50 and 85 degrees Fahrenheit. Although it is quite tolerant to cold temperatures, cilantro can bolt at around 80 degree Fahrenheit.

Transplanting in February gives you a harvest in April, and planting in September gives a harvest in November. It can be planted directly from seed, keeping 12-15 inches between each seed. A soil pH of 6.2-6.8 is ideal for plant growth. Water the young plants abundantly, but when the plant grows to a certain height, it may not require as much water.

Use a nitrogen fertilizer in the ratio 21-0-0 or 34-0-0. A serious problem comes from aster yellows, carried by leafhoppers. To get rid of leafhoppers, sprinkle diatomaceous earth around plants, and pull out plants infected by aster yellows.

Cilantro can be harvested in 40-75 days after planting. Simply pinch off fresh immature leaves on stems that are 6 inches tall. Wait for a few days between harvests. When plants bolt, the green seeds can be harvested for their sharp flavor. Alternatively, the mature seeds can be harvested by cutting off the seed head along with the stalk, and hanging them upside down in a paper bag.

Dill: Dill is widely used in Asian and Mediterranean cuisine. It has soft, ferny, feathery greenish-blue leaves, and grows to about 3-4 feet. Dill flowers are bright yellow, and come in flattened clusters or umbels measuring about 6 inches. Dill has a strong aroma and soothes the stomach. It also has antimicrobial, antioxidant and antifungal properties.[75] Seeds may be sown in spring when temperatures are above 25 degrees Fahrenheit.

Dill seeds self-sow, and you can get a good supply of dill just by sowing it once. When planting for the first time, it's always best to sow seeds rather than transplant, as it has a sensitive tap root, and tends to bolt when transplanted. Planting soil must contain compost, and about 2-3 seeds must be planted 4-6 inches apart in rows spaced 12 inches apart.[75] Soil pH must be 5.6-6.5, and the temperature should be about 70 degrees Fahrenheit. Hot temperatures will cause it to bolt. Soils with a high clay content require compost to be added. Dill also does well with companion plants, including leeks, onions and garlic.

Water daily for germination, which takes about 10-14 days. Thereafter, the plants require about an inch of water every week. Use drip irrigation, as sprinklers may encourage infection. Organic fertilizer with vermicompost increases yield. Thin out the seedlings to achieve a plant after every 4 inches in dry climate, and 6 inches when the environment is humid. Plant in an area with 6-8 hours of sunlight, allow good air circulation, and remove weeds regularly.[75]

Watch out for aphids, and repel them with beneficial insects and companion plants. Black swallowtail caterpillars often munch on the herb, and gardeners often relocate them to have the beautiful black swallowtail butterflies in their garden. Problems may arise from root-knot nematodes, which may stunt plant growth. Solarizing and growing cover crops helps to get rid of the problem. Humid climates make the plant susceptible to a number of diseases, including downy mildew and root rot. [75]

Dill can be harvested when its stems are a few inches tall. Harvesting regularly makes the plants bushier. The best time to harvest the leaves is when flower buds form. Cutting flower heads allows foliage to grow. You could also choose to make the plant go to seed, which encourages seed production rather than foliage.

Tarragon: The delicate leaves of tarragon are a part of many cuisines worldwide. It adds a unique flavor to vinegar, salad dressing, beverages, poultry and fish. It does well in cool temperatures, and gives a steady supply of leaves in well-drained soil and sunny areas that have been watered well. It may require a water-soluble fertilizer, but cannot withstand high heat. It has rapidly growing roots that spread quite fast.[78]

Enrich the soil for planting with worm castings, peat moss, bone meal, mature compost, and well-rotted manure. To plant tarragon, simply place the root ball in the soil, and water gently. The plant may require fish fertilizer during its growing season, and may go dormant in the cold season, when stems may have to be cut back few inches and covered with compost. Plants propagate by stem cuttings or root division. To plant by root division, divide the root into half, a third, or quarter sections, and replant. Late spring and early summer is a good time for stem division, when the base of the stem has become sturdy. 6-inch stems may be planted after dipping them in root hormone in an area with enough sunlight and water. To harvest, cut the stem to 5-6 inches, and take off its leaves.[78] Tarragon comes in several different varieties, and is good for the stomach.

Parsley: Parsley is rich in vitamins, minerals and antioxidants, and is often grown with roses and other vegetables. Its lacy bright green leaves add a rich flavor to many preparations. Unlike other herbs, parsley gives the sweetest leaves in its first year, and the sweetness begins to decline from the second year onwards. Pinching off the sweetstack keeps the flavor intact, and also promotes longevity. It germinates slowly but self-seeds, saving you a lot of effort for the coming year. It can successfully survive very cold winter temperatures (as low as 10 degrees Fahrenheit), which may cause the leaves to fall, only to reappear when conditions become favorable. Adding mulch works well with parsley in the cold months.[76]

Seeds may be sown when the soil temperature reaches about 70 degrees Fahrenheit. Germination happens in 4 weeks, and you can speed it up by soaking the seeds for 24 hours in lukewarm water. If you plan to start the seeds indoors, it has to be done 8-12 weeks before the last frost. When planting in your raised bed, add rotted manure and compost, and maintain a soil pH of 6.0-7.0 to help absorb nutrients. Sow seeds ¼ inch deep, and leave an inch of space between them. [76] Thinning is a good practice after the second leaves have grown, so the plants are 6 inches apart. Use the nitrogen-phosphorus-potassium fertilizer in the 1-1-1 ratio, or the foliage formula in the 3-1-2 or 5-1-1 proportion. Soil may also be enriched with fish fertilizer.

Leaf spot and root rot are common problems that occur when the soil is wet and acts as a medium for the growth of fungi and bacteria. To solve the problem, use drip irrigation, improve air circulation, and get rid of the damaged plants. Check soil drainage often to prevent problems. It is time to harvest the leaves as soon as you see three separate segments on the stem, which may be cut from the outside to allow the inner part to mature.

Rosemary: Rosemary has a piney, bittersweet flavor, and was originally found in the Mediterranean basin. There are multiple species of rosemary, including the upright, clumping, and creeping varieties. It has inch-long narrow leaves shaped like a lance, and the plant reaches a height of 6-8 feet when it matures. Flowers resembling whorls are colored pink, blue, mauve and white, and appear from late winter until late spring. Another bloom appears in late summer, going all the way to fall and winter. Rosemary essential oil is used extensively, and the herb is known to cure skin problems and anxiety, can be used as a mouthwash, to treat asthma, and to ease numerous other medicinal issues.[77]

Propagation is mainly through seeds that germinate slowly, with a 50%success rate. Seeds can be collected in summer. When starting the seeds indoors, the time to do so is mid-to-late winter. Use a seed starting mix, and cover them lightly with soil. Make sure the soil is moist, and provide heat so a consistent temperature of 80-90 degrees Fahrenheit is maintained. Water with a spray after germination, maintain 6-8 hours of sunlight, and make sure there is enough air circulation.[77] Transplant the seedlings when they are about 3-4 inches in length. Protect the plants during the first winter, and plant during the following spring.

Rosemary can also be propagated from 6-8 inch long stem cuttings. Dip them in a rooting hormone, and plant them in well-drained soil. Make sure you water them well. Rosemary requires full sun exposure and a pH of 6.0-7.8. Add a mixture made up of coarse sand and organic matter, and firm the soil over the roots.[77] Water the plants well, and use an all-purpose fertilizer in the proportion 10-10-10 for a good supply of nutrients.

Prune plants after they flower (between late spring and midsummer), taking off a third of their growth. Avoid pruning in late autumn or winter, allowing the plants to harden and survive cold temperatures. To protect against freezing temperatures, add 4-6 inches of mulch.

The two main problems to tackle when growing rosemary are aphids and root rot. While the former requires a jet of water to get rid of the pests, the latter can be overcome by watering optimally so there is no water logging. Rosemary can be planted with cruciferous vegetables, beets and carrot,s and attracts pollinators like humming birds and bees.[77] Harvesting is possible the full year round. Stems may be picked between morning and afternoon before the temperature rises. 8-10 inch stems may be pruned for use.

Sage: Sage is a perennial Mediterranean herb with green-gray leaves and a strong aroma. Sage blossoms attract a variety of beneficial insects that take over pests in the garden and allow pollination. The herb requires well-drained soil and full sunlight. An ideal soil pH of 5.6-7.8 must be maintained. Mature stalks grow to 12 inches tall and 36 inches wide. Sage may be propagated by stem cuttings or from seeds.[81]

When starting seeds indoors, sow them 8 weeks before the last frost date, or sow them ⅛ inch deep in the soil. Seeds may be sown directly by sprinkling them on moist soil and allowing them to germinate. Alternatively, you could use 4-6 inch long stem cuttings with the growing tip, pinch off the bottom leaves, and dip them in rooting hormone. Put the stalks in water (changing water daily) in a location where they receive indirect sunlight. Transplant when you see roots on the stalks. You can also propagate the plant by uprooting and dividing the plant.

Sage grows well in full sun. Soil must be well-drained and contain compost, and the outside temperature must be above 50 degrees Fahrenheit. Transplant in warm temperatures. Sage can be grown with other vegetables and rosemary. Mature plants reach a height of 18-24 inches, and a variety of species are available. The crop may be affected by powdery mildew, aphids and slugs, which can be easily taken care of by watering the soil well, maintaining good air circulation, and using water jets to get rid of the pests on the leaves. Weeds can be prevented by adding mulch over the soil. Harvesting is a matter of pinching off the leaves or snipping off the flower. Harvesting about half of the plant encourages growth of the foliage.

8

RAISED BED MAINTENANCE: WATERING, WEEDING, AND PEST CONTROL

Preparing the Soil

Preparing the soil is one of the most important aspects of raised bed gardening. To keep up your produce year after year, it is important to cultivate healthy soil. Here are a few tips to help you prepare your soil well every spring before planting.[89]

- Avoid stepping on the soil in your raised bed when working with it. As mentioned in the previous chapters, this will avoid soil compaction and facilitate good airflow for a well-drained soil bed. Soil that is not compacted encourages the growth of microorganisms and allows plants to grow well.
- Plant cover crops between crop rotations to add organic matter to the soil. Also add a nitrogen-rich fertilizer. Turn them under before they go to seed by

cutting with shears close to ground level, chopping the stubble, and turning it under with a hoe. Use the cuttings for mulch or compost. Alternatively, smother the cover crop by adding a layer of mulch followed by a black plastic sheet. This breaks down the cover crops in about 2-3 weeks.

- Look for roots from weeds, and pull them out in the direction from which they originated. You may have to go all the way to the root ball to pull it out. Also check to see if there are any tree roots in the vicinity, in which case you want to dig up the root, cut it, and install an appropriate barrier. Avoid laying a blanket barrier at the bottom of the raised bed, as this may interfere with water drainage. Instead, dig a trench, about 8 inches wide and 3-4 inches deep around the bed to prevent the roots from encroaching.

Check the soil in spring to see if it is still crumbly. If it is, add peat, and make it fluffy. If you don't want to till the soil, just add a top dressing of rock phosphate, compost, peat and lime, and cover it up with mulch. When lime is added to soil with a pH of 6.2, it reaches an ideal pH of 6.5-6.8. Add dolomite to achieve this, as opposed to quick lime. To feed the soil, till in compost, and add manure about 2 weeks prior to seeding

- Cover the soil with mulch after adding amendments in spring time. Covering helps retain warmth and break down amendments before the seeds are planted. The cover prevents the nourishment from being washed away, and prevents the growth of weeds.

- To prepare new beds for perennial flowers, spread 6-inch deep organic matter, and work it deep into the soil. Apply mulch all around the root mass that is sprouting, avoiding covering the whole area.
- Do not start working on the soil when it is too wet, as your seeds may rot or suffocate from lack of aeration. The ideal temperature for sowing most seeds is 60 degrees Fahrenheit, and about 68-80 degrees Fahrenheit is good for germination. However, peas need a temperature of 75 degrees Fahrenheit.

Other best practices include:

- Before you start planting, look for any imperfections from pressure on the raised bed structure, and fix them. The weight of the soil tends to loosen the corners, and you may have to use screws to lock them in place. Commercially available raised beds are generally tougher, as the manufacturers use interlocking hardware to keep the seams in place.
- Use poles and trellises to grow tall crops such as pole beans, peas and tomatoes. Build a structure around tomatoes, and cover it with corrugated plastic sheets to keep the rain off. The shelter should be removed to allow winter rain to nourish the plant and encourage beneficial microorganisms and worms.

- Avoid watering the foliage by using soaker hoses, and add mulch to retain moisture for longer periods.

Mulching

Mulch is a layer of covering for the exposed soil. Biodegradable materials such as straw, pine bark, chips, and grass clippings are best choices for mulch in your garden, as they decompose easily and nourish the soil. Other products that can be used as mulch include shredded paper, cocoa mulch (cocoa shell and cocoa beans), and cover crops. Stones and shells or rubber and plastic are not mulch, as they are not biodegradable.[88] Using mulch has several benefits for your raised bed garden:

- Mulch retains moisture, insulating the soil against wind and heat.
- It decreases the number of times you have to water your crop.
- It protects the feeder roots just beneath the soil surface against extreme temperatures, and keeps the plants healthy.
- It gives the bed an aesthetic look, and protects the soil surface from erosion.
- It reduces germination of weeds, and prevents soil-borne diseases.
- It improves the health of the soil when it breaks down.
- Using bark, leaves, and other wood products as mulch cuts down on landfill waste.

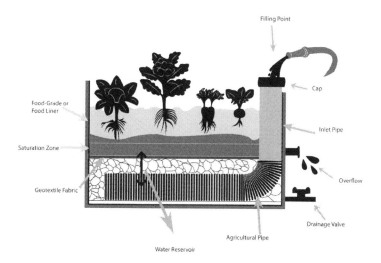

Applying mulch the right way is important in order to obtain the desired benefits. Do not apply it too thinly, as it cannot protect against erosion, heat, or weed growth. Do not apply a thick layer of mulch, however, as it may smother the crop and prevent water from getting into the soil. The ideal depth of mulch is 2-4 inches. Mulch should be applied so that it does not make contact with the trunk of the shrubs, as this can promote rot or allow pests and diseases to infest the crop.[88] Seeds that are about to germinate should not be mulched, as it may become an impediment for their healthy growth. When it is time, fertilizer and compost can also be applied over the mulch, as it tends to seep in as you irrigate the raised bed. Compost can also be applied by pulling off the layer of mulch and then restoring it after adding the compost.

Watering

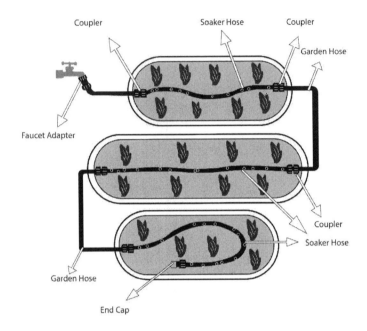

Coupler · Soaker Hose · Coupler · Garden Hose · Faucet Adapter · Coupler · Soaker Hose · Garden Hose · End Cap

There are many different watering techniques, and the plants you use and the climate you live in determine the ideal way to water your raised bed garden. Raised beds need holes at the bottom to allow water drainage. Plants have different water requirements, so knowing them well is important when you start your garden. When you decide on the method to water your plants, keep your materials and equipment handy, use a rain gauge to check rainfall, and use a ruler to check the moisture content in the soil. Finally, add mulch to retain the moisture.[87]

Benefits of Hand Watering

Although automation saves time and increases the efficiency of watering your garden, there are good reasons that you may want to hand water[90]:

- Hand watering means your plants always receive the required amount of water, and there is no under-watering or over-watering. This method caters to the needs of individual plants, and also preserves soil amendments.
- Hand watering prevents water from spilling onto the foliage, and reduces chances of fungal disease.
- Your entire bed receives an even soaking, and your pathways remain dry and devoid of weed growth.
- You get to watch your plants closely as they grow, allowing you to spot problems sooner rather than later. These issues may be related to pests such as aphids, installing stakes for plants, or checking blossoms.
- Hand-held sprayers cost less and require minimal maintenance, in contrast with sprinkler and drip irrigation systems, which often require their parts to be replaced.

Benefits of Drip Irrigation

Drip irrigation is a system that allows water to trickle near the base of the plant using pipes, valves, tubing and emitters. Drip irrigation also has its benefits, as described below[84] [90]:

- Drip irrigation allows roots to absorb water gradually, and is a more effective and efficient means of watering your beds.
- Considerably less water is wasted, even when compared to sprinklers, as 90 percent of the water is absorbed into the soil, and very little water evaporates.
- It reduces chances of water runoff and erosion, as a gradual and measured quantity of water is delivered.
- It requires minimal manual intervention, and it is also possible to set up timers to monitor the process. The effectiveness of the system also saves money.
- It does not water the foliage like a sprinkler, and this prevents diseases like powdery mildew from developing on the leaves.
- It just waters the, which means that the weed seeds do not receive water, and this controls weed growth.

Whichever method you choose to water the garden, it is essential you stay there when the watering takes place, even when it is automated. This allows you to check problems with your growing plants, and also helps to detect flooding.

Watering is not the same in all conditions. To achieve optimal plant growth, check the season, and decide on the appropriate frequency of watering. Also make sure you understand how much water each plant variety needs, and provide the required hydration. Over-watering, as well as under-watering, can damage the crop. The best way to add the right amount of moisture to the soil is to water it deeply but less frequently.[82] Consistency is important, and a good time to water is in the morning when plants absorb moisture more effectively.

Weeding

Weeds are unwanted plants such as pigweeds, dandelion and purslane. Weeds may become a source of diseases and pests, and also take nutrients, water and sunlight from the plant. Some weeds also produce seeds, and may live as parasites in your garden for many years.[86] Here are a few strategies to adopt to keep your garden free from weeds:

- Pull out weeds promptly, as they are much easier to remove when they are young. Pull them out regularly to stop them from spreading. Some of the most effective tools for weeding are the Cobrahead weeder and cultivator, a hori hori knife (which is a trowel with a serrated edge on one side), and a hand trowel to lift off weeds.
- Use mulch to keep your garden free from weeds. Mulch blocks sunlight from reaching the soil, and prevents the germination of weeds. 2-3 inches of mulch is ideal to stop the proliferation of weeds.
- Weed seeds can remain dormant in your garden for many years under the right conditions. When you see flowers on the weeds, snip them off, and do not allow seeds to get into the soil. You can also reduce weeds by hand-tilling the soil.
- Use a dense cover crop like buckwheat or a perennial

cover crop like clover to keep the weeds from growing.

- Cover all bare soil with mulch, plant quick-growing crops in between slow-growing crops, and use high-intensity planting to prevent weeds from growing.
- When you get new plants, check the roots and soil for weeds, and remove them before planting.
- Healthy plants can compete with the weeds, and to grow well, they require soil enriched with organic matter like compost or manure.
- Use watering techniques that deliver water to the plant, such as soaker hoses, and restrict weed growth.

Natural Pest Control

Pests can be a big threat to your healthy plants, and although raised beds provide some protection against pests by raising the plants off the ground, you still want to address a few concerns to keep pests away naturally[83]:

- Use companion plants, beneficial predators, and good microorganisms in your raised bed to deter pests. Choose natural treatments before using pesticides for best results. You can also install barriers such as meshes and fences to keep pests away. Organic sprays to leaves and soil are effective treatments. A few of treatments that prevent insect damage include:
- Diatomaceous earth, made from crushed exoskeletons of freshwater plankton, essentially

silica, which deters pests. This material is applied all along the perimeter of the raised bed, and prevents pests from entering it.

- Neem oil, extracted from the neem tree contains salannin, which kills insects and their larvae and eggs. It serves as a good treatment for aphids, beetles, spiders and the like.
- Sticky traps capture insects and help you understand what pests are causing problems in a specific area.
- Adding beneficial nematodes to your garden makes it resistant to over 200 different species of insects, including cabbage maggots, beetles and root weevil larvae. They do not affect the growth of earthworms or interfere with pollinators.
- Thin white fabric stretched over a frame is known as a floating row cover, and protects plants against pests.
- Besides insects, plants need to be protected from slugs and snails, which can be accomplished using diatomaceous earth, ferric phosphate, or copper mesh.
- Copper mesh tape may be stretched along the perimeter of the bed, as slugs do not cross copper. For a more aggressive approach, you could also attach a battery to the copper mesh so the slugs get a tiny zap when they're trying to cross the barrier.
- Adding ferric phosphate kills the slugs but does not harm birds, insects, earthworms or most pets. It could, however, be harmful for dogs.

Other strategies to prevent pests include the following[91]:

- Choosing the right plants: Avoid varieties that are prone to pests and could be replaced by a pest-resistant variety. Besides, some plant characteristics may also deter pests, such as the presence of hairy leaves. Choosing these plants acts as a natural barrier against pests.
- Using intercropping: Intercropping increases diversity and confuses pests, as they find it difficult to locate the host plant.
- Keeping the plants healthy: Healthy plants have a sound chemical defense system, and can prevent pests on their own.
- Allowing beneficial pests to thrive: Beneficial insects such as ladybugs, damsel bugs, and the like keep the harmful insects under check by acting as predators.

Extra Tips for Southern Gardeners

If you're growing a raised bed garden in the south, then you're probably dealing with clay, which is difficult to work with in spite of the generous amount of minerals it contains. It is, therefore, a good idea to first check if more amendments are required. When soil is saturated and summer has frequent rainfall, your raised beds serve as an ideal growth medium to drain excess water and prevent the roots from rotting. Use soaker hoses to avoid wetting the foliage and inviting diseases and pests. When the sun is too hot, use a shade cloth to protect your plants.[85]

Extra Tips for Northern Gardeners

On the other hand, if you're setting up a raised bed in the northern region, then your soil will warm up faster, and productivity is increased to give you a longer growing season. In the northern region, an effective orientation for your raised bed is north to south so your plants get the morning and the afternoon sun. Line the bottom of your raised bed with poultry wire or hardware cloth to keep rodents away. To support plants, use trellises and keep the beds covered with clear plastic during weather changes, folding it back when the warm sun reappears.[85]

9

REAPING YOUR REWARDS: EVERYTHING YOU NEED TO KNOW ABOUT HARVESTING

The way you harvest depends on the type of plant. Planning your raised bed was covered in Chapter Four, and harvesting for individual plants is also covered in Chapter Five to Seven. This chapter covers some general tips you may want to incorporate when it's time to harvest your favorite fruits, vegetables and herbs in your raised bed garden. Harvesting is an important part of your crop cycle, as it influences the yield and quality of your crop.[93]

Harvesting Dos and Don'ts

You want to keep the following important aspects of harvesting in mind in order to get the most of the time and effort you spend tending to your garden[92] [93]:

- Many vegetables taste best when they are immature, and this is the best time to harvest them. Examples include cucumber, zucchini, potatoes and turnips. Others taste best when ripe, such as watermelons and tomatoes.

- Avoid harvesting when the weather is wet and humid, or in the morning when you see dew covering the leaves. This is true especially for crops prone to disease.
- Frequent harvesting gives better quality vegetables that also taste good. It also enhances the yield. Most vegetables can be harvested daily, as soon as they are ripe, to increase the production.
- You may sometimes need tools such as pruning shears to make a clean cut and allow the plants to regrow. Damage to plants must be avoided, as it may become an entry point for disease. Always place the harvested vegetables and fruits in a basket to avoid damaging them.
- Keep track of the timing for planting your vegetables so you know when they are ready for harvesting.
- Look for signs of diseased vegetables, such as rotting or yellowing, and remove the affected parts.

Tips for Harvesting Common Vegetables

Finally, here are a few tips to help you harvest some classic vegetables[93]:

- Snap Beans: Harvest slightly immature snap beans for crisp and firm pods every day or on alternate days. Avoid harvesting when you see morning dew or when it is raining.

- Green Beans: Pick green beans when they have immature seeds and are tender. Delaying the harvest makes the pod tough.
- Beets: Beets are ready 2 months after you plant them. Harvest when roots are 1-1.5 inches in width. Avoid leaving them in the ground for long, or else they will turn woody.
- Cucumbers: Harvest cucumbers when they are immature to avoid the bitter taste and ensure that they retain their crispiness. To avoid disease, cut the cucumbers from their vines, and do not pull them out.
- Sweetcorn: To check if sweetcorn is ready, feel the rounded kernels under the husk. Other signs that corn is ready to harvest include the drying silk at the top of the ear. Also test to see if milky sap comes out when you squish a kernel.
- Peas: Different varieties of peas need to be harvested at different stages. Harvest snow peas when pods are tiny. For snap peas, wait until the pods are crisp and plump. Harvest shell peas when pods are fat and contain sweet and tender peas. Pick them every day to make sure production continues.
- Eggplant: Eggplants that have crossed maturity tend to be seedy and bitter. Eggplants come in several varieties, and the best time to harvest them is when the skin is glossy.
- Carrots: Harvest carrots when they grow to ½ inch

in diameter. This is the average size for the baby roots. If you want to store them for later, allow them to grow to their full size. Taste them to check if they are crisp and sweet, as that is the time when they are ready for harvest. To avoid breaking off the carrot tops, loosen the earth beneath them.

- Sweet Peppers: Harvest sweet peppers when they're green, or when they get the final color (yellow, red or purple) and taste. Clip them using a shears to avoid damaging them.

- Lettuce: Pick lettuce before it bolts due to hot weather. Bolting imparts a bitter taste to the leaves. Cut young and tender leaves when they are 5 inches long. Sow seeds every two weeks for a sumptuous harvest.

- Tomatoes: Cherry tomatoes are ready to harvest when they get a good ripe color and are slightly firm. Some varieties of tomatoes are ripe as soon as they can be released from the stem. The two most common types of tomatoes are determinate and indeterminate. The determinate variety stops producing fruit after a few weeks, and the indeterminate variety continues to produce fruit until frost sets in. When it is a week before the first frost is due to set in, pick your green tomatoes, and allow them to ripen indoors.

- Turnips: The roots and leaves of turnips can be eaten. Make sure the roots of turnips are harvested when they are an inch across. Growing successive crops every few weeks is a good practice.

- Zucchini: The best time to pick zucchini is when it is immature and firm. Elongated zucchinis grow to about 4-6 inches when they're ready to be picked, and other varieties may be as big as 0.5-3 inches across.
- Herbs: Cut back the herbs to make sure their production increases.
- Melons: To know when to harvest a melon, thump it to see if you can hear a hollow sound, and sniff it to see if you get a sweet smell. Cut the stem and let the fruit ripen for a day or two. Breaking the stem may create a wound and cause the plant to rot.
- Watermelon: Check to see if the part touching the ground has turned yellow, and if the rind is tough. Cut one of the watermelons to see if it is ripe (this also applies to all other melons).

Storing Abundant Produce

When it is time for harvesting, you stand a good chance of having an abundant supply of vegetables that you, your family, or your neighbors cannot consume. Here are a few ways to store them for later.[94]

- Peas and beans can be blanched and frozen in bags.
- Blackcurrants and blackberries can be frozen.
- Soft vegetables such as tomatoes and chillies can be used to make soups.
- Use tomatoes to make pasta sauce.
- Make jams, chutneys, and pickles from apples and courgettes.
- Store potatoes in hessian sacks in a cool and dark place.
- Either dry the fruits or vegetables, or dry a layer of puree to make fruit leathers and store them.
- Chop vegetables, and fry them with chopped onion and soy sauce to make pancake fillings.

CONCLUSION

The Suburban Grower is a comprehensive book on creating and maintaining your very own raised bed garden. It covers important information on the history and benefits of raised bed gardening, and allows you to understand the different materials available to set up your own raised bed. Several strategies to plan and prepare your raised beds have been presented, including selecting the right time and choice of plants for a thriving garden. It also contains detailed information on vegetables, fruits and herbs you may wish to include in your garden. Details on sowing, pruning and harvesting are included for the curious gardener. Several other facts on watering, weeding, pest control and harvesting are included to provide complete information on growing your raised bed garden. This book is available online on Amazon, and if you have found it helpful, please feel free to leave a review – doing so will help other gardeners with their own raised bed projects.

NOW FOR THE BEST PART!

You get to help our community by giving a 1-click review.

Many gardeners, just like you, know how hard it is to find current, concise, and useful information, especially when starting. Your review will help them find the type of book they are looking for and the information they are seeking.

Do a fellow gardener a favor and leave a review talking about the information you found, what you liked about the book, and how it helped you... even if it just a sentence or two!

Customer Reviews

★★★★★ 2
5.0 out of 5 stars ▾

5 star		100%
4 star		0%
3 star		0%
2 star		0%
1 star		0%

See all verified purchase reviews ›

Share your thoughts with other customers

Write a customer review ⬅

I am so very appreciative of your review, as it truly makes a difference in our community.

Thank you from the bottom of my heart for purchasing this book. I hope our paths cross again in the future.

Scan this QR code and leave a brief review on Amazon.

A SPECIAL GIFT TO MY READERS

If you haven't already, don't forget to access your free
Gardening Planner

Follow the link below to receive your free copy:
www.marissaclemont.com
Or by accessing the QR code:

You can also join our Facebook community **Homegrown Sustainable Gardening,** or contact me directly via
marissa@marissaclemont.com.

REFERENCES

[1] The Editors of Garden Variety, "A Brief History of Intensive Gardening," *Garden Variety*, 2013. https://gardenvarietynews.wordpress.com/2013/12/27/a-brief-history-of-intensive-gardening/.

[2] "A History of Vegetable Gardening: Grok's Berries to the Victory Garden," *Vegetable Garden Guru*. https://www.vegetablegardenguru.com/history-of-vegetable-gardening.html.

[3] "Raised Beds - Vegetable Growing in Raised Beds," *Allotment & Gardens*. https://www.allotment-garden.org/gardening-information/raised-beds/ (accessed 2021).

[4] "10 alpines to grow," *BBC Gardeners' World Magazine*, 2020. https://www.gardenersworld.com/plants/10-alpines-to-grow/.

[5] Andrew, "How to use Raised Beds For Vegetable Gardening," *Quickcrop.co.uk*, 2017. https://www.quickcrop.co.uk/blog/raised-bed-vegetable-gardening-2/.

[6] DaNelle, "The Best Material for Raised Garden Boxes," *Weed 'em & Reap*, 2014. https://www.weedemandreap.com/best-material-for-raised-garden-boxes/.

[7] "Douglas-Fir," *The Wood Database*, 2021. https://www.wood-database.com/douglas-fir/#:~:text=Rot%20Resistance%3A%20Douglas-Fir%20heartwood.

[8] N. Faires, "10 Excellent Reasons to Use Raised Beds in Your Garden," *Eartheasy Guides & Articles*, 2017. https://learn.eartheasy.com/articles/10-excellent-reasons-to-use-raised-beds-in-your-garden/.

[9] Jonathon David Madore, "Best Material for Raised Garden Beds (4 Choices To Make Them Last!)," *GreenUpSide*. https://greenupside.com/best-material-for-raised-garden-beds-make-them-last/.

[10] "Learn the Difference Between Garden Soil and Raised Bed Soil," *Kellogg Garden Organics™*, 2020. https://www.kellogggarden.com/blog/soil/difference-between-garden-soil-and-raised-bed-soil/.

[11] Mother Earth News, "Earth-Sheltered Home Kits for Owner-Builders - Green Homes," *Mother Earth News*. https://www.motherearthnews.com/green-homes/earth-sheltered-home-kits.

[12] S. O'Connor, "What is an Engineering Brick and what are the applications of an Engineering Brick," *Likestone*, 2018. https://likestone.ie/2018/08/23/purpose-and-specification-of-an-engineering-brick/.

[13] "Raised beds," *www.rhs.org.uk*, 2021. https://www.rhs.org.uk/advice/profile?pid=428.

[14] "Raised Beds: Benefits and Maintenance - Gardening Solutions - University of Florida, Institute of Food and Agricultural Sciences," *gardeningsolutions.ifas.ufl.edu*, 2021. https://gardeningsolutions.ifas.ufl.edu/design/types-of-gardens/raised-beds.html.

[15] Ryan, "Black Locust: the Sustainable Hardwood of our Future?," *Metropolis*, 2012. https://www.metropolismag.com/uncategorized/black-locust-the-sustainable-hardwood-of-our-future/.

[16] Z. Wasielewski, "Cedar Decking Pros and Cons," *JAY-K Lumber*. https://www.jay-k.com/cedar-decking-pros-cons/.

[17] A. White, "Raised Bed Gardening Benefits: What do they actually do?," *Gardener's Path*, 2016. https://gardenerspath.com/gear/enclosures/the-benefits-of-raised-bed-gardening/.

[18] "Who Is Your Garden For - You Or Your Neighbors?," *Smiling Gardener*, 2015. https://www.smilinggardener.com/introduction/who-is-your-garden-for/.

[19] T. Besemer, "14 Common Raised Bed Mistakes You Must Avoid," *Rural Sprout*, 2021. https://www.ruralsprout.com/raised-bed-mistakes/.

[20] "Soil Calculator," *www.gardeners.com*. https://www.gardeners.com/how-to/soil-calculator/7558.html.

[21] "How to Build Raised Garden Beds," *DIY*. https://www.diynetwork.com/how-to/outdoors/gardening/how-to-build-raised-garden-beds.

[22] T. Nolan, "6 things to think about before preparing a raised bed garden," *Savvy Gardening*, 2017. https://savvygardening.com/preparing-a-raised-bed-garden/.

[23] T. Nolan, "4x8 Raised Bed Vegetable Garden Layout Ideas," *Savvy Gardening*, 2020. https://savvygardening.com/4x8-raised-bed-vegetable-garden-layout/.

[24] "Rise Above Challenges with Raised Garden Beds, How to Build DIY," *Earth's Ally*, 2019. https://earthsally.com/gardening-basics/rise-above-challenges-with-raised-garden-beds.html.

[25] M. Thoma, "How To Avoid 5 Common Mistakes And Build The Best Raised Garden Beds," *Healthy Fresh Homegrown by Tranquil Urban Homestead*, 2020. https://tranquilurbanhomestead.com/raised-garden-beds/.

[26] C. Boeckmann, "Vegetable Gardening for Beginners," *Old Farmer's Almanac*, 2021. https://www.almanac.com/vegetable-gardening-for-beginners.

[27] D. Cat, "Choosing the Best Materials for Raised Garden Beds," *Homestead and Chill*, 2021. https://homesteadandchill. com/materials-raised-garden-beds/.

[28] S. Cowan, "How to Build a Raised Garden Bed: Best Kits and DIY Plans," *learn.eartheasy.com*, 2020. https://learn. eartheasy.com/articles/how-to-build-a-raised-garden-bed-best-kits-and-diy-plans.

[29] "Gardening tips for raised beds," *BBC Gardeners' World Magazine*, 2019. https://www.gardenersworld.com/plants/ gardening-tips-for-raised-beds/.

[30] "Guide to Raised Garden Beds: Plans, Timing, Tending," *Gardeners Supply*, 2019. https://www.gardeners.com/how-to/raised-bed-basics/8565.html.

[31] J. Hall, "Hardscaping 101: Raised Garden Beds," *Gardenista*, 2020. https://www.gardenista.com/posts/ hardscaping-101-raised-garden-bed-how-to/.

[32] "How to Build a Super Easy 4x8 Raised Bed," *Bonnie Plants*. https://bonnieplants.com/gardening/super-easy-4-x-8-raised-bed/.

[33] M. Iannotti, "15 Raised Bed Garden Design Ideas," *The Spruce*, 2018. https://www.thespruce.com/raised-bed-garden-ideas-4172154.

[34] J. Lamp'l, "Raised Bed Garden from A - Z," *joe gardener®*, 2018. https://joegardener.com/podcast/raised-bed-gardening-pt-1/.

[35] S. Lyons, "What Is a Permaculture Garden and How Do I Start One?," *The Spruce*, 2021. https://www.thespruce.com/how-to-start-a-permaculture-garden-4050110.

[36] "Raised Garden Beds: How to Build & Where to Buy," *learn.eartheasy.com*. https://learn.eartheasy.com/guides/raised-garden-beds/.

[37] S. DeJohn, "New USDA Plant Hardiness Map - Zone Finder," *Gardeners Supply*, 2021. https://www.gardeners.com/how-to/new-hardiness-map/7887.html.

[38] J. Engels, "Intercropping: What It Is, What It Isn't, and Why We Do It," *The Permaculture Research Institute*, 2016. https://www.permaculturenews.org/2016/08/12/intercropping-what-it-is-what-it-isnt-and-why-we-do-it/.

[39] "Gardening Encyclopedia," *www.gardeners.com*. https://www.gardeners.com/gardening-encyclopedia.

[40] M. Iannotti, "How to Use Succession Planting in Your Garden," *The Spruce*, 2019. https://www.thespruce.com/succession-planting-1403366.

[41] N. Jabbour, "A Vegetable Garden Planner for High Yields & Healthy Plants," *Savvy Gardening*, 2019. https://savvygardening.com/vegetable-garden-planner/.

[42] K-State Research and Extension, "Intensive Spacing for Raised Beds,." [Online]. Available: https://www.johnson.k-state.edu/docs/lawn-and-garden/in-house-publications/vegetables/Intensive%20Spacing%20for%20Raised%20Beds_13.pdf.

[43] Project Diaries, "How to: Start Square Foot Gardening," *www.youtube.com*, 2017. https://www.youtube.com/watch?v=n9mA0VELRMs.

[44] L. Seaman, "Vegetable Garden Seed Ordering Tips," *learn.eartheasy.com*, 2011. https://learn.eartheasy.com/articles/vegetable-garden-seed-ordering-tips/.

[45] Old Farmer's Almanac, "Marigolds," *Old Farmer's Almanac*, 2019. https://www.almanac.com/plant/marigolds.

[46] H. Buckner, "How to Plant and Grow Arugula: Add 'Rocket' Greens to Your Garden," *Gardener's Path*, 2019. https://gardenerspath.com/plants/vegetables/grow-arugula.

[47] H. Buckner, "How to Plant and Grow Turnips for Roots and Greens," *Gardener's Path*, 2019. https://gardenerspath.com/plants/vegetables/grow-turnips.

[48] B. L. Grant, "StackPath," *www.gardeningknowhow.com*, 2020. https://www.gardeningknowhow.com/edible/vegetables/beans/growing-pole-beans.htm.

[49] C. Groom, "How to Grow Bok Choy," *Gardener's Path*, 2019. https://gardenerspath.com/plants/vegetables/grow-bok-choy.

[50] "Grow Kale in India with these easy steps," *AllThatGrows*. https://www.allthatgrows.in/blogs/posts/grow-kale-in-india-with-these-easy-steps.

[51] G. Heber, "Gardener's Path," *Gardener's Path*, 2019. https://gardenerspath.com/plants/vegetables/grow-peas/.

[52] G. Heber, "How to Grow Cucumbers," *Gardener's Path*, 2019. https://gardenerspath.com/plants/vegetables/cucumbers/.

[53] K. Hicks-Hamblin, "How to Grow Bush Beans | Gardener's Path," *Gardener's Path*, 2020. https://gardenerspath.com/plants/vegetables/grow-bush-beans.

[54] N. Jabbour, "Plant fast growing vegetables for a homegrown harvest in 6 weeks or less," *Savvy Gardening*, 2014. https://savvygardening.com/one-month-or-less-super-speedy-vegetables/.

[55] N. Jabbour, "6 high-yield vegetables," *Savvy Gardening*, 2016. https://savvygardening.com/6-high-yield-vegetables/.

[56] N. Jabbour, "The Easiest Vegetables to Grow in Garden Beds and Containers," *Savvy Gardening*, 2019. https://savvygardening.com/easiest-vegetables-to-grow/.

[57] R. Kennedy, "How to Plant and Grow Zucchini Squash | Gardener's Path," *Gardener's Path*, 2020. https://gardenerspath.com/plants/vegetables/grow-zucchini.

[58] L. Knerl, "How to Grow Spinach," *Gardener's Path*, 2019. https://gardenerspath.com/plants/vegetables/grow-spinach.

[59] L. Knerl, "How to Grow Summer Squash," *Gardener's Path*, 2019. https://gardenerspath.com/plants/vegetables/grow-summer-squash.

[60] L. Kring, "How to Grow Radishes in Your Veggie Patch," *Gardener's Path*, 2019. https://gardenerspath.com/plants/vegetables/grow-radishes.

[61] L. Kring, "How to Grow Cherry Tomatoes," *Gardener's Path*, 2020. https://gardenerspath.com/plants/vegetables/growing-cherry-tomatoes.

[62] A. Shidler, "How to Plant and Grow Leaf Lettuce," *Gardener's Path*, 2018. https://gardenerspath.com/plants/vegetables/grow-leaf-lettuce.

[63] B. Vanheems, "Growing Asian Greens from Sowing to Harvest," *GrowVeg*, 2018. https://www.growveg.com/guides/growing-oriental-leaves-from-sowing-to-harvest/.

[64] A. White, "How to Plant and Grow Garlic," *Gardener's Path*, 2019. https://gardenerspath.com/plants/vegetables/growing-garlic.

[65] D. Grist, "Protecting Berries from Birds: Blueberries, Raspberries, Strawberries," *www.gardeners.com*, 2021. https://www.gardeners.com/how-to/protecting-berries-from-birds/7532.html.

[66] "Growing Berries and Asparagus in Raised Beds," *www.gardeners.com*, 2021. https://www.gardeners.com/how-to/berries-asparagus-raised-beds/7562.html

[67] K. Lofgren, "How to Grow Gooseberries," *Gardener's Path*, 2020. https://gardenerspath.com/plants/fruit/grow-gooseberry.

[68] J. Mcintosh, "Grow Juicy Blackberries for Smoothies, Pies, and Jams," *The Spruce*, 2020. https://www.thespruce.com/how-to-grow-and-care-for-blackberries-4589374.

[69] A. Shilder, "How to Grow Your Own Raspberries," *Gardener's Path*, 2019. https://gardenerspath.com/plants/fruit/grow-raspberries.

[70] A. Shidler, "How to Plant and Grow Strawberries," *Gardener's Path*, 2019. https://gardenerspath.com/plants/fruit/grow-strawberries.

[71] B. Vanheems, "Easy-Peasy Soft Fruits for Beginners to Grow," *GrowVeg*, 2018. https://www.growveg.com/guides/easy-peasy-soft-fruits-for-beginners-to-grow/.

[72] Andrew, "How To Create A Raised Bed Herb Garden With This Guide from Quickcrop," *Quickcrop blog*, 2017. https://www.quickcrop.ie/blog/2017/05/how-to-create-a-raised-bed-herb-garden/.

[73] G. Heber, "Learn How to Grow Cilantro and Coriander," *Gardener's Path*, 2018. https://gardenerspath.com/plants/herbs/grow-cilantro/.

[74] G. Heber, "How to Grow Mint in the Garden (Without It Taking Over)," *Gardener's Path*, 2020. https://gardenerspath.com/plants/herbs/grow-mint.

[75] K. Hicks-Hamblin, "How to Plant and Grow Dill Weed," *Gardener's Path*, 2020. https://gardenerspath.com/plants/herbs/grow-dill.

[76] L. Kring, "How to Grow Parsley in Your Home Herb Garden," *Gardener's Path*, 2020. https://gardenerspath.com/plants/herbs/grow-parsley.

[77] L. Kring, "How to Grow Rosemary in the Home Herb Garden," *Gardener's Path*, 2020. https://gardenerspath.com/plants/herbs/grow-rosemary.

[78] L. Kring, "How to Grow Tarragon in Your USDA Hardiness Zone," *Gardener's Path*, 2017. https://gardenerspath.com/plants/herbs/how-to-grow-tarragon.

[79] M. G. Leslie, "How to Plant and Grow Basil," *Gardener's Path*, 2018. https://gardenerspath.com/plants/herbs/homegrown-basil.

[80] A. Shidler, "How to Grow Chives in the Herb Garden," *Gardener's Path*, 2019. https://gardenerspath.com/plants/herbs/grow-chives.

[81] N. Schiller, "Grow Common Sage, a Mediterranean Culinary Staple," *Gardener's Path*, 2020. https://gardenerspath.com/plants/herbs/common-sage/.

[82] Angela, "Best Way to Water Raised-Bed Gardens," *Growing In The Garden*, 2019. https://growinginthegarden.com/best-way-to-water-raised-bed-gardens/.

[83] "Control Pests Naturally in Your Raised Garden Beds," *learn.eartheasy.com*. https://learn.eartheasy.com/guides/control-pests-naturally-in-your-raised-garden-beds/.

[84] M. H. Dyer, "Benefits of Drip Irrigation," *Gardening Know How*, 2016. https://blog.gardeningknowhow.com/trends/benefits-of-drip-irrigation/.

[85] "How to Maintain a Raised Garden Bed," *The Home Depot.* https://www.homedepot.com/c/ai/how-to-maintain-a-raised-garden-bed/9ba683603be9fa5395fab90b72df4a4.

[86] N. Jabbour, "A Weed Free Garden: 9 Strategies for Reducing Weeds," *Savvy Gardening,* 2020. https://savvygardening.com/weed-free-garden/.

[87] D. Johnson, "How to Water 12-Inch Raised Vegetable Beds," *Home Guides,* 2020. https://homeguides.sfgate.com/water-12inch-raised-vegetable-beds-35252.html.

[88] J. Lamp'l, "Why Mulch Matters," *joe gardener®,* 2019. https://joegardener.com/podcast/110-why-mulch-matters/.

[89] G. Seaman, "Raised Beds: Preparing your Garden Beds for Spring," *learn.eartheasy.com,* 2011. https://learn.eartheasy.com/articles/raised-beds-preparing-your-garden-beds-for-spring/.

[90] G. Seaman, "7 Reasons to Hand Water your Garden," *learn.eartheasy.com,* 2015. https://learn.eartheasy.com/articles/7-reasons-to-hand-water-your-garden/.

[91] J. Walliser, "Preventing Pests in Your Garden: 5 Strategies for Success," *Savvy Gardening,* 2016. https://savvygardening.com/preventing-pests-in-your-garden/.

[92] "How to Harvest Vegetables," *www.burpee.com.* https://www.burpee.com/gardenadvicecenter/standard-articles-and-videos/gardening-how-to-articles/harvesting-vegetables/article10387.html.

[93] N. Jabbour, "A Handy Guide to Harvesting Vegetables," *Savvy Gardening*, 2017. https://savvygardening.com/harvesting-vegetables/.

[94] Piper Terrett, "Dealing with a vegetable glut," *The Frugal Life*, 2009. https://piperterrett.wordpress.com/2009/07/16/dealing-with-a-vegetable-glut/.

[95] "Trees for smaller gardens," *www.rhs.org.uk*. https://www.rhs.org.uk/advice/profile?pid=117.

[96] "Which shrubs to grow in raised beds," *Love The Garden*. https://www.lovethegarden.com/uk-en/article/which-shrubs-grow-raised-beds#:~:text=There%20are%20several%20winter%2Dflowering.

[97] J. Harrington, "How to Get Rid of Grass for a Raised Garden," *Home Guides*. https://homeguides.sfgate.com/rid-grass-raised-garden-68416.html.

[98] "Grow a Good Life," *Grow a Good Life*, 2015. https://growagoodlife.com/vegetable-garden-map-garden-beds/.

[99] "Non Toxic Surface Treatments," *www.rainforestinfo.org.au*. https://www.rainforestinfo.org.au/good_wood/ntox_trs.htm.

[100] "Raised Beds: Soil Depth Requirements," *Eartheasy Guides & Articles*. https://learn.eartheasy.com/guides/

Every Psalm

for

Easy Singing

A translation for singing
arranged in daily portions

Verse only edition

Prepared and translated by

C.W.H. Griffiths, M.A.

pearlpublications.co.uk

Contact: info@pearlpublications.co.uk

Every Psalm for Easy Singing: A translation for singing arranged in daily portions. Verse only edition

Paperback: ISBN 978-1-901397-06-2
Hardback: ISBN 978-1-901397-07-9
E Book: ISBN 978-1-901397-08-6

British Library CIP Data available.

BISAC: REL006120; REL006770; REL055020

We acknowledge with thanks permission from Christian Focus Publications to quote Alec Motyer, *Psalms by the Day* and also Alec Motyer, Journey. *Psalms for Pilgrim People*.

The help of David Legg, Margaret Maclean, Hendrik van der Poel, Angharad Griffiths and Margaret Watkinson in the completion of this book is gratefully acknowledged.

Dedicated to the memory of

my beloved daughter,

Naomi

who now sings a new song

CONTENTS

PREFACE

Personal and family praise and worship has been neglected by Christians and Churches for generations. For most Christians the 'voice of praise' at home now comes from our favourite singers and groups at the press of a button. Perhaps we even leave the choice to a Christian radio station or Alexa. If we sing God's praise at all at home, it is a sort of sing-along karaoke to our CD player or iPad.

When Governments introduced restrictions in response to the Covid 19 pandemic Churches closed their doors. When restrictions were eased, they re-opened, but with congregations gagged by face coverings, and forbidden to sing. Churches turned for solutions, not to the old paths of family and personal worship under the supervision of the local Church, but to untried and untested innovation. For many people, the local 'body of Christ' was replaced by virtual association with Churches in distant places, and perhaps even distant lands. Congregational singing was lost.

This reinforced the idea that praise is something that we listen to, rather than 'the fruit of our lips' - what is pleasing to the ear, rather than 'teaching and admonishing one another in psalms and hymns and spiritual songs, singing, with grace in your hearts, to the Lord'.

We hope that this Psalm book in 365 portions for singing; together with its companion *A Help for Using the Psalms in Personal and Family Worship* will encourage the old habit and discipline of personal and family worship that includes singing. If it does, that will help to build a stronger defence against future State restrictions, or even persecution of the Church.

Chris Griffiths, February 2023

INTRODUCTION TO THIS EDITION

This edition of *Every Psalm for Easy Singing* gives the entire Book of Psalms in verse. The translation has been divided into 365 portions intended for daily use by individuals, or for family worship. The portions vary in length as they follow the subject matter and structure of each Psalm.

This Psalm book can be used with *A Help for using the Psalms in Personal and Family Worship*, (also published by Pearl Publications), which gives devotional and expository comment on each of the same 365 portions.

The object of Psalm-singing is to sing words given by the Holy Spirit for use in worship. What we sing should therefore be as close as possible to the original, in a form that anyone can sing. That is the aim of this translation.

To sing inspired words requires concentration of the mind. It should, indeed, at times be joyful, but the Psalms are not simple choruses, or repetitive 'worship songs'. We must therefore sing the Psalms thoughtfully at a measured speed, looking to the Lord to bless and instruct us. It is a different worship-form from that used in almost all modern Churches.

All the Psalms are set to one metre in this translation. This means that the whole book can be sung to a single tune, for example, the tune to 'Abide with me'.

In Appendix 1 we suggest suitable tunes for use with this Psalm book. These are also on the Pearl Publications website, together with audio files that can be played to assist familiarisation with the tunes.

An Expanded Study Edition of *Every Psalm for Easy Singing* has been published. That edition explains the approach adopted in translation. It has extensive exegetical footnotes and appendices. See the note in the Advertisement at the end of this book.

CORE PRINCIPLES

This book grew from the following convictions.

1. That the Psalms, as inspired writings, are fundamentally different from hymns, choruses and worship songs (2 Sam 23:2).

2. That Scripture requires God's people in the New Testament (1 Corinthians 14.26) as well as in the Old Testament (Psalm 105:2) to sing the Psalms.

3. That it is 'profitable' to sing all the Psalms (2 Timothy 3:16).

4. That by singing the Psalms the believer glorifies God, is instructed in the will and purposes of God (Psalm 101:1, Colossians 3:16), and expresses his or her own spiritual aspirations - mourning and joy - in the words of Scripture (Psalm 22:1, James 5:13).

5. That praise to God is essentially 'the fruit of our lips' (Hebrews 13:15). All the Psalms should be singable without needing knowledge of dozens of metres and hundreds of tunes, and without needing musical accompaniment.

6. That any translation of the Scriptures, whether for reading or for singing, should keep as close to the inspired words as possible (Jeremiah 36, Revelation 22:19).

7. That any translation should be transparent regarding the translation decisions made (Acts 17:11). We have been guided in our translation primarily by the translators of the Reformation period.

8. That a translation of the Scriptures should avoid novelty or originality (2 Peter 1:20). We have constantly consulted well-respected expositors of a previous age (see Appendix 2).

Book 1

Psalms 1 - 41

1   Psalm 1

[1] Blessings and happiness are on that man
who does not walk as wicked ones advise,
who does not linger in the sinners' path,
who does not sit down in the scorners' seat.

[2] But in the LORD's Law he has his delight:
That Law, his constant thought both day and night.
[3] He's like a tree by streams of water set,
Which fruits in season, and its leaves don't fade.

Whatever work he does shall prosper well;
[4] Not so the wicked - they are like the chaff,
Which wind blows from the harvest threshing floors.
[5] Therefore, in judgment, wicked ones won't stand.

Sinners will not rise up. They will not stand
within the company of righteous ones.
[6] The LORD well knows the path the righteous take;
The path the wicked take will pass away.

2   Psalm 2:1-6

[1] Why do the nations gather in their rage?
Why do the peoples make such foolish plans?
[2] Earth's kings have set themselves in readiness;
Together rulers meet to plot and plan -

Against the LORD and his Anointed One!
[3] Saying, 'Let's break their chains and ties from us'.
[4] But he who sits in heaven will just laugh;
My Lord will mock them, and treat them with scorn.

[5] Then in his anger he will speak to them
And in his fury will strike them with fear.
[6] 'I have anointed and set my own King
On Zion, mountain of my holiness'.

3   **Psalm 2:7-12**

⁷ I will declare the LORD's decree to me,
'I have begotten you, my Son, this day;
⁸ Ask me, I'll give you an inheritance -
The nations! You'll possess earth's farthest lands'.

⁹ 'You shall, as with a rod of iron, break
And you will smash them like a potter's jar'.
¹⁰ So, kings be wise. Earth's judges all be warned.
¹¹ Rejoice, with trembling. Serve the Lord with fear.

¹² O kiss the Son, lest he should be enraged
And you will then be cut off from the way,
For soon and quickly does his anger burn.
Blest are all those who take refuge in him.

4   **Psalm 3**

¹ O LORD how many are my enemies!
Many are those who rise up against me!
² So many people say about my soul
'There's no deliverance for him in God'.

³ But yet, O LORD, you are a shield for me
My glory and the lifter of my head.
⁴ My voice has cried aloud unto the LORD;
From his own holy hill he answered me.

⁵I lay down and I slept; and then I woke,
Because the LORD upholds me. ⁶I'll not fear
10,000 set against me round about.
⁷Arise, O LORD, and save me, O my God.

For all my foes you have hit on the cheek;
Broken in pieces are the wicked's teeth.
⁸ Deliverance belongs unto the LORD.
Upon your people will your blessing rest!

5   Psalm 4

1 Answer me when I call, my righteous God.
You gave relief when I was in distress
When I was hemmed in, you then gave me room
Be gracious to me. Listen to my prayer!

2 O you great men, just how long will it be?
For how long will my glory be disgraced?
How long will you love what is vanity?
How long will you seek what are only lies?

3 Know this: the LORD selects the one he loves
The LORD will hear me when I call to him
4 Tremble in awe and see that you don't sin.
Speak to your heart upon your bed. Be still.

5 Give offerings of righteous sacrifice.
And place your confidence upon the LORD.
6 Many are saying, 'Who will show us good?'
O Lift the light of your face on us, LORD!

7 You have bestowed more gladness to my heart,
More than the time their corn and wine increased.
8 In quiet peace I will lie down and sleep;
For you alone LORD, make me dwell secure.

6   Psalm 5:1-6

1 Incline your ear unto my words O LORD.
My inmost thoughts O do consider now!
2 O heed my cry, my King, my God, I pray.
3 LORD, in the morning, you will hear my voice.

I will prepare at morning, and keep watch,
4 You're not a GOD, who takes delight in sin.
You will not harbour any wickedness
5 The boastful shall not stand before your eyes.

[Continued →

You hate all those who work iniquity.
6 You will destroy all those who speak a lie.
The LORD abhors the man who would shed blood.
The LORD abhors the man who would deceive.

7   Psalm 5:7-12

7 But, as for me, through your great steadfast love,
I'll come into your house. And in your fear
I will bow down toward your holy place:
Even the Temple of your holiness.

8 O lead and guide me in your righteousness,
Because my foes do lie in wait, O LORD.
Before me make your pathway smooth and straight.
9 For nothing in their mouth is fixed or sure

Inside they are so full of wickedness;
Their mouth is like a yawning open grave;
Their tongue they use to flatter and deceive.
10 Charge guilt upon them - punish them, O God.

By their own wicked counsels make them fall.
For all their trespasses thrust them away
Because it is against you they rebelled.
11 But let all those who trust in you rejoice.

Let them for ever sing: you'll shelter them.
Let them that love your name rejoice in you.
12 Because you'll bless the righteous one, O LORD.
Surround him with your favour as a shield.

8   Psalm 6:1-5

1 Do not rebuke me in your anger, LORD,
Nor in your hot displeasure chasten me.
2 Be merciful, O LORD, for I am weak.
My very bones are aching. Heal me LORD!

[Continued →

³ My soul is greatly troubled and dismayed.
How long? How long? O LORD, I cry to you!
⁴ Return again, O LORD, rescue my soul,
And for your mercy's sake, O LORD save me.

⁵ For your remembrance is not there in death
And there is no memorial to you.
In Sheol who is there that gives you thanks?
In Sheol who will offer thanks to you?

9   Psalm 6:6-10

⁶ I am worn out with all my sighs and groans.
I cry and weep through each and every night.
I make my bed to swim with all my tears.
My couch I water as my tears do fall.

⁷ Because of grief my eyesight wastes away.
Through all of my oppressors it grows old.
⁸ Depart from me, all who do wickedness.
The LORD has listened to my tearful cry.

⁹ The LORD has heard my earnest cry for grace.
So, therefore, will the LORD accept my prayer.
¹⁰ All those who hate me shall be shamed and vexed.
They shall turn back; at once be put to shame.

10   Psalm 7:1-8

¹ O LORD, my God, in you I put my trust.
Save me from all who hunt me and pursue.
Deliver me. ² Lest he should rend my soul,
Lest lion-like he tears with none to help.

³ O LORD my God, if I have done this thing;
And if injustice be upon my hands;
⁴ If I rewarded evil to my friend;
(I rescued him who wrongly was my foe).

[Continued →

5 Then let the enemy pursue my soul,
And overtake it, and tread down my life.
Let him tread down my life into the ground
And lay my honour down unto the dust.

6 O LORD, rise up and show your anger now.
Stand up against the fury of my foes.
Wake as from sleep - arouse yourself for me,
For you command that judgment should be done.

7 Around you will the peoples congregate
And for their sake return to the high place
8 Judge peoples, LORD and justly treat me, LORD.
After my righteousness and uprightness.

11   Psalm 7:9-17

9 Oh, make the evil of the wicked cease.
Confirm the righteous. You search mind and heart.
O righteous God, 10 My shield is upon God.
He saves the men of honest, upright hearts.

11 God - righteous Judge! GOD - outraged every day!
12 If one will not turn back, he'll whet his sword.
He's surely bent his bow, ready to shoot
13 With deadly weapons and with bolts of fire.

14 Behold! one travails to bear wickedness
Conceiving mischief, gives birth to a lie.
15 He made a pit, and when he'd dug it out
He fell into the ditch that he'd prepared.

16 His mischief shall return on his own head,
And on his skull will violence descend.
17 My thanks will answer the LORD's righteousness.
Sing psalms unto his name - the LORD Most High.

12   Psalm 8

¹ O LORD, our Lord, how splendid is your name -
How splendid is your name in all the earth!
Over the heavens you your glory set.
Display your glory over them above!

² Out of the mouth of infants and of babes
You have established strength, perfected praise.
Because of those who are your hurtful foes,
To still the enemy and vengeful one.

³ Seeing your heavens that your fingers made,
The moon and stars that you have put in place
⁴ What is frail man that you remember him?
The son of man that you would visit him?

⁵ You've made him little less than the angels are.
Honour and glory gave him, as a crown
⁶ Over your handiwork you gave him rule.
You have set all things underneath his feet.

⁷ All sheep and cattle; wild beasts; ⁸ birds that fly;
Fish and all creatures that swim in the sea.
⁹ O LORD, our Lord, how splendid is your name -
How splendid is your name in all the earth!

13   Psalm 9:1-10

¹ I will praise you, O LORD, with all my heart.
I will declare the wonders you have done.
² I will be glad and will rejoice in you.
Sing psalms unto your name. You are Most High!

³ Because my enemies are driven back
They shall be cast down, cut off from your sight.
⁴ You have upheld my judgment and my cause.
You are enthroned and judge in righteousness.

[*Continued* →

⁵ You censured nations: crushed the wicked one.
You blotted out their name for evermore.
⁶ Ruined for ever is the enemy.
Forgotten are the cities you plucked up.

⁷ The LORD will take his seat for evermore.
He has set up his throne, his judgment seat.
⁸ He'll judge and rule the world with righteousness.
In uprightness the peoples he will judge.

⁹ The LORD's a refuge for all those oppressed:
A place of refuge in distressing times.
¹⁰ And those who know your name will trust in you.
You've not abandoned those who seek you, LORD.

14   Psalm 9:11-20

¹¹ Sing praises, sing with psalms, unto the LORD,
Unto the LORD, he who in Zion dwells!
Among the peoples make known what he's done.
¹² He who avenges blood remembers them!

The LORD does not forget the anguished cry,
When the afflicted ones call out for help.
¹³ See my affliction LORD, and pity me,
For it was from my hateful enemies

You raise me from the very gates of death:
¹⁴ In Zion's daughter's gates, I will praise you.
In your deliverance I will rejoice.
¹⁵ The nations are sunk in the pit they made.

Their foot's caught in the net that they had hid.
¹⁶ The Lord is now made known. Judgment is done!
The wicked one is trapped in his own schemes.
Higgaion. Selah. Think upon these things!

[Continued →

¹⁷ The wicked ones to Sheol shall descend,
All nations who do not remember God.
¹⁸ The needy shall not always be forgot,
The hope of the afflicted shall not cease.

¹⁹ Arise, O LORD, and let not man prevail!
Bring judgment to the nations in your sight.
²⁰ Cause them to know your terror and your fear,
So shall the nations know they are but men.

15   Psalm 10:1-11

¹ Why do you stand so far away, O LORD?
Why hide yourself in times of great distress?
² The wicked in his pride hunts down the poor,
And they are caught in schemes that they devised.

³ The wicked one boasts of his soul's desire,
Blesses the greedy and reviles the LORD.
⁴ In angry pride the wicked does not seek -
In all his thoughts there is no room for God.

⁵ And yet his ways at all times do succeed
(Your judgments are on high, out of his sight).
He scorns all foes, ⁶ and says within his heart
'Nothing will shake me. Always trouble-free!'

⁷ His mouth is full of curses, lies, and threats,
Under his tongue vexatious vanity.
⁸ In villages in ambush he awaits.
The innocent he murders secretly.

His eyes watch slyly for the helpless one.
⁹ He lies in wait as in a lion's den.
He lies in wait that he may catch the poor;
Seizes the poor and draws him in his net.

[Continued →

¹⁰ He crouches, and he gets himself down low.
Thus do the helpless fall down by his power.
¹¹ 'GOD has forgot' he says unto his heart,
'He's hid his face, and he will never see'.

16   Psalm 10:12-18)

¹² Arise, O LORD! Lift up your hand, O GOD!
Do not forget the ones who are oppressed.
¹³ Why does the wicked one disparage God?
And, in his heart, say 'You will not enquire!'

¹⁴ But you have seen, and you yourself regard
Trouble and grief, to pay back by your hand.
The helpless one commits himself to you.
You are the helper of the fatherless.

¹⁵ Break the arm of the wicked evil one.
Seek out his wickedness till you find none.
¹⁶ The LORD is king for ever, evermore:
The nations have been cut off from his land.

¹⁷ O LORD you heard the longing of the poor.
Strengthen their heart. Incline your ear to them
¹⁸ To vindicate the orphan and oppressed
To end the terror of the man of earth.

17   Psalm 11

¹ I trust the LORD, so why say to my soul
'Flee to your mountain as a bird takes flight'?
² For, surely, look - the wicked bend their bow.
See! - how they set their arrow on the string.

They darkly shoot at men of upright heart.
³ Whatever should a righteous person do
If the foundations are to be destroyed?
⁴ The LORD is in his holy temple still.

[Continued →

It's in the heavens the LORD has his throne.
His eyes behold. He tries the sons of men.
5 The righteous the LORD tries: but his soul hates
He who is wicked and loves cruelty.

6 He will make snares fall on the wicked ones -
Fire, brimstone, tempest! This shall be their lot.
7 The LORD is righteous and loves righteousness;
He who is upright shall behold his face.

18   Psalm 12

1 Save LORD! The gracious man is at an end,
The faithful from the sons of men are gone.
2 Each one unto his neighbour speaks vain things.
They speak so smoothly with a double heart.

3 O may the LORD cut off all smooth lips now.
May he cut off the tongue that speaks great things.
4 Those who have said, 'We'll triumph by our tongues,
These are our lips, so who will master us?'

5 'Because the poor are plundered and laid waste;
Because the needy do lament and sigh',
'I will rise up' is what the LORD now says.
'From him who shows contempt I'll make them safe'.

6 The LORD's words are words that are pure and clean,
As silver melted when it's purified,
As passing through a furnace seven times,
As in a melting pot they are refined.

7 You will protect and you will keep them, LORD.
You will preserve him now and evermore.
8 On every side the wicked strut about
When vileness is exalted among men.

19   **Psalm 13**

¹ How long? Will you forget me always, LORD?
How long will you conceal your face from me?
² How long shall I keep scheming in my soul?
How long will daily sorrow grieve my heart?

And how long will my enemy rise up?
³ Look on me, answer me, O LORD, my God.
Lighten my eyes, lest I should sleep in death.
⁴ My enemy will say, 'I have prevailed!'

When I should fall, my foes would then rejoice,
⁵ But in your mercy I have put my trust.
In your salvation my heart will rejoice.
⁶ I'll sing unto the LORD. He's good to me!

20   **Psalm 14**

¹ 'There is no God'. The fool says in his heart.
They are corrupt and what they do is vile.
No one does good, no not a single one.
² The LORD from heaven sees the sons of men.

He looks to see if any understand,
If there are any who seek after God.
³ They've turned away. They're all together foul.
No one does good, no not a single one.

⁴ Do those who work such wickedness not know?
Who eat my people just as they eat bread -
These are the ones who don't call on the LORD.
⁵ But there they were, afraid with trembling fear.

For God is with the righteous company.
⁶ Though you deride the counsel of the poor,
Yet, nonetheless, his refuge is the LORD.
⁷ O give salvation unto Israel!

[Continued →

Salvation out of Zion may he give,
The LORD will bring his people back again.
When he shall turn them from captivity.
Jacob will joy and Israel be glad.

21   Psalm 15

¹ LORD, who will be a guest within your tent?
Who will abide upon your holy hill?
² It is the one whose walk is blemish-free,
For he does right and truth speaks in his heart.

³ He does not utter slander with his tongue
Harms not his friend, nor slurs one near to him,
⁴ But in his eyes the vile one is despised.
He honours those who truly fear the LORD.

He keeps his word, though it should cost him dear.
⁵ He does not lend his money at a price.
Nor takes reward to hurt the innocent.
He never shall be moved who does such things.

22   Psalm 16:1-6

¹ O GOD preserve me, please do keep me safe.
You are my refuge and in you I trust.
² 'You are My Lord' I say unto the LORD,
The good I do brings nothing unto you.

³ Saints of the earth are truly excellent,
All my delight is in those holy ones;
⁴ But sorrows will be multiplied to those
Who hastily run after other gods.

Their offerings of blood I will not make,
Nor will I take their names upon my lips
⁵ The LORD's my portion and he is my cup.
He takes good care of what he's given me.

[Continued →

6 In pleasant places the lines have been cast.
They measured out a pleasant place for me.
Yet more than that is my inheritance
It is a bright and pleasing thing for me.

23   Psalm 16:7-11

7 I'll bless the LORD, the one who counsels me.
Indeed, my heart instructs me in the night!
8 I keep the LORD before me all the time.
I'll not be moved with him at my right hand.

9 My heart is glad. My glory full of joy.
For yet my flesh shall dwell secure in hope.
10 To Sheol you will not forsake my soul,
Nor give the One you love to see the Pit.

11 You will reveal - you will make known to me
The path that leads to everlasting life.
Abundant joy is there before your face.
At your right hand are pleasures evermore.

24   Psalm 17:1-7

1 Hear a just cause. Attend, LORD, to my cry.
Please hear my prayer from lips free of deceit.
2 Send judgment out for me before your face -
Your eyes behold things that are true and right.

3 You tried my heart, examined me by night.
You tested and found nothing that was wrong.
I purposed that my mouth should not transgress.
4 The word you spoke kept me from things men do.

Thus, I avoided the Destroyer's ways.
5 Sustain me as I follow in your paths.
O keep my footsteps, so they may not slip.
6 To you I call. You'll answer me, O GOD.

[Continued →

Incline your ear to what I have to say.
7 Display the wonder of your steadfast love.
O Saviour of those seeking for refuge,
Save from those rising against your right hand.

25   Psalm 17:8-15

8 O keep me as the apple of your eye.
Hide me beneath the shadow of your wings,
9 From wicked ones who hurt me and oppress,
From deadly foes who circle me around.

10 Closed to all feeling, shut up in their fat,
They speak: their mouth is lifted up with pride.
11 We are beset by them at every step.
Their eyes are set to cast us to the ground.

12 He, like a lion, longs to rip and tear:
Like a young lion crouching in its hides.
13 Arise, O LORD, confront him, bring him down.
Save my soul from the wicked by your sword.

14 From mortal men, LORD, rescue with your hand,
From earthly men, whose portion is this life.
For with your treasure you fill up their womb.
With children in abundance they're supplied.

They leave their goods unto their little ones.
15 But I will see your face in righteousness.
I shall be satisfied when I awake,
For, in your likeness, I shall then appear.

26   Psalm 18:1-6

1 I love you fervently, O LORD, my strength.
2 The LORD's my rock, a fortress unto me.
He's my deliverer. He is my GOD.
He's my strong rock. I take my refuge there.

[Continued →

He is my shield - my buckler for the fight:
Horn of salvation and my high stronghold.
[3] I'll call upon the LORD, for praise is due,
I will be saved from all my enemies.

[4] Twined round about me were the cords of Death.
Belial's torrents made me so afraid.
[5] Sheol had cords around about me bound.
I was confronted by the snares of death.

[6] In my distress I cried unto the LORD.
I cried aloud for help unto my God.
Within his Temple he then heard my voice.
My cry before his face came to his ears.

27   Psalm 18:7-15

[7] His anger burned. The earth then shook and quaked.
To their foundations, hills were moved and shook.
[8] Smoke from his nostrils, and fire from his mouth!
By it were burning coals of fire consumed.

[9] He bowed the heavens, and he then came down:
Darkness - thick darkness - underneath his feet!
[10] Mounted upon a cherub he flew down.
Yes, he flew swiftly on the wings of wind.

[11] Darkness his secret place, his booth around
Darkness of waters, thick clouds of the skies
[12] Out of his brightness, his thick clouds went forth.
They went with hailstones and with coals of fire

[13] The LORD in heaven sent forth thunder's sound.
The Highest gave his voice: hail, coals of fire!
[14] He sent his arrows, and he scattered them:
Abundant lightnings, and he panicked them.

[15] The channels of the waters were then seen.
Foundations of the earth were then revealed.
All this occurred at your rebuke, O LORD.
It was accomplished by your nostrils' breath.

28   Psalm 18:16-19

16 He sent down from on high - took hold of me;
And from great waters he then drew me out.
17 Delivered me from my strong enemy:
Stronger than I, were those who hated me.

18 They had opposed in my day of distress,
But still the LORD was a support to me.
19 He brought me out into a spacious place.
He rescued me, for I was his delight.

29   Psalm 18:20-26

20 Therefore the LORD gave his reward to me:
According to my righteousness he gave.
Just as my hands were clean, as they were pure,
His recompense he rendered unto me.

21 For I have kept the pathways of the LORD.
And did not wickedly go from my God.
22 All of his judgments are before me set.
And his decrees I have not turned away.

23 I was without a blemish before him.
I kept myself from my iniquity.
24 Therefore the LORD rewarded righteousness:
Just as my hands were clean before his eyes

25 You will show mercy to the merciful,
Act without blame unto the blameless man.
26 He who is pure will know your purity.
The stubborn one will find you hostile too.

30   Psalm 18:27-36

27 You - you yourself - the humble people save.
But haughty and conceited looks bring down.
28 You are the one who lights my lamp, O LORD.
Into my darkness, my God will shine light!

[Continued →

²⁹ For by you, LORD, I run against a troop,
And by my God can even jump a wall.
³⁰ GOD's way is perfect; the LORD's word is tried.
He is a shield to all who trust in him.

³¹ For who is God except the LORD alone?
Who is a rock of refuge, but our God?
³² He is the God who clothes me round with strength.
He gives to me a perfect, blameless way.

³³ He makes my feet just like the feet of deer.
On my high places he makes me to stand.
³⁴ He trains my hands for battle and for war.
So, with my arms, I can press down the bow.

³⁵ To me you've given your salvation's shield.
It is your right hand that has held me up.
Your lowly gentleness has made me great.
³⁶ You gave a wide place, lest my feet should slip.

31   Psalm 18:37-45

³⁷ I chased my foes - have overtaken them;
Did not turn back until they were destroyed.
³⁸ I cut them through so that they could not rise,
And they were cast down underneath my feet.

³⁹ For you have bound me round with strength for war.
Those who rose up against me you subdued.
⁴⁰ You made my foes to turn their backs in flight,
So those that hate me I might then destroy.

⁴¹ They cried for help - there was no-one to save -
- cried to the LORD - but he no answer gave.
⁴² I beat them fine as dust, blown by the wind;
I cast them out, like dirt of muddy streets.

[Continued →

⁴³ You've saved me from the strifes the people make.
Over the nations you have made me head.
Even a people that I have not known -
That people will give service unto me.

⁴⁴ They will obey when they shall hear of me,
And strangers will submit themselves to me.
⁴⁵ The strangers will lose heart and fade away,
And come with trembling from where they have hid.

32   Psalm 18:46-50

⁴⁶ The LORD most surely lives! Blest be my Rock!
Lift up the God of my salvation high.
⁴⁷ He is the GOD who thus avenges me,
Who makes the peoples subject under me.

⁴⁸ He sets me free from all my enemies.
Above my foes you have exalted me,
And from the cruel man you rescued me.
⁴⁹ Among the nations I will thank you, LORD!

I will, with psalms, sing praises to your name.
⁵⁰ Great victories the LORD gives to his king.
To his Anointed he shows steadfast love;
To David and his offspring evermore.

33   Psalm 19:1-6

¹ The heavens do declare - GOD's glory tell;
The sky above shows what his hand has done.
² From day to day continually they speak;
Fresh knowledge night to night they do declare.

³ Though they are without speech and without words,
and (even though their voice cannot be heard)
⁴ Their line's extended throughout all the earth -
Their words unto the limit of the world.

[Continued →

23

He set in them a dwelling for the sun.
5 It is just like a bridegroom coming forth.
The sun comes forth out of his canopy -
Glad, like a strong man, now to run his course.

6 He rises from the heavens' farthest end;
Completes the circuit to its end again.
And there is nothing hidden from its warmth,
No-one is hidden from its scorching heat

34   Psalm 19:7-14

7 The LORD's, full, perfect Law restores the soul.
Sure is his Testimony. It makes wise.
8 Right precepts of the LORD rejoice the heart.
The LORD's command is pure - lights up the eyes.

9 Fear of the LORD is clean and it endures.
The judgments of the LORD are true and right.
10 Desirable much more than gold – pure gold.
Sweeter than honey and the honeycomb.

11 Moreover by them is your servant warned.
The keeping of them gives a great reward.
12 As for his errors - who can understand?
From hidden faults declare me innocent!

13 Keep back your servant from presumptuous sins.
Let them not have dominion over me.
Then I will be both blameless and complete.
From great transgression I shall be kept free.

14 O may the words I utter with my mouth,
The meditation of my heart in me,
Make it accepted - pleasing in your sight.
Be my strong Rock, Kinsman-Redeemer, LORD.

35   Psalm 20

¹ The LORD reply to you when trouble comes
And by the name of Jacob's God keep safe.
² Send you your help out of the Holy Place.
And out of Zion may he give you strength.

³ Remember all the offerings you made,
And your burnt sacrifice may he accept.
⁴ Give you according to your heart's desire;
Bring to completion all you plan to do.

⁵ We'll shout for joy in your deliverance!
And set our banners up in our God's name!
All your petitions may the LORD fulfil.
⁶ I know the LORD saves his Anointed One!

He, from his holy heaven, answers him,
With all the saving strength of his right hand.
⁷ Some put their trust in chariot, or horse;
The LORD's name we'll recall. He is our God.

⁸ Though they're brought down unto their knees and fall;
We have arisen and we stand upright.
⁹ O LORD, give your deliverance, and save.
The king will answer in the day we call.

36   Psalm 21:1-7

¹ The king rejoices in your strength, O LORD.
In your salvation he'll be full of joy.
² You've given to him what his heart desired,
What he requested you did not withhold.

³ You meet him with the blessings of what's good.
You put a crown of pure gold on his head.
⁴ He asked for life and you gave it to him -
Days that will last for ever, evermore

[Continued →

[5] Great is his glory through your saving work.
Majestic splendour you bestow on him.
[6] You have made him most blest for evermore.
You gladden him with joy before your face.

[7] Because the king is trusting in the LORD -
Because he rests in his unfailing love
(The loving-kindness of the Most High God) -
So, he shall not be shaken or removed.

37   Psalm 21:8-13

[8] Your hand will find out all your enemies.
Yes, those who hate you, your right hand will find.
[9] And you will make them as a blazing fire,
When it is time for you to show your face.

The LORD will then engulf them in his wrath;
And with a fire he will devour them up.
[10] Their offspring he'll destroy out of the earth;
Their issue from among the sons of men.

[11] For they intended evil against you.
They made a plot that they could not perform.
[12] For you will make them back away from you,
When in their sight you shall prepare your bow.

[13] O be exalted; LORD, be lifted high!
O be exalted in your strength and might!
So, we will sing, and surely we will praise,
And, singing psalms, will celebrate your power.

38   Psalm 22:1-5

[1] My GOD, my GOD, why have you left me so?
Far off from helping: from my groaning words!
[2] My God, I cry by day. You answer not.
There is no quiet for me in the night.

[Continued →

³ But you are holy: throned in Israel's praise.
⁴ Our fathers trusted: You delivered them.
⁵ They cried to you: and then they were set free
In you they trusted: They were not ashamed.

39   Psalm 22:6-13

⁶ I am a worm, and I'm not like a man:
Reproach of men, and by the people scorned.
⁷ All those who see me laugh at me and mock:
Make mouths at me, and joking shake their head

⁸ 'He cast himself, and trusted, on the LORD.
Let him deliver, since he pleases him!'
⁹ But you are he who took me from the womb,
And made me hope upon my mother's breasts.

¹⁰ I was cast forth upon you from my birth:
And from my mother's womb you've been my GOD.
¹¹ O be not distant or remote from me!
Trouble is near, and there's no-one to help.

¹² There are so many bulls surrounding me.
Strong bulls of Bashan circle me around.
¹³ And they have gaped upon me with their mouth,
Just as a lion goes to tear and roar.

40   Psalm 22:14-21

¹⁴ Poured out like water; bones all out of joint.
My heart within me melted, just like wax.
¹⁵ My strength is dried up, like an earthen pot.
My tongue just sticks and cleaves against my jaws.

By you I'm brought unto the dust of death,
¹⁶ For dogs surrounded and encompassed me.
A crowd of evil men are all around,
By them my hands and feet were pierced right through.

[Continued →

¹⁷ I count my bones. They look and stare at me.
¹⁸ They part my garments; cast lots for my clothes.
¹⁹ Do not be far away from me, O LORD.
You are my Strength. Come quickly to give aid!

²⁰ My soul - my life - deliver from the sword.
From the dog's grip, O save my precious life!
²¹ Give me salvation from the lion's mouth:
From the fierce oxen's horns. You've answered me!

41   Psalm 22:22-31

²² Unto my brothers, I will tell your name.
In the assembly, I'll give praise to you.
²³ Give praise to him all you who fear the LORD.
Offspring of Jacob, glory give to him.

All Israel's offspring, stand in awe of him.
²⁴ He did not scorn the humbling that he bore,
Did not abhor, nor hide his face from him.
But, when he cried to him for help, he heard.

²⁵ You'll be my praise in the great gathering.
I'll pay my vows before those who fear him.
²⁶ The meek ones eat, and they are satisfied.
And those who seek him, they shall praise the LORD!

Your heart will be alive for evermore.
²⁷ Earth's ends remember, and turn to the LORD!
Tribes of all nations shall before you bow.
²⁸ The kingdom is the LORD's for him to reign!

He rules the nations. He is over them.
²⁹ Earth's favoured ones shall eat and worship too.
All who go down to dust, before him bow!
Each one who cannot make his own soul live.

[Continued →

³⁰ There is an offspring that shall serve the LORD;
The generation for the LORD they'll be.
³¹ They shall come and proclaim his righteousness,
And tell an unborn people he did this.

42   Psalm 23

¹ The LORD's my Shepherd. There's nothing I'll lack.
² For in fresh pastures he makes me lie down
He guides me where the restful waters flow.
³ He gives refreshment, and restores my soul.

He leads me in right paths for his name's sake.
⁴ Though through a valley deathly dark I go,
I fear no evil, for you are with me.
Your rod, your staff, they comfort and console.

⁵ Before my foes, you set my table out.
Anoint my head, and my cup overflows.
⁶ Goodness and mercy all my days attend,
 In the LORD's house I shall dwell endless days.

43   Psalm 24

¹ The earth and all that fills it is the LORD's;
The world, and everything that dwells therein.
² For it was founded by him on the seas,
And he established it upon the floods.

³ Who shall go up the mountain of the LORD?
And who shall stand within his holy place?
⁴ The one who has clean hands and a pure heart:
Not vainly lifted up, nor telling lies.

⁵ He shall receive the blessing from the LORD;
And righteousness have from his saving God.
⁶ This is the generation who seek him,
Even the Jacob - those who seek your face.

[Continued →

7 Gates, raise your heads up! Be raised, ancient doors!
So that the King of Glory may come in.
8 Who is this King of Glory? - It's the LORD!
The mighty LORD. Strong. Mighty in the fight!

9 Gates, raise your heads up! Rise up, ancient doors!
So that the King of Glory may come in
10 Who is this King, the King most glorious?
The LORD of Hosts the King of Glory is!

44　　　　　Psalm 25:1-7

1 To you, O LORD, do I lift up my soul.
2 My God in you I trust. Keep me from shame.
Don't let my enemies joy over me.
3 Let no-one be ashamed who waits on you.

They shall be shamed who, without cause, deceive.
4 Show me your ways, O LORD. Teach me your paths!
5 Cause me to tread your way of truth. Teach me!
I long for you all day, my saving God.

6 Your tender mercies call to mind, O LORD,
Remember too your loving-kindnesses,
For they have been for ever, from of old.
7 Remember not my sins and faults of youth.

Remember not my sins and faults of youth.
My plea is that you will remember me
According to your loving-kindnesses,
And, LORD, because you are so very good.

45　　　　　Psalm 25:8-14

8 The LORD is good and upright, and therefore,
He will instruct - teach sinners in the way.
9 In judgment he will make the meek to walk.
And to those who are meek he'll teach his way.

[Continued →

¹⁰ All the LORD's ways are steadfast love and truth
To those who keep his covenant and laws.
¹¹ Pardon my sin, LORD, for your own name's sake.
Forgive my very great iniquity.

¹² What man is this, the man who fears the LORD?
He will direct him in his chosen way.
¹³ In good prosperity his soul shall dwell.
The land shall be his children's heritage.

¹⁴ The secret counsel of the LORD will be
To those who fear him with a godly fear.
The LORD will cause such ones to understand.
He will make known his covenant to them.

46   Psalm 25:15-22

¹⁵ My eyes are ever, always, on the LORD,
For he will draw my feet out of the net.
¹⁶ O turn to me. Have mercy upon me.
For I'm afflicted, desolate, alone.

¹⁷ The troubles of my heart are multiplied.
From my distresses, O do bring me out!
¹⁸ Behold and see my trouble and my pain.
O do forgive my sins: bear them away.

¹⁹ See how my enemies are multiplied,
And how they hate me with a cruel hate.
²⁰ O keep my soul! O do deliver me!
Keep me from shame. I put my trust in you.

²¹ Let my integrity and uprightness
Preserve and guard me, for I wait on you.
²² Redemption give to Israel, O God!
From his afflictions, O do set him free!

47   Psalm 26:1-7

[1] O vindicate! Give justice unto me.
For, LORD, I've walked in my integrity.
Upon the LORD I also put my trust.
I have not wavered, and I shall not slip.

[2] O prove me, LORD, and put me to the test.
My inner man and heart refine and try.
[3] Your loving-kindness is before my eyes.
Therefore, I've walked the way your truth directs.

[4] I do not stay or sit with false, vain men;
Nor will I go among the hypocrites
[5] I hate the evildoers' company.
I will not stay or sit with wicked men.

[6] To show my innocence I'll wash my hands.
So I will go about your altar, LORD.
[7] So I'll proclaim with voice of thankfulness,
And tell the wondrous works that you have done

48   Psalm 26:8-12

[8] LORD, I have loved the place where you reside:
That habitation is your house, O LORD.
I love the place, for there your glory is:
The tabernacle where your honour dwells.

[9] With sinners do not gather up my soul,
Nor with blood-guilty men my life remove.
[10] For in their hands there is a wicked plan.
Their right hand's full of gifts of bribery.

[11] But I will walk in my integrity.
Redeem me and be merciful to me!
[12] My foot stands on an even, level place.
In the assemblies I will bless the LORD.

49   Psalm 27:1-6

[1] LORD - Saviour - Light to me: Whom shall I fear?
Strength of my life. Who will make me afraid?
[2] When wicked men came up to eat my flesh -
My enemies and foes - they slipped and fell!

[3] If against me an army should encamp,
My heart within me will not be afraid.
For, though a war should break out against me,
In spite of this I shall be confident.

[4] One thing I asked, requested, of the LORD,
And for that thing I surely will enquire:
That all my life I may dwell in his house,
Gaze on his beauty, in his Temple seek.

[5] For he will hide me in the evil day.
He will conceal me in his sheltered place.
And secretly will hide me in his tent.
And he will lift me high upon a rock.

[6] My head shall also now be lifted up
Above my foes who have surrounded me.
I'll sacrifice with joy within his tent.
Unto the LORD I'll sing; I'll sing with psalms.

50   Psalm 27:7-14

[7] LORD, answer me, for I cry with my voice.
Be gracious and give answer unto me.
[8] 'Go seek my face' you said. My heart repeats,
'Your face, O LORD, I earnestly will seek'.

[9] Do not conceal, or hide, your face from me,
Nor put away your servant in your wrath.
O leave me not! For you have been my help
Do not forsake me, O my Saving God!

[Continued →

¹⁰ The LORD will take me in, though I should be -
Forsaken by my father, mother too.
¹¹ Teach me your way, LORD. In a plain path lead,
Because of those who lie in wait for me

¹² Don't give me up to my oppressors' will.
False witnesses rise up: breathe cruelty.
¹³ Unless I'd trusted that I yet would see -
His goodness in the land of those who live!

¹⁴ Wait on the LORD and take encouragement.
Your heart he'll strengthen. He will make it strong.
Again, I say 'Wait' - 'Wait upon the LORD'.
And wait for him in earnest, patiently.

51 Psalm 28

¹ I'll cry to you, O LORD. You are my rock.
Do not be deaf to me, nor silence keep,
Lest I be like those who go to the Pit.
² My pleas for mercy hear. I cry for help.

I lift hands to your Holy Inner Place.
³ With evildoers don't drag me away,
And with the workers of iniquity,
Who speak in peace with friends, with evil hearts.

⁴ Give them according to what they have done.
Give them according to their wicked deeds.
Repay them for the things their hands have done.
Return the recompense that they deserve.

⁵ They don't regard the things the LORD has done.
And don't regard the working of his hands.
He will destroy them and not build them up.
⁶ Blest be the LORD! He heard my cry for grace!

[Continued →

7 The LORD's my strength and shield. I trust in him.
In him my heart trusts, and I have been helped.
Therefore, my heart is jubilant with joy,
And with my song I will give thanks to him.

8 Their mighty strength is only in the LORD.
He's strong to save for his Anointed One.
9 O save your people! Bless your heritage!
Shepherd and carry them for evermore!

52   Psalm 29

1 Sons of the mighty give unto the LORD.
Give to the LORD the glory and the power.
2 Give to the LORD the glory due his name.
In lovely holiness bow to the LORD.

3 Upon the waters the LORD's voice sounds out.
The thunders of the GOD of Glory roar.
The LORD is on the mighty waters now.
The LORD is on the mighty waters now.

4 Mighty and strong is the voice of the LORD.
Voice of the LORD! It's full of majesty.
5 Voice of the LORD! It breaks the cedars down.
Lebanon's cedars broken by the LORD!

6 He makes the Lebanon skip like a calf.
Sirion skips as if a wild young bull.
7 The LORD's voice is dividing flames of fire.
8 The LORD's voice makes the wilderness to shake.

The wilderness of Kadesh the LORD shakes,
9 And the LORD's voice now makes the deer give birth.
The forests are laid bare at the LORD's voice.
Throughout his Temple 'Glory!' is declared.

[Continued →

¹⁰ The LORD has sat enthroned upon the flood.
He sits enthroned as King for evermore.
¹¹ The LORD will give unto his people strength.
The LORD will bless his people with his peace.

53   Psalm 30:1-5

¹ I will exalt you, LORD. You drew me up.
You did not let my foes rejoice at me.
² O LORD my God, I cried to you for help,
And you have been a healer unto me.

³ LORD, up from Sheol you have brought my soul:
Revived, and kept from falling in the Pit.
⁴ Those whom he loves, Sing psalms unto the LORD!
Give thanks when you recall his holiness.

⁵ His anger lasts for just a moment long,
But his good favour lasts a whole life through.
Weeping may lodge, and for an evening stay,
But shouts of joy will be at break of day.

54   Psalm 30:6-12

⁶ In my security and ease I said
'I shall be never shaken or be moved'.
⁷ And 'LORD, your favour made my mountain strong'.
You hid your face, and then I was dismayed.

⁸ I cried to you, LORD, and your favour sought.
⁹ What is the benefit of my shed blood
When I descend and go down to the pit?
Will dust give praise? Will it declare your truth?

¹⁰ Please hear, O LORD. Have mercy upon me.
O LORD, do be a helper unto me.
¹¹ You turned my mourning into dance for me;
Took off my sackcloth and clothed me with joy,

[Continued →

12 My glory will praise you with psalms,
So that I'll not be silent any more.
O LORD my God I will give thanks to you -
Give thanks to you for ever, evermore.

55 Psalm 31:1-8

1I put my trust in you for refuge, LORD,
Let me not be ashamed for evermore
But in your righteousness deliver me.
2 Incline your ear and rescue speedily.

Be for me as a rock - a rock of strength
A fortress house so that I may be saved,
3 You are my stronghold, fortress of defence,
For your name's sake lead me and guide me through.

4 Release me from the net they hid for me,
Because you are the one who gives me strength.
5 Into your hand my spirit I commit.
You have delivered me, LORD, GOD of truth.

6 I hate those who respect false empty things,
For in the LORD I place my confidence.
7 I will be joyful in your steadfast love,
And in your loving-kindness I'll be glad.

For my affliction has been seen by you,
And you have known my soul in its distress.
8 You did not give me into my foe's hand,
But in the roomy place you set my feet.

56 Psalm 31:9-15

9 Be gracious to me, LORD, for I'm pressed in:
My eye, my soul, my body, waste with grief.
10 My life is spent with grief, my years with sighs:
Strength fails because of sin and bones decay.

[Continued →

¹¹ For all my enemies I'm a reproach
And even more to those who dwell near me,
To my acquaintances a thing of dread.
And those who saw me fled when I went out.

¹² 'Dead and forgotten, mad, a broken pot!'
Thus I have heard the slander of the crowd.
¹³ Fear-all-around while they against me plot,
And seek somehow to take my life away.

¹⁴ But as for me, I trusted in you, LORD,
And do declare to you, 'You are my God'.
¹⁵ My times are in your hand - Deliver me!
Save from my foes, from those pursuing me!

57   Psalm 31:16-20

¹⁶ Upon your servant cause your face to shine,
And save me for your loving-kindness' sake.
¹⁷ Keep me from shame, LORD, for I called on you.
But shame the wicked. Hush them in the grave.

¹⁸ Let lying lips be dumb that speak hard things
Against the righteous, proudly, with contempt.
¹⁹ For those who fear you, bounty is in store!
Prepared for those who trust you, before men

²⁰ You hide them in your secret hiding place -
Hide in your presence from the schemes of man,
And in a shelter keep them secretly
From the contention of accusing tongues.

58   Psalm 31:21-24

²¹ Blest be the LORD, who in a fortress town
With wonders showed his kindness unto me
²² Though he did this, I spoke when I made haste,
'I've been cut off before your very eyes!'

[Continued →

Yet nonetheless, you heard my pleading voice -
My supplications - when I cried to you
23 O love the LORD, all who partake his grace,
Those who are faithful are kept by the LORD.

The LORD will deal with those who act in pride.
The LORD will fully give to them their due.
24 Be of good courage! Let your heart be strong
All you who on the LORD wait patiently.

59   Psalm 32:1-6

1 What blessedness belongs to him who has
transgression pardoned - covering for sin!
2 Blest man to whom the LORD imputes no sin! -
And in whose spirit there is no deceit.

3 When I kept silence, then my bones decayed
With cries of anguish I let out all day.
4 For day and night your hand weighed hard on me.
Gone is my moisture, as in summer drought.

5 My sin I then acknowledged unto you,
And did not cover my iniquity.
Said, 'I'll confess my sins unto the LORD'.
'The guilt of sin you then forgave for me'.

6 All who you love shall pray because of this
Pray to you when it's time for finding you.
Be sure when floods of many waters come,
The waters shall not go as far as him.

60   Psalm 32:7-11

7 You are for me a secret hiding place.
You will preserve me from adversity.
You will surround me with glad shouts of joy,
With celebration of deliverance

[Continued →

⁸ 'Yes, I'll instruct and teach the way to go,
And I'll advise you with my eye on you.
⁹ Be not like undiscerning horse or mule,
Unless they're bridled, they will not approach'.

¹⁰ The sorrows of the wicked one are great.
Mercy surrounds him who trusts in the LORD!
¹¹ Joy in the LORD! Be glad you righteous ones!
And shout for joy all you of upright heart!

61   Psalm 33:1-6

¹ You righteous, shout for joy unto the LORD!
Praise is a thing that suits the upright well.
² Give praise unto the LORD upon the harp;
Upon a ten-stringed lyre sing psalms to him.

³ Sing unto him a rare and choice new song.
Play skilfully, and with a shout of joy.
⁴ For the LORD's word is right; because it's true,
And all his works are done in faithfulness.

⁵ Justice and righteousness are what he loves.
The mercy of the LORD fills all the earth.
⁶ By the LORD's word the heavens have been made
The breathing of his mouth made all their host.

62   Psalm 33:7-11

⁷ He heaped together waters of the sea,
And in the storerooms he laid up the deeps.
⁸ All earth shall be afraid - shall fear the LORD.
All dwellers in this world shall stand in awe.

⁹ For he just spoke, and then it came to pass;
As he commanded it was set in place.
¹⁰ The nations' purposes the LORD makes naught,
And he frustrates what peoples planned to do.

[Continued →

[11] The counsel of the LORD forever stands.
Even the purposes his heart has planned
Unto all generations they shall be.
Unto all generations they shall be.

63   Psalm 33:12-17

[12] Blest be the nation whose God is the LORD -
The people chosen for his heritage.
[13] The LORD has from the heavens looked about,
And all the sons of men he has beheld.

[14] From where he dwells, he surveys all around,
He looks upon all those who dwell on earth.
[15] He forms and fashions all their hearts alike,
And all the things they do he understands.

[16] No king is saved by his great army's size;
No mighty man escapes by his great strength.
[17] It's vain to trust for safety in a horse.
It can't deliver, though it has great strength.

64   Psalm 33:18-22

[18] See! - The LORD's eye is on those who fear him.
On those who in his loving-kindness hope.
[19] To give their soul deliverance from death,
And in the famine to keep them alive.

[20] Our soul waits for the LORD - our Help and Shield.
[21] Because of this, our heart will joy in him.
Trusting his holy name our heart is glad.
[22] Your mercy's on us, LORD: we wait for you.

65   Psalm 34:1-6

[1] In every season, I will bless the LORD.
His praise shall constantly be in my mouth.
[2] And in the LORD my soul will make its boast.
The humble ones will hear and will be glad.

[Continued →

³ O come and magnify the LORD with me.
Let us together lift his name on high.
⁴ I sought the LORD and he has answered me,
And out of all my fears he rescued me.

⁵ They looked to him and they were radiant.
Their faces shall not ever be ashamed.
⁶ This poor one cried: the LORD listened to him.
And out of all his troubles rescued him.

66 Psalm 34:7-15

⁷ The angel of the LORD encamps around
The ones who fear him. He delivers them.
⁸ O taste and see, because the LORD is good.
Blest is the man who puts his trust in him.

⁹ O fear the LORD, you saints - his holy ones -
For there is nothing those who fear him need.
¹⁰ Young lions may have need, and long for food,
But those who seek the LORD lack nothing good.

¹¹ O children come and listen unto me
And I will teach you how to fear the LORD.
¹² What man seeks life, and loves to see good days?
¹³ Then guard your tongue from wrong, your lips from lies.

¹⁴ Depart from evil, and do what is good.
Seek after peace and be pursuing it.
¹⁵ The LORD's eyes are upon the righteous ones,
Just as his ears are open to their cry.

67 Psalm 34:16-22

¹⁶ But the LORD's face is set against all those
Who practice evil and do wickedly.
To cut off every memory of them
Even removing it from off the earth.

[Continued →

¹⁷ The righteous cry for help, and the LORD hears -
From out of all their troubles rescues them.
¹⁸ The LORD is near to those with broken heart;
Those with a contrite spirit he will save

¹⁹ The troubles of the righteous one abound
And yet he's rescued by the LORD from all
²⁰ He takes good care - protecting all his bones:
Not one is broken – not a single one!

²¹ Evil shall bring the wicked one to death.
Condemned are they who hate the righteous one.
²² Because the LORD redeems his servants' soul,
None are condemned who take refuge in him.

68   Psalm 35:1-8

¹ LORD put on trial those who would try me;
Wage war on those who go to war with me.
² Take buckler and great shield. Rise for my help!
³ Take out the spear. Stop them pursuing me.

Say to my soul, 'I'm your deliverance'.
⁴ Confound, bring shame, to those who seek my soul.
Turn back, confuse them, who devise my hurt.
⁵ The angel of the LORD chase them like chaff.

⁶ O make their pathway dark and prone to slip -
The angel of the LORD pursuing them.
⁷ For, without cause, they hid their net for me,
And without cause dug for my soul a pit.

⁸ And let destruction come like this to him
As unexpected, when he does not know.
And let the net he hid entangle him;
Into that same destruction let him fall.

69   Psalm 35:9-16

[9] My soul shall be so joyful in the LORD.
In his salvation shall my soul delight
[10] My bones all say, 'O LORD, who is like you?'
Who is like you, LORD, rescuing the poor?

You rescue him from one stronger than him.
The poor you rescue, and the one in need
From him who comes to plunder and despoil
[11] The witnesses arise for violence.

They ask of me such things I do not know.
[12] Evil for good repay. My soul bereave.
[13] Yet I wore sackcloth when they were unwell,
And with the fasting I humbled my soul.

So may my prayer return unto my breast!
[14] I went as for my brother or a friend.
Bowed down as one who for his mother mourns,
[15] But, when I fell, they met to show their joy.

Yes, and the smiters gathered against me.
I knew them not - they tore unceasingly.
[16] Like godless mockers, slandering for gain,
Against me grinding, gnashing with their teeth.

70   Psalm 35:17-23

[17] My Lord, how long will you just look and watch?
From their destructions, O restore my soul!
My precious life save from the lions' young.
[18] I'll thank you in the great assembled throng.

Among much people I will give you praise.
[19] Keep my false foes from being glad at me.
Let them not wink that hate me without cause.
[20] They don't speak peace, but make deceitful plans,

[*Continued* →

Deceiving peaceful people in the land.
21 They opened up their mouth against me wide,
'Aha! Aha!', they said, 'our eye has seen'.
22 But you have seen, LORD. Do not silence keep!'

My Lord do not be far away from me.
23 Awake! Rouse up yourself, as out of sleep.
Awake yourself to judgment, O my God:
My Lord, for vindication of my cause.

71   Psalm 35:24-28

24 Judge me according to your righteousness.
O LORD my God, give them no joy from me.
25 Let not their heart say, 'We would have it so!'
Let them not say 'We have swallowed him up!'

26 Make them ashamed, confound them every one
Who find their joy in my calamity.
And clothe them with dishonour and with shame
Who over me do magnify themselves.

27 But those delighting in my righteousness -
Let them shout joyfully! Let them be glad!
Let them say always, 'Magnify the LORD!'
'For he has pleasure in his servant's peace'.

28 My tongue will tell, and speaking, meditate,
And it shall talk about your righteousness.
And all the day it shall tell out your praise.
Your praise shall be its theme continually.

72   Psalm 36:1-4

1 Thus spoke transgression to the wicked one
(and it declared to me within my heart)
'There is no fear of God before his eyes'.
2 Self-flattery is all his eyes can see.

[Continued →

Self-flattery until his wickedness ...
has been found out, its hatefulness made known.
[3] Words of his mouth are wicked and deceive.
He ceases to act wisely or do good.

[4] When he is on his bed, he plots and plans,
Devising wickedness upon his bed.
He sets himself a path that is not good,
And what is evil he does not refuse.

73   Psalm 36:5-12

[5] Your steadfast love is in the heavens, LORD:
Your faithfulness extends unto the clouds:
[6] Like GOD's own mountains is your righteousness:
Your judgments like unto a mighty deep.

O LORD, preserver of both man and beast,
[7] How precious is your steadfast love, O God!
Therefore, the sons of men their refuge take,
And trust, beneath the shadow of your wings.

[8] They feast on the abundance of your house.
You make them drink your river of delights.
[9] For with you is the very fount of life,
And, in your light, we surely shall see light.

[10] Prolong your mercy to those who know you;
Your righteousness to the upright in heart.
[11] The foot of pride, let it not come to me.
Nor let the wickeds' hand drive me away.

[12] There fell the workers of iniquity.
There they have fallen, and been overthrown.
They have been thrust down, and are cast away.
So that they can no longer rise again.

74   Psalm 37:1-6

[1] Don't fret yourself because of wicked men.
Do not have envy of those who do wrong.
[2] For they will soon be cut down like the grass,
And wither as the greenness of the herb.

[3] Trust in the LORD and labour to do good.
Dwell in the land and surely you'll be fed.
[4] Enjoy the LORD and make him your delight.
So he will give your heart's desires to you.

[5] Roll your way over; cast it on the LORD.
Just trust in him and he will make it so.
[6] He'll bring your righteousness out as the light.
He'll bring your judgment out like midday sun.

75   Psalm 37:7-15

[7] Rest in the LORD, wait patiently for him.
Fret not at one who makes his way succeed -
Because a man fulfils his evil plans.
[8] Do not be angry. Go away from wrath.

Fret not yourself lest you do wickedly.
[9] Those who do wicked things shall be cut off.
Those who, expecting, wait upon the LORD
They'll gain the earth as their inheritance.

[10] In a short while the wicked shall not be.
You'll seek his place, but it will be no more.
[11] Those who are meek shall yet possess the earth,
Peace in abundance will be their delight.

[12] The wicked plots against the righteous one.
Gnashes his teeth at him - [13] but the Lord laughs!
For he foresees the coming of his day.
[14] The wicked ones draw sword and bend their bow.

[Continued →

The poor and needy they seek to cast down -
To slay those who are upright in the way.
15 Their sword shall enter into their own heart.
Broken and ruined and shall their bows be too.

76 Psalm 37:16-22

16 Better the little of the righteous one
Than the great wealth of many wicked men.
17 Broken shall be the arms of wicked men,
Those who are righteous the LORD will uphold.

18 The LORD knows all the days of blameless men.
Their heritage shall be for evermore.
19 They will not be ashamed when evil comes.
In days of famine they will have their fill.

20 As for the wicked, they will be destroyed;
And the LORD's enemies will pass away -
Just like the preciousness – the fat – of lambs,
For into smoke they shall consume away.

21 The wicked borrows but does not give back.
The righteous has compassion and he gives.
22 Those whom he blesses will possess the earth
But those he curses, they shall be cut off.

77 Psalm 37:23-28

23 A good man's steps are ordered by the LORD;
And in his way he places his delight.
24 Though he should fall, he will not be cast down,
Because the LORD upholds him with his hand.

25 I was once young, but now I'm an old man.
I have not seen the righteous destitute,
Nor have I seen his children begging bread.
Nor have I seen his children begging bread.

[Continued →

26 All day he's merciful and freely lends.
His offspring will give blessing and be blest.
27Depart from evil and do what is good
And then you will abide for evermore.

28 The LORD loves judgment, and will not forsake.
The ones on whom he sets his steadfast love.
For ever they will be kept and preserved.
The offspring of the wicked are cut off.

78   Psalm 37:29-34

29 Those who are righteous shall possess the earth,
And they will dwell in it for evermore.
30 The righteous one speaks wisdom with his mouth,
And, with his tongue, of judgment he will speak.

31 The Law of God abides within his heart,
None of the footsteps that he takes will slip.
32 The wicked waits to kill the righteous one,
33 The LORD won't leave him in the wicked's hand.

The LORD will not condemn him when he's judged.
34 Wait on the Lord, and keep upon his way!
He will exalt you to possess the earth.
You'll see the wicked when they are cut off.

79   Psalm 37:35-40

35 I've seen the wicked - ruthless, in great power,
Spreading just as a green and native tree.
36 He passed away. Behold, he was no more!
I sought for him, but he could not be found.

37 Mark him who's blameless. See the upright one.
For that man's destiny is one of peace.
38 Together shall transgressors be destroyed:
The wicked's destiny - to be cut off!

[Continued →

³⁹ The righteous have salvation from the LORD.
He is their strength when trouble is at hand.
⁴⁰ The LORD will help and rescue from bad men:
Rescue and save them, for they trust in him.

80   Psalm 38:1-8

¹ O LORD, do not rebuke me in your wrath,
And in your anger do not chasten me -
² Because your arrows sink down deep in me -
Because your hand is pressing on me hard.

³ Your wrath has left no soundness in my flesh.
My bones are without rest because of sin.
⁴ Iniquities have gone over my head:
A heavy burden - far too much for me.

⁵ My wounds are stinking, and they are corrupt.
It is because of this - my foolishness.
⁶ I'm twisted up. I'm brought down very low.
I go about a mourner all the day.

⁷ My loins are full of burning, searing heat,
And there is left no soundness in my flesh.
⁸ I am made feeble, crushed, and broken down,
Because of turmoil in my heart, I groan.

81   Psalm 38:9-14

⁹ All that I long for is before you, Lord,
Also, my groaning is not hid from you.
¹⁰ My heart is beating fast, and my strength fails.
Light has gone from me, even from my eyes.

¹¹ My friends and loved ones stand back from my plague.
My neighbours and my kinsmen stand far off.
¹² And those who seek my life lay snares for me.
Those who speak ruin; plan deceits all day.

[Continued →

13 But I am like one deaf; I do not hear,
And as one dumb who opens not his mouth.
14 I have become as one who does not hear,
And in whose mouth there are no arguments.

82 Psalm 38:15-22

15 O LORD, I wait in patient hope for you.
You'll hear and answer me, My Lord, my God.
16 Because I said, 'Lest they rejoice at me,
Or, over me exalt, if my foot slips'.

17 I'm almost falling. I have constant pain!
18 I own my guilt. I'm sorry for my sin.
19 My enemies are full of life and strength,
And there are many hate me without cause.

20 Evil for good my adversaries pay,
Because I follow after what is good.
21 Don't leave me, or be distant, LORD my God.
22 Lord, My Salvation, hurry for my help.

83 Psalm 39:1-6

1 I said, I'll place a guard upon my ways,
So that I'm kept from sinning with my tongue.
I'll guard my mouth, and I will muzzle it,
While the ungodly are within my sight.

2 So I kept silence; dumb from speaking good,
And pain and sorrow were stirred up in me.
3 My heart was hot; within me the fire burned.
After such thinking, I spoke with my tongue,

4 'O LORD, cause me to know my mortal end.
Help me to know the limit of my days -
What is their measure, and how frail I am.
Help me to know how fleeting are my days.

[Continued →

⁵ 'See how, you've made my days so very short.
They are just like the handbreadths of a man.
For my whole life is nothing in your sight
Yes, even one who stands is but a breath' -

'And every man is wholly vanity
⁶ Man's going to and fro, a shadow cast.
Indeed, in vain they are disquieted.
They heap up wealth they know not who will gain'

84   Psalm 39:7-13

⁷ 'And now, what am I waiting for, My Lord?
My hope, my expectation, is in you.
⁸ From all of my transgressions rescue me.
Don't set me so a fool can mock at me'.

⁹ So I was dumb; I opened not my mouth,
Because the doer of this thing was you.
¹⁰ O take from me the plague that you have sent,
For I am wasted by your hostile hand

¹¹ Rebukes from you correct a man for sin.
What he desires you melt just like a moth,
For a mere vanity is every man.
¹² LORD, hear my prayer. Give ear unto my cry!

Answer my tears, for I'm your stranger here.
A sojourner as all my fathers were.
¹³ O spare me that I may recover strength,
Before I go away and am no more.

85   Psalm 40:1-4

¹ I waited patiently upon the LORD.
He reached to me and listened to my cry -
² Brought from roaring pit, the mire and mud
My feet set on a rock - my steps made sure.

[Continued →

³ And he has put a new song in my mouth -
Even a song of praise unto our God.
Many will see, and will have godly fear,
And they will set their trust upon the LORD.

⁴ How blesséd is the man - the mighty man -
The one who sets his trust upon the LORD -
Who does not turn himself unto the proud -
Nor unto those who turn aside to lies

86   Psalm 40:5-10

⁵ You've done so many things, O LORD my God -
Your wonders and the things you've planned for us
They can't be set in order unto you
They're numberless if I should tell and speak

⁶ Sacrifice, offering, you don't desire.
(My ears you've dug and opened up for me:
even a body you've prepared for me).
Burnt-, and sin-offering you don't require.

⁷ Then I said, 'Lo I come! Within the scroll -
Within the book - it is written of me.
⁸ I take delight to do your will my God.
Your Law is in the very midst of me'.

⁹ Within the great assembly I proclaimed.
I did not put restraint upon my lips.
Behold, O LORD, these things you truly know.
¹⁰ Your righteousness I've not hid in my heart

For I have told of your sure faithfulness,
And your deliverance I did relate.
I haven't hid your mercy and your truth,
Even before the great assembled throng.

[Continued →

87   Psalm 40:11-17

[11] Do not withhold your mercies from me, LORD.
Your steadfast love, and truth my constant guard.
[12] Evils past counting have surrounded me.
My sins have gripped me so I can't look up.

My sins are more than hairs upon my head.
My heart fails in me - [13] O please help me LORD!
Make haste, O LORD, to come and give me help.
[14] For some are seeking to destroy my soul

Let them together be shamed and confused -
Those who would harm me - turn back - put to shame!
[15] Let desolation recompense their shame.
- All those who jeer at me, 'Aha!' 'Aha!'

[16] But let all those who earnestly seek you -
Let them exult with joy - be glad in you.
Those who love your salvation, let them say -
Continually, 'The LORD be magnified!'

[17] But as for me, I'm poor and I have need.
Yet, even so, My Lord thinks upon me.
You are my Help and my Deliverer.
You are my God, so please make no delay.

88   Psalm 41:1-6

[1] He who attends the poor one shall be blest!
The LORD will save him in an evil day.
[2] The LORD shall keep him, and preserve his life,
He will have blessedness upon the earth.

You will not leave him to his foes' ill-will.
[3] The LORD will strengthen when he's sick in bed.
And all his sickbed he will turn for him.
[4] I said, 'Be gracious unto me, O LORD!'

[Continued →

'Please heal my soul for I've sinned against you'.
5 My enemies in malice speak of me,
'When will he die, and his name pass away?'
6 And if he comes to me speaks emptiness.

Yes he speaks falsehood when he comes to me.
His heart goes gathering iniquity,
Unto itself collecting wickedness.
When he goes out, he tells it in the street.

89   Psalm 41:7-13

7 All those who hate me join in whispering,
Devising ways how they can do me harm.
8 'A cursed thing has taken hold on him'.
'Now he lies prostrate he shall rise no more!'

9 My own familiar friend I trusted in -
Who ate my bread - against me raised his heel!
10 LORD, will you please be merciful to me,
And raise me up to pay them back in full.

11 By this I know that I am your delight.
My foe is not in triumph over me.
12 But as for me - in my integrity -
You give me your support and hold me up.

You make me stand before your face always.
13 The LORD be blest - the God of Israel!
From one eternity unto the next.
Amen. So be it, and again Amen!

Book 2

Psalms 42 - 72

90　　　　Psalm 42:1-5

1 Just as a deer pants for the water streams,
Likewise, my soul pants after you, O God!
2 My soul is thirsting for the Living GOD.
When shall I come - be seen before God's face?

3 My tears have been my food both day and night.
They say to me all day, 'Where is your God?'
4 Recalling this I then pour out my soul,
For I once travelled with the thronging crowd.

I went and led them to the House of God -
With shouts of gladness and with thankful praise -
A multitude of those who kept the feast -
The company of those on pilgrimage.

5 Why, O my soul, do you cast yourself down?
Why so disturbed and troubled within me?
Wait. Hope in God, for I shall praise him yet.
For his salvation, when he shows his face.

91　　　　Psalm 42:6-11

6 My God, my soul is cast down within me,
So from the land of Jordan I'll recall;
From Hermon's peaks and from the mount Mizar;
7 Deep calls to deep as noise of waterfalls.

Your rolling waves have all gone over me.
8 His mercy the LORD will command by day;
And in the night his song will be with me -
Even a prayer to the GOD of my life

9 I'll say unto the GOD who is my rock,
'Why is it that you have forgotten me?'
'Why do I go out just as one who mourns,
Because the enemy oppresses me?'

[Continued →

¹⁰ As if they put a sword into my bones;
As if they struck, so shattering my bones.
My adversaries cast reproach on me.
They say to me all day 'Where is your God?'

¹¹ Why, O my soul, do you cast yourself down?
Why so disturbed and troubled within me?
Wait. Hope in God: for I shall praise him yet.
He is my Saviour, and he is my God.

92   Psalm 43

¹ O vindicate me, God. Take up my cause,
Against a nation without godliness.
Deliver from the unjust, crafty man.
² God of my strength, why have you cast me off?

Why do I go about as one who mourns
Through the oppression of the enemy?
³ Send out your light and truth. Let them lead me,
To bring me where you dwell, your holy hill.

⁴ Then I will go unto God's altar there -
To God - the GOD of my exultant joy.
And I will offer thanksgiving to you
Upon the harp to God - to my own God.

⁵ Why, O my soul, do you cast yourself down?
Why so disturbed and troubled within me?
O hope in God, for I shall praise him yet.
He is my Saviour and he is my God.

93   Psalm 44:1-8

¹ Our ears have heard, O God - our fathers told:
The work you worked in their days - days of old.
² You drove out nations, but did plant them in;
Afflicted peoples, but them you spread out.

[Continued →

3 They did not get the land by their own sword;
Their arm did not save them, but your right hand,
Even your arm, and the light of your face;
Because you showed your favour unto them.

4 You are the one who is my king, O God.
Command for Jacob your deliverance.
5 By you our adversaries we'll push down;
We'll trample down insurgents in your name.

6 My bow I will not trust - nor sword - to save.
7 From enemies you saved. Shamed those who hate.
8 In God we'll boast and glory all day long,
Give thanks unto your name for evermore.

94   Psalm 44:9-19

9 But you have cast us off: made us ashamed,
And you do not go with our armies now.
10 You make us turn back from the enemy,
And those who hate us spoil us at their will.

11 Like sheep for meat; among the nations strewn;
12 You sell your people at such a low price.
Yes, you have sold them, without any gain.
13 You made us, to our neighbours, a reproach -

Scorn and derision to those round about.
14 A byword to the nations we've become -
Among the peoples - they just shake their head!
15 Confusion is before me all day long!

Covered with shame; 16 by taunts and blasphemies
Before the foe, and him who seeks revenge.
17 All this came on us; we did not forget.
Nor were we false unto your covenant.

[Continued →

18 Despite all this, our heart did not turn back:
Our step has not departed from your path,
19 But, where the jackals are, you've crushed us down,
And with the shade of death you've covered us.

95 Psalm 44:20-26

20 If the name of our God we had forgot -
If we'd spread out our hands to a strange GOD -
21 Would God not then be sure to find this out?
Because he knows the secrets of the heart.

22 But, for your sake, we're slain all the day long.
We are as sheep appointed to be slain.
23 Awake, My Lord, why are you sleeping still?
Arise! Do not for ever cast us off.

24 Why do you hide your face, and why forget?
We are afflicted, and we are oppressed.
25 Our very soul is bowed down to the dust;
Our body is as fastened to the earth

26 O do rise up for us, to be our help;
And do redeem us for your mercy's sake.
Yes, do rise up for us to be our help;
Yes, do redeem us for your mercy's sake.

96 Psalm 45:1-8

1 My heart boils over with a pleasing theme.
I speak the things that I've done for the king.
My tongue is as a ready writer's pen.
2 'Fair, fair are you, more than the sons of men!'

'Such graciousness is poured upon your lips!
Therefore has God blest you for evermore.
3 Gird your sword on your thigh, O mighty one.
Gird on your glory and your majesty'.

[Continued →

⁴ 'Yes, in your majesty, prosper - ride on!
For truth and meekness, and for righteousness.
Your right hand will teach you things that cause fear.
⁵ Sharp arrows pierce the heart of the king's foes -

'Therefore, the peoples fall down under him.
⁶ Your throne, O God, abides for evermore;
Your kingdom's sceptre is of uprightness.
⁷ You have loved justice: hated wickedness'.

'Therefore, has God, your God, anointed you -
More than your fellows - with the oil of joy.
⁸ All your clothes are myrrh - aloes - cassia,
Made glad from palaces of ivory'.

97   Psalm 45:9-17

⁹ 'Daughters of kings are with your favoured ones.
At your right hand the queen in Ophir's gold.
¹⁰ O daughter, hear, consider, and give ear:
Forget your people and your father's house'.

¹¹ 'So will the king desire your beauty well.
He is your lord: Bow down yourself to him.
¹² There with a gift is the daughter of Tyre.
The richest of the people seek your face'.

¹³ 'Resplendent is the king's daughter within.
Her clothing is with gold embroidery.
¹⁴ With coloured robes she's brought unto the king.
The virgins, her companions, follow her'.

'In train to her, they will be brought to you.
¹⁵ They will be led with gladness and with joy,
They'll enter to the palace of the king.
¹⁶ In place of fathers shall your children be -

[Continued →

'You'll make them princes over all the earth.
¹⁷ I'll set your name as a memorial,
To every generation it shall be.
Peoples shall give you thanks for evermore!'

98   Psalm 46

¹ God is to us our refuge and our strength:
A very present help in time of need.
² Therefore, we will not fear though earth be changed
Though mountains be removed into the seas -

³ Although their waters foam, although they roar;
Though mountains tremble at its surging tide.
⁴ There is a river whose streams will make glad
The holy dwelling place of the Most High.

⁵ God in the midst of it: it won't be moved.
And God will help it when the morning breaks.
⁶ The nations were in tumult; kingdoms moved.
The earth did melt when he raised up his voice.

⁷ The LORD of Hosts is present with us now.
The God of Jacob. He is our high tower.
⁸ Come and behold the things the LORD has done.
He has made desolations in the earth.

⁹ To earth's remotest end he makes wars cease.
He breaks the bow, and cuts the spear in two.
The chariots he burns up in the fire.
¹⁰ 'Be still and surely know that I am God!'

'Among the nations I'll be lifted up.
I will be lifted up in all the earth'.
¹¹ The LORD of Hosts is present with us now.
The God of Jacob, he is our high tower.

99   Psalm 47

¹ O all you peoples, join in clapping hands.
Shout out to God with a triumphant voice.
² Because the LORD Most High is to be feared,
He is a great King over all the earth.

³ He makes the peoples subject unto us;
And he puts nations underneath our feet.
⁴ He chooses our inheritance for us:
The excellence of Jacob whom he loves.

⁵ God is gone up; ascended with a shout!
Even the LORD with sound of the shofar.
⁶ Sing psalms to God. Sing psalms of praise to him.
Sing psalms unto our king. Sing praise with psalms!

⁷ Because God is the King of all the earth.
Sing psalms with understanding, and with skill.
⁸ Over the nations, God now reigns as king.
God sits upon his throne of holiness.

⁹ The princes of the peoples gathered round
The people of the God of Abraham.
Because the shields of earth belong to God,
So he has been exalted very high.

100   Psalm 48:1-8

¹ Great is the LORD and greatly to be praised
In our God's city - on his holy hill!
² In beauty raised up, and the whole earth's joy
Is Zion's mount upon its northern sides.

It is the city of the mighty King,
³ And in its palaces, God is made known
As a high tower for refuge and defence.
⁴ Behold! - the kings joined! They passed by as one.

[Continued →

5 They saw it, and therefore they were amazed.
They were astounded. They fled in alarm.
6 For trembling fear took hold upon them there;
As anguish of a woman giving birth.

7 You wrecked the ships of Tarshish with east wind.
8 Just as we heard, so we have seen it there -
The city of the LORD of hosts, our God,
God will establish it for evermore.

101   Psalm 48:9-14

9 Upon your mercy we have thought, O God,
Within your Temple, in its inner parts.
10 According to your name, so is your praise.
It reaches to the ends of all the earth.

Well-filled with righteousness is your right hand.
11 Rejoice, Mount Zion, and be very glad!
Let Judah's daughters now exult with joy,
Because of the right judgments made by you.

12 Walk about Zion. Circle it around.
Go and encompass it all round about.
And then the number of its towers count.
13 Set your heart on its ramparts and defence.

Mark well its palaces, so you can tell -
Recount to generations following -
14 That this is God, our God for evermore!
And he will guide us even unto death.

102   Psalm 49:1-5

1 Hear all you peoples, and listen to this!
Give ear to this all dwellers in this world!
2 Both common men and men of noble birth,
The rich man and the one who is in need.

[Continued →

³ My mouth will speak with words of wisdom now;
My heart will ponder on discerning things.
⁴ Unto a parable I'll turn my ear.
I'll open up my puzzle on the harp.

⁵ Why should I be afraid in evil days?
When I'm supplanted by my wicked foes;
When I'm surrounded by iniquity,
though it's behind me, even at my heels.

103   Psalm 49:6-15

⁶ They trust in wealth, of their great riches boast -
⁷ And yet a man his brother can't redeem,
Nor give a ransom unto God for him -
⁸ (Their soul is priceless. They cannot redeem) -

⁹ Redeem to ever live; not see the Pit.
¹⁰ For he must see it - wise men also die.
They, with the fool and stupid, pass away.
They leave their wealth to others after them.

¹¹ Their heart is that their houses always last -
Dwellings for generations yet to come!
Therefore, they name their lands after themselves.
¹² Yet man with honour will not stay for long.

He's like the beasts. For they are cut off too.
¹³ This is the way of those with foolish hope -
Their followers approve the things they say.
¹⁴ As sheep for Sheol they have set themselves.

And death shall be a shepherd unto them.
By morning shall the just ones tread them down.
Their beauty is for Sheol to consume
So they no longer have an honoured place.

[Continued →

¹⁵ But God will make a ransom for my soul,
Redeem me from the grasp of Sheol's power.
For he will take and keep me in his care.
He will receive me so I am with him.

104   Psalm 49:16-20

¹⁶ Be not afraid when someone becomes rich,
Or if the glory of his house increase.
¹⁷ For, when he dies, he takes nothing away.
His glory won't descend down after him.

¹⁸ Though, while he was alive, he blest his soul
(And when you prosper, men will give you praise).
¹⁹ Yet he shall go to where his fathers are,
And they shall never see the light again.

²⁰ The man who is in honour and admired
(If he is one who does not understand)
He may be likened to the senseless beasts.
They also perish, and they are cut off.

105   Psalm 50:1-6

¹ The Mighty GOD of gods, the LORD, thus spoke;
Called earth from sun's rise to its going down.
² From Zion - faultless beauty - God shined out.
³ Our God will come. He will not hold his peace.

A fire will go before him to devour.
Around him will a mighty tempest rage.
⁴ He'll call unto the heavens from above
And to the earth, to judge his people's cause.

⁵ Assemble unto me those whom I love,
Who made a covenant by sacrifice.
⁶ The heavens shall declare his righteousness,
For it is God himself who is the Judge.

106   Psalm 50:7-15

[7] Hear, O my people, I will speak to you!
O Israel, I bring my charge to you!
For I myself am God, even your God
[8] (Your sacrifices - I will not reprove

I'll not reprove for your burnt offerings
They also are before me constantly).
[9] I would not take a young bull from your house,
Nor would I take the he-goats from your folds,

[10] For every forest animal is mine,
Even the cattle on a thousand hills.
[11] The mountain birds are all well-known to me;
With me is every thing that moves in fields.

[12] If I were hungry, I would not tell you.
The world and all its fullness is for me.
[13] Would I eat up the flesh of mighty bulls?
Or take the blood of he-goats for a drink?

[14] Make sacrifice to God by giving thanks.
Perform your vows to Him who is Most High,
[15] And call on me in the day of distress.
I'll rescue you, and you will honour me.

107   Psalm 50:16-23

[16] God speaks these things unto the wicked one:
'What right have you repeating my decrees?
Taking my covenant into your mouth?
[17] You are the person who hates discipline',

'And you have put my words behind your back.
[18] You saw a thief, and were well-pleased with him,
And with adulterers you cast your lot.
[19] Your mouth you have let loose in wickedness.

[Continued →

'Your tongue contrives to carry out deceit.
[20] You sit down and against your brother speak.
You bring a slander on your mother's son.
[21] Yet I kept silence when you did these things!'

'You thought that I was such a one as you!
I will reprove, set out before your eyes!
[22] You who forget God, Oh consider this,
Lest I should tear, and none delivers you.

[23] The one who offers this for sacrifice -
Who offers thanks - will give glory to me;
And, to the one who orders his way well,
Salvation - God's salvation - I will show.

108 Psalm 51:1-6

[1] According to your steadfast love, O God,
Be gracious - show your favour unto me;
According to your mercies, which are great,
Blot out the sins in which I have transgressed.

[2] O wash me well from my iniquity;
And purify - yes, cleanse me from my sin.
[3] For my transgressions are well-known to me;
Constantly I'm confronted by my sin.

[4] Against you, and you only, have I sinned,
And I have done this evil in your sight:
So that you may be just when you declare:
So you are blameless when you act as judge.

[5] Yes, I was in iniquity when born;
I was in sin when my mother conceived.
[6] Yes, you delight in truth in inner parts;
You'll teach me wisdom in the hidden part.

109   Psalm 51:7-15

7. You'll purge with hyssop, that I may be clean;
You'll wash, so I'll be whiter than the snow.
8 Rejoicing, gladness, you will make me hear;
So bones that you have broken may rejoice.

9 O hide your face away from these my sins
And wipe away all my iniquities.
10 A heart that's pure, create for me, O God;
A steadfast spirit make anew in me.

11 Do not discard and cast me from your sight!
Your Holy Spirit do not take from me!
12 Give your salvation's joy to me again;
And with a willing spirit hold me up.

13 Then I'll instruct transgressors in your ways,
And sinners will return again to you.
14 Deliver from blood-guiltiness, O God.
You are the one who is my saving God.

My tongue will then shout loudly and will sing -
With joy it will sing of your righteousness.
15 My Lord, will you just open up my lips,
Then my mouth also will declare your praise.

110   Psalm 51:16-19

16 You do not take delight in sacrifice:
If that were so, I would give it to you.
You take no pleasure in burnt offering.
17 A broken spirit is God's sacrifice.

A broken spirit is God's sacrifice -
A broken, contrite, heart you'll not despise.
18 Do good to Zion as it pleases you,
And build the walls up of Jerusalem.

[Continued →

¹⁹ Then with the sacrifices you'll be pleased -
Even with sacrifice of righteousness.
With sacrifices burnt, and offered whole,
Bulls will be offered on your altar then.

111 Psalm 52

¹ Why do you boast of evil, mighty man?
GOD's loving-kindness lasts all the day long.
² Your tongue devises such malicious things.
Like a sharp razor, you work your deceit.

³ You love what's evil, more than what is good;
And falsehood, more than speaking righteousness.
⁴ Deceitful tongue; you love words that devour.
⁵ GOD also will destroy you evermore.

He'll seize you, and will tear you from your tent.
Uproot you from the land of those who live.
⁶ The righteous then shall see, and fear, and laugh.
⁷ 'Behold! The man who made not God his strength'!

'He put his trust in his abundant wealth,
And, in his malice, he made himself strong!'
⁸ But as for me, I'm like an olive tree
That flourishes within the house of God.

I trust God's steadfast love for evermore.
⁹ Because you've done this, I'll give endless praise.
And I'll wait on your name, for it is good -
Before those who are your beloved ones.

112 Psalm 53

¹ 'There is no God!' the fool says in his heart.
They are corrupt, and what they do is vile.
No one does good, no not a single one,
² From heaven God looks on the sons of men.

[Continued →

He looks to see if any understand;
If there are those who will seek after God.
3 They've turned away. They're all together foul.
No one does good, no not a single one.

4 Do those who work such wickedness not know?
Who eat my people as a loaf of bread!
These are the ones who do not call on God.
5 Great fear was on them - when there was no fear!

God scattered round about the bones of him
Who camped against you. You put them to shame.
They were rejected, and despised by God.
6 O, please, grant that deliverance may come!

Israel's salvation shall from Zion come,
When God restores, and brings his people back.
He will return them from captivity.
Jacob will joy, and Israel be glad.

113 Psalm 54

1 Save me, O God. O save me by your name,
And by your strength give judgment on my cause.
2 O be attentive to my prayer, O God,
And listen to the words that my mouth speaks.

3 Strangers rose up against me - ruthless foes
Sought for my soul - had no regard for God.
4 But surely God's a helper unto me.
My Lord is with those who support my soul.

5 He will requite the evil of my foes.
O, in your truth, be sure to cut them off!
6 With willing heart I'll sacrifice to you;
A freewill offering to you I'll bring.

I'll praise your name, O LORD, for it is good!
I'll praise your name, O LORD, for it is good!
7 Because he rescued me from all distress.
My eye has looked upon my enemies

114   Psalm 55:1-8

[1] Incline your ear unto my prayer, O God,
And from my supplication do not hide.
[2] Take notice, and give answer unto me.
I mourn in my lament and I'm distraught.

[3] Because the enemy is crying out;
Because the wicked are oppressing so.
For they would throw iniquity on me,
And in their anger keep their hate for me.

[4] My heart writhes as in travail within me.
Terrors of death have fallen upon me.
[5] Trembling and fearfulness have come on me,
And so with horror I am overwhelmed.

[6] I said, 'O had I wings just like a dove
Then would I fly away and be at rest.
[7] Yes! I would leave and wander far away,
And I would lodge within the wilderness'.

[8] 'I would make haste to find a sheltered place
I would make haste, and so make my escape
Far from the tempest and the stormy wind
Yes from the tempest and the stormy wind'.

115   Psalm 55:9-15

[9] 'My Lord, destroy them, and divide their tongue!
For I have seen the city's savage strife'.
[10] By day and night they go around its walls,
Iniquity and sorrow are within.

[11] Destruction is within the midst of it.
Deceit and guile do never leave its streets.
[12] It was no enemy brought me reproach,
For that is something that I then could bear.

[Continued →

72

He who rose up was not my hating foe,
For then I would have hid myself from him.
13 But it was you, a man, ranked just like me.
You, my companion, my familiar friend.

14 Together once we had sweet fellowship,
In company we walked unto God's house.
15 Death seize them! Take them down to Sheol live!
For wickedness is in their homes and heart.

116   Psalm 55:16-23

16 I'll call to God. The LORD will save me then.
17 I'll pray at evening, morning, and at noon.
I'll cry aloud, and he will hear my voice.
18 He has redeemed my soul to be at peace.

Saved from the battle that against me raged,
For there were many who stood on my side.
19 For GOD will hear, and he will answer them.
He is the one who sits enthroned of old.

Because their life continues without change;
Therefore, because of this, they don't fear God.
20 This one laid hands on those at peace with him,
And he defiled and broke his covenant.

21 Mouth smooth as butter, yet war in his heart -
Soft oily words, yet they were like drawn swords.
22 Cast your lot on the LORD. He will sustain.
He will not let the righteous man be moved.

23 But you, O God, will surely cast them down -
Thrown for destruction to the lowest pit.
False, bloody men not living half their days.
But as for me, I'll put my trust in you.

117   Psalm 56:1-7

[1] O do be gracious unto me, O God,
For mortal man would hound and harry me.
He daily fights, and he oppresses me.
[2] My enemies would hound me all the day.

Against me many fight, O God Most High.
[3] When I'm afraid I'll put my trust in you -
[4] In God I'll praise his word - in God I trust.
I will not fear what flesh can do to me.

[5] Yet all the day they twist and wrest my words.
Against me are their thoughts - their evil plans.
[6] They come together, and they hide themselves.
They mark my steps, when they wait for my soul.

[7] Shall they escape by their iniquity?
Shall they escape by their iniquity?
O in your anger make them to sink down.
In anger cast the nations down, O God.

118   Psalm 56:8-13

[8] You keep a count of all my wandering.
Into your bottle put the tears I shed,
For are they not recorded in your book?
[9] My foes will turn back in the day I call.

For this I know, that God is on my side.
[10] In God I'll praise the word; The LORD's word praise.
[11] In God I put my trust, I'm not afraid,
For what then can a man do unto me?

[12] Your vows are binding upon me, O God.
Thanksgivings I will render unto you.
[13] You freed my soul from death. You kept my feet.
So in the light of life I'll walk with God.

119 Psalm 57:1-5

[1] Be gracious, God, be gracious unto me.
My soul has fled for refuge unto you.
In shadow of your wings I'll take refuge,
Till these calamities have passed away.

[2] I will cry out unto the Most High God.
GOD brings to pass his purposes for me.
[3] He'll send from heaven, and he will save me.
The one who hounds me he will put to shame.

God shall send forth his mercy and his truth -
His loving-kindness and his faithfulness.
[4] For roaring lions are all round my soul,
And I lie down with those who flame with fire -

Men who have spears and arrows for their teeth -
With those whose tongue is like a sharpened sword.
[5] High above heaven be exalted, God.
Above the whole earth let your glory be.

120 Psalm 57:6-11

[6] They have prepared a net for where I walk.
Because of this my soul has been bowed down.
In front of me they went and dug a pit,
But they have fallen into it themselves.

[7] My heart is fixed, O God, my heart is fixed.
And I will sing; with psalms I will give praise.
[8] Awake my glory! Wake up lyre and harp!
Yes, I would even wake the morning dawn!

[9] Among the peoples, I will thank you Lord;
Among the nations I'll sing psalms to you.
[10] Your loving-kindness is so very great,
Even unto the heavens it extends.

[Continued →

Likewise, your truth extends unto the clouds.
^{11} Above the heavens, be exalted, God!
Above the whole earth may your glory be.
Above the whole earth may your glory be.

121   Psalm 58:1-5

^{1} O congregation, do you speak what's right?
Do you judge uprightly, you sons of men?
^{2} No. In your heart you work iniquities;
Your hands deal injury upon the earth.

^{3} The wicked are as strangers from the womb.
They go astray as soon as they are born.
And from the time they're born they speak a lie.
And from the time they're born they speak a lie.

^{4} For they have venom, venom like a snake;
Like the deaf cobra, shutting up its ear,
^{5} which does not hear the sound the charmers make
Though they should do their charming skilfully.

122   Psalm 58:6-11

^{6} Shatter, O God, their teeth within their mouth!
Tear out the great teeth of young lions, LORD!
^{7} As water let them quickly flow away,
And blunt his arrows when he draws his bow.

^{8} Let them go like a snail that melts away;
Like one misborn who does not see the sun.
^{9} Before your pots can feel the heat of thorns,
Both green and burning, he'll sweep them away.

^{10} The just, when seeing vengeance, will rejoice,
And in the wicked's blood he'll wash his feet.
^{11} A man will say, 'the just have a reward'.
'There is a God who judges in the earth!'

123   Psalm 59:1-9

¹ Deliver from my enemies, my God;
Defend from those who rise up against me.
² Deliver from those who do wickedness;
And from bloodthirsty men, O do save me!

³ For - See! - they lie in ambush for my soul.
The mighty ones are gathered against me,
For no offence or sin of mine, O LORD.
⁴ They run, make ready, though I'm not at fault.

Stir up yourself up to help me - Look and see! -
⁵ O LORD of hosts, the God of Israel -
To punish all the nations - rouse yourself!
Spare none of those who transgress wickedly.

⁶ Each evening they come back. Just like a dog
They howl. Around the city prowl about.
⁷ See! - from their mouths such gushing talk flows out.
Swords in their lips, they question 'Who will hear?'

⁸ But you yourself, O LORD, will laugh at them;
And all the nations you will mock in scorn.
⁹ (O his great strength!). For you I will keep watch,
Because God is my tower and my defence.

124   Psalm 59:10-17

¹⁰ God in his kindness will come to meet me,
And let me look on those who wait for me.
¹¹ 'Don't let them die, lest my people forget.
By power scatter, sink them, Lord, Our Shield'.

¹² 'For their sin of mouth, word of their lips
Let them be taken in their arrogance;
And for the curse and lie that they repeat
¹³ Consume in wrath! Consume!' They are no more!

[Continued →

And let them know that God in Jacob reigns.
He rules unto the very ends of earth.
14 Let them come back at evening like a dog -
They'll howl. Around the city prowl about.

15 Make them to wander round about for food,
And let them pass the night and not be filled.
16 But as for me, I'll sing about your strength.
At morning will I sing your love with joy.

For you have been my tower and defence,
And, in the day of trouble, my refuge.
17 I will sing psalms of praise to you, my Strength.
For God is my defence: my gracious God.

125   Psalm 60:1-5

1 O God, you have cast off and scattered us.
You have been angry. Turn to us again!
2 You caused the land to shake. You broke it up.
Mend where it's broken. It's about to fall.

3 You've made your people to see what is hard.
The wine of shaking you've made us to drink.
4 You give a banner to those who fear you,
That it may be displayed because of truth.

5 For those who are so very dear to you -
For your beloved - give deliverance.
O give salvation with your own right hand!
And please do hear, give answer unto me.

126   Psalm 60:6-12

6 God has declared this in his holiness.
'I will rejoice, and Shechem I'll divide.
The valley of Succoth I'll measure out.
7 Gil-e-ad and Manasseh are both mine.

[Continued →

Ephraim's the strong defence unto my head.
Judah's my sceptre; 8 Moab's my wash-pot.
And over Edom I will throw my shoe.
Shout out Philistia, because of me!'

9 O who will bring me to the fortress-town?
And who will guide me unto Edom's land?
10 Is it not you, O God, who cast us off?
For with our armies you no longer go.

11 From out of tribulation give us help.
Deliverance from man is all in vain.
12 Through God we will contend courageously.
For he himself will trample on our foes.

127   Psalm 61

1 God, hear my cry; attend unto my prayer:
2 From the earth's utmost end I'll call to you.
Yes, I will call when my heart's overwhelmed.
Lead to the rock that is too high for me.

3 For you have been a refuge unto me,
A tower of strength before the enemy.
4 For ever I will dwell within your tent,
And I will trust the cover of your wings.

5 You heard my vows, O God, and gave to me
The heritage of those who fear your name.
6 Days upon days yet add unto the king!
Let his years be as generations long!

7 He will abide for ever before God.
Set truth and mercy to watch over him.
8 So I'll sing psalms for ever to your name,
As I perform my vows from day to day.

128　　　　Psalm 62:1-7

¹ On God alone my soul waits silently.
It is from him that my salvation comes.
² My rock and my salvation - only him!
He's my stronghold, and I will not be moved.

³ 'How long will you rush in upon a man?'
(You'll all be slain and you'll be broken down,
Just like a bowing wall, or shaky fence).
⁴ Though he be high they plan to bring him down.

Though their mouth blesses, they delight in lies,
And, in their heart, they're cursing inwardly.
⁵ My soul, in silence wait for God alone,
Because my expectation is from him.

⁶ My rock and my salvation - Him alone!
He is my stronghold, and I'll not be moved -
⁷ On God my glory and salvation rest.
Rock of my strength - my refuge is in God.

129　　　　Psalm 62:8-12

⁸ O people, put your trust in him always.
Pour out your heart to him - God's our refuge.
⁹ Men are but breath - the best of men a lie -
Put in the scales, they are as light as breath.

¹⁰ Don't put your trust in what oppression gains,
Nor vainly hope in spoils of robbery.
And, if you find that riches do increase,
Let not your heart depend upon such things.

¹¹ Once God has spoken - and twice I have heard -
That power and great strength belong to God.
¹² That steadfast love belongs to you My Lord.
Repaying every man for what he does.

130   Psalm 63:1-5

1 I'll seek you early, God - you are my GOD.
For you my soul thirsts. My flesh longs for you
In a dry, weary land that's waterless.
2 Thus in the Holy Place I gazed on you

I looked to see your glory and your power,
3 For better is your love than life itself.
Therefore, my lips will utter praise to you.
4 Thus will I magnify you while I live

I'll bless you for as long as I shall live,
And, in your name, I will lift up my hands.
5 My soul is filled with fatness and with fat.
With joyful lips my mouth shall bring you praise.

131   Psalm 63:6-11

6 When in my bed I do remember you;
In the night-watches meditate on you.
7 For you have been a helper unto me.
In your wings' shadow I will sing for joy.

8 My soul is clinging closely after you,
And by your right hand you do hold me up.
9 Those who are seeking to destroy my soul -
they shall go down into the depths of earth.

10 They shall fall by the power of the sword.
The jackals' portion is what they shall be.
11 The king shall joy in God. And all shall praise
who swear by him; the mouths of liars stopped.

132   Psalm 64:1-6

1 O God, my voice hear in my private prayer.
And guard my life from terror of the foe.
2 Hide me from what the wicked ones conspire -
From raging workers of iniquity

[Continued →

³ Who sharpen up their tongue, just like a sword,
And they, like arrows, aim their bitter word,
⁴ To shoot in secret at the blameless one.
Fearless they shoot to take him by surprise.

⁵ They make each other strong for what is bad.
They talk of hiding snares - 'For who will see?'
⁶ Plan evil. Say, 'We have a perfect plan!'
The inner man, the heart, is O so deep!

133   Psalm 64:7-10

⁷ But, with an arrow, God will shoot at them.
And then they will be wounded suddenly.
⁸ They're made to stumble: their tongue makes them fall.
All those who look on them will flee away.

⁹ All men shall fear, and shall declare God's work,
And they shall understand what he has done.
¹⁰ The righteous one joys in the LORD, and trusts.
All those of upright heart shall offer praise.

134   Psalm 65:1-8

¹ Praise is awaiting you in Zion, God;
And unto you the vow will be performed.
² Hearer of prayer, all flesh shall come to you.
Hearer of prayer, all flesh shall come to you.

³ Iniquities have been too strong for me.
Atone for our transgressions. Cover them!
⁴ Blest is the one you choose and cause to come;
He is the one who'll dwell within your courts.

We're filled with all the goodness of your house -
Even the Temple - your own holy place.
⁵ By awesome things performed in righteousness,
God, our salvation, you will answer us.

[Continued →

You are the trust of all the ends of earth,
and of those who are distant on the sea.
⁶ Who firmly sets the mountains by his strength,
And who is girded round about with power.

⁷ He stills the roar of seas, the roar of waves,
And the disturbance that the peoples make.
⁸ Dwellers in distant lands will fear your signs.
The springs of dawn, and sunset, shout for joy.

135   Psalm 65: 9-13

⁹ You visit and give water to the earth:
It is abundantly enriched by you.
For God's own river is with water filled.
When you've prepared it, you prepare their corn.

¹⁰ Its furrows you do water copiously;
By this its ridges you do settle down;
By heavy showers you then make it soft;
You bless its increase and its springing up.

¹¹ And with your goodness you have crowned the year.
Your paths with plenty and with fatness flow.
¹² They flow to pastures of the wilderness,
The little hills do gird themselves with joy.

¹³ The meadows are arrayed and clothed with flocks.
The valleys also are decked out with corn.
They shout for joy, and they together sing.
They shout for joy, and they together sing.

136   Psalm 66:1-9

¹ All earth as one shout joyfully to God!
² Sing out with psalms the glory of his name,
And celebrate his glory in his praise,
³ Say unto God, 'How awesome are your works!'

[Continued →

For through the greatness of your strength and power
Your enemies shall yield themselves to you.
4 All earth shall worship, and sing psalms to you;
Yes, they will sing with psalms unto your name.

5 Come and behold the things that God has wrought:
Fearful in deed toward the sons of men.
6 He did convert the sea into dry land.
Through flood they trod. There we rejoiced in him

7 By his great power, he forever rules.
His eyes upon the nations will keep watch
So let the rebels not exalt themselves.
So let the rebels not exalt themselves.

8 You peoples, bless the one who is our God!
And make the voice of his praise to be heard.
9 He is the one who keeps our soul alive,
And he does not allow our feet to slip.

137   Psalm 66:10-15

10 For you, O God, have proved and tested us:
Refining us as silver is refined.
11 You made us go into the hunter's net:
You laid affliction heavy on our loins

12 You caused man to ride roughshod on our heads;
Through fire, and through the waters, we did come.
Into abundance you have brought us out.
13, 14 Burnt offerings I'll bring into your house!

The vows my lips expressed I'll pay to you,
Which my mouth spoke when I was in distress.
15 I'll offer you fat beasts as offerings;
With smoke of rams; I'll offer bulls and goats.

138   Psalm 66:16-20

[16] Come here and listen, all you who fear God.
I will declare what he did for my soul.
[17] Unto him with my mouth I cried aloud,
And his high praise was underneath my tongue.

[18] If, in my heart, I have regard for sin,
Then My Lord will not listen unto me.
[19] But God has heard! He heard my prayer. [20] Blest God!
Turned not away his mercy, or my prayer.

139   Psalm 67

[1] God shall bless and be gracious unto us;
And on us he will make his face to shine.
[2] So shall your way be known upon the earth,
and your salvation to all nations then.

[3] The peoples shall give thanks to you, O God;
Yes, all the peoples shall give thanks to you.
[4] The nations shall rejoice and shout for joy.
The peoples you will judge with equity.

For you will govern nations on the earth,
And you will lead and be the nations' Guide.
[5] The peoples will give thanks to you, O God;
Yes, all the peoples shall give thanks to you!

[6] The earth shall then deliver its increase.
God, even our own God, will bless us then.
[7] We shall be blessed by God. He shall be feared
By all the ends of earth he shall be feared.

140   Psalm 68:1-6

[1] Let God arise! Scatter his enemies!
Let them that hate him flee before his face!
[2] As smoke is driven, so drive them away,
Like melting wax when put before the fire.

[Continued →

3 So let the wicked perish before God,
But let the righteous ones be filled with joy.
Let them exult before the face of God,
And in their joyfulness they will be glad.

4 Sing unto God. Sing psalms unto his name.
In deserts run a road for him who rides.
His name is JAH! Exult before his face!
5 Father to orphans, and the widows' judge

God is within his holy dwelling place.
6 God makes the lonely to dwell in a home;
Frees prisoners to great prosperity.
But rebels shall dwell in an arid land.

141   Psalm 68:7-14

7 O God, before your people you went out.
When you were marching through the desert waste
8 Earth quaked. The heavens poured out before God;
This Sinai faced by God, by Israel's God.

9 Abundant rain you will send down, O God.
Establishing your weary heritage.
10 Your company of people lived in it,
Set by your goodness for the poor, O God.

11 My Lord will give the word - it is announced.
A mighty troop of women make it known.
12 The kings of armies flee; they surely flee,
And she that stays at home divides the spoil.

13 Will you lie down among the cattle pens
Silver-winged dove; feathers of yellow gold?
14 In the Almighty's scattering of kings,
On dark Zalmon you shall be white as snow.

142   Psalm 68:15-23

¹⁵ A mighty mountain is the mount Bashan;
Mountain of high peaks is the mount Bashan.
¹⁶ Why look in envy, mountains of high peaks,
Upon the mount where God desired to dwell?

Truly the LORD will dwell there evermore.
¹⁷ Double ten thousand are God's chariots,
The number swelled, yes, many thousand times:
Among them is the One who is My Lord

Sinai is now within the holy place.
¹⁸ You did go up - ascended up on high -
And you did lead captive captivity.
You have received and given gifts to man.

Yes, for the rebels he has given gifts,
That God whose name is JAH might dwell with them.
¹⁹ Blest be My Lord who bears us day by day -
The GOD who is salvation unto us.

²⁰ GOD of deliverances is our GOD.
Ways out from death are from My Lord, the LORD.
²¹ But God will smite his foes upon the head -
His head of hair that goes on in his guilt.

²² My Lord has said, 'From Bashan I will bring -
And from the depths of sea I'll bring them back;
²³ So that your foot may paddle in the blood.
Your dogs' tongue finds its portion from your foes'.

143   Psalm 68:24-35

²⁴ They've seen your ways of going forth, O GOD.
My God, My King's ways in the Holy Place;
²⁵ Singers before, musicians after them,
Among them young girls beating tambourines.

[Continued →

26 In the assemblies, O bless God, My Lord!
You who are from the fount of Israel!
27 There's little Benjamin, he who subdues;
With Judah's princes and their company.

Princes of Zebulun and Naphtali -
28 God gave you strength. Make strong your work, O God!
29 Your Temple is found at Jerusalem.
Therefore, a gift shall kings bring unto you.

30 Rebuke the living creature of the reeds,
The herd of bulls, the peoples' calves with them.
With gifts of silver they prostrate themselves.
He scattered nations that delight in wars.

31 The foremost men shall out of Egypt come,
And Cush shall haste to stretch its hands to God.
32 O kingdoms of the earth, sing unto God,
And sing with psalms to him who is My Lord.

33 To him who on the highest heaven rides -
The heavens which are from the ancient times.
See, he gives voice. It is a voice of strength.
34 Ascribe the strength and power unto God.

His majesty is over Israel.
His strength is in the skies. 35 God to be feared!
'Out of your holy places - Israel's GOD!'
He gives the people strength and might. Bless God!

144   Psalm 69:1-5

1 Save me, O God. The waters reach my soul.
2 I sink in a deep mire. I cannot stand.
I have now come where the deep waters are:
The overwhelming flood sweeps over me.

[Continued

³ I faint with crying out. My throat is dry.
My eyes have failed, while I wait for my God.
⁴ Those who have hatred for me without cause
Are more in number than hairs of my head.

My strong destroyers - lying enemies -
Though I stole nothing, yet I must repay.
⁵ You, you O God have known my foolishness;
My trespasses have not been hid from you.

145   Psalm 69:6-12

⁶ Those who wait for you, My Lord - LORD of Hosts,
Let them not be ashamed because of me.
And those who seek you, God of Israel,
Let them not be perplexed because of me.

⁷ It's for your sake that I have borne reproach.
Shame and perplexity covered my face.
⁸ From my own brothers I am now estranged:
A foreigner unto my mother's sons.

⁹ The zeal for your house has consumed me so,
Reproaches cast at you now fall on me.
¹⁰ And so I wept, and my soul kept the fast,
And yet it brought reproaches upon me.

¹¹ I put on sackcloth to show my remorse,
And I became a by-word unto them.
¹² I am the talk of all those at the gate,
Yes, even drunkards make their song of me.

146   Psalm 69:13-21

¹³ But, as for me, my prayer is to you, LORD,
At such a time as pleases you, O God.
In your great loving-kindness answer me -
Give answer in your saving faithfulness.

[Continued →

¹⁴ Rescue me from the mire (don't let me sink) -
From those who hate me - from the waters deep.
¹⁵ Let not the flood engulf me, nor the deep;
Let not the pit close up its mouth on me.

¹⁶ Give answer LORD - your steadfast love is good -
In your abundant mercies turn to me.
¹⁷ I am your servant. Do not hide your face.
I am in trouble. Answer speedily.

¹⁸ Draw near unto my soul and ransom it.
Deliver me from those who are my foes.
¹⁹ You know how I'm reproached, shamed and perplexed
All those who trouble me are seen by you.

²⁰ My heart is heavy. Broken by reproach.
No one to pity or to comfort me.
²¹ They gave me bitter poison for my food;
They gave me vinegar to quench my thirst.

147   Psalm 69:22-28

²² As for their table, let it be a snare.
To those in peace cause it to be a trap.
²³ Darken their eyes so that they cannot see,
And make their loins to shake unceasingly.

²⁴ Pour out your indignation upon them,
And let your burning anger overtake.
²⁵ Make desolate the place in which they live;
Let no one dwell within their tents at all.

²⁶ For they pursue the one whom you did smite.
They tell the pain of those whom you did wound.
For they pursue the one whom you did smite.
They tell the pain of those whom you did wound.

[Continued →

27 Add unto their iniquity yet more
Let them not enter to your righteousness
28 Put them out of the book of those who live
And with the righteous do not write them down

148   Psalm 69:29-36

29 But still I am afflicted and in pain.
O God, let your salvation lift me up.
30 I will give praise unto God's name with song,
And magnify it with my grateful thanks.

31 This also is more pleasing to the LORD
Than is an ox, a bull with horns and hooves.
32 The humble ones shall see this and be glad.
Your heart shall live, who thus seek after God.

33 The needy and the poor the LORD will hear.
He won't despise his people when they're bound.
34 The heavens and the earth give praise to him,
The seas and every moving thing in them.

35 For God saves Zion. Judah's cities builds
So they may stay and take possession there.
36 His servant's seed shall then inherit it;
In it will dwell all those who love his name.

149   Psalm 70

1 O God, to rescue and deliver me;
O LORD, unto my help; Act speedily!
2 Shame, and confuse, those who seek for my soul;
Turn back, disgrace, those who wish harm to me.

3 And may their shame cause them to be turned back
All those who jeer at me, 'Aha!' 'Aha!'
4 Let all who seek you be glad and rejoice.
And let those who love your salvation speak.

[*Continued* →

'God be exalted' may they ever say.
5 I'm poor and needy. Hasten to me, God!
You are my Help and my Deliverer;
You are the LORD, so please make no delay.

150   Psalm 71:1-8

1 In you, the LORD, I've taken my refuge,
So do not let me ever be ashamed.
2 Deliver; rescue, in your righteousness.
O turn your ear to me. Deliver me!

3 Be a stronghold where I may always go.
You gave commandment that I should be saved,
For you're a rock and fortress unto me.
4 Rescue me from the wicked's hand, my God.

Rescue me from the cruel and unjust,
5 Because you are my hope, My Lord - the LORD -
My trust from youth - 6 My mainstay from the womb.
You, from my mother's body, drew me out

My praise shall be of you continually.
7 To many I've become a prodigy,
You are my sure refuge - 8 my mouth is filled -
Filled with your praise, your honour, all day long.

151   Psalm 71:9-18

9 Don't cast me off in the time of old age;
When my strength fails, do not forsake me then.
10 Because my enemies against me speak,
And those who watch my soul confer as one.

11 They say of me, that God's forsaken him,
'Pursue and seize him. None will rescue him!'
12 O God, do not be far away from me.
My God, unto my help; Act speedily!

[Continued →

¹³ Shame, and consume, those who oppose my soul;
With scorn and shame clothe those who would harm me
¹⁴ But as for me - I'll always wait in hope;
I'll add to all your praise yet more and more.

¹⁵ My mouth will tell about your righteousness,
And tell of your salvation all the day
For the numbers of them I don't know!
¹⁶ I'll come with My Lord's strength, even the Lord's.

I will commemorate your righteousness,
Even the righteousness of you alone.
¹⁷ O God, you have instructed me from youth;
Since then I have declared your wondrous works.

¹⁸ And to old age, as well (when I'm grey-haired).
O God, I ask, do not forsake me then!
Till to the generation I declare
Your arm, your might, to all who are to come.

152   Psalm 71:19-24

¹⁹ Your righteousness, O God, is very high.
You've done great things. O God, who is like you?
²⁰ Great, grievous troubles you have made me see,
You will return and give me life again.

And from earth's depths you'll raise me up again.
²¹ You'll make me greater. Turn to comfort me.
²² I will give thanks to you upon the lyre,
And for your truth I'll thank you, O my God.

I will sing psalms unto you with the harp,
To you, the Holy One of Israel.
²³ My lips will sing for joy when I sing psalms
Together with my soul, which you've redeemed.

[Continued →

²⁴ My tongue will meditate all the day long
All day it will speak of your righteousness.
For they are put to shame, and are confused,
Who tried to find a way to do me harm.

153   Psalm 72:1-7

¹ Give your right judgments to the king, O God;
And give your righteousness to the king's son.
² Your people's cause he'll judge with righteousness,
Judge with right judgment your afflicted ones.

³ The mountains will bring to the people peace.
The hills will do the same by righteousness.
⁴ The poor ones of the people he'll judge right;
The children of the needy he will save.

And the oppressor he will break and crush,
⁵ They'll fear you just as long as there is sun.
While shines the moon; through generations long.
⁶ He shall come down as rain on the mown grass.

He'll come as showers watering the earth.
⁷ So shall the righteous flourish in his days;
Abundant peace shall then be multiplied,
Until the time the moon shall be no more.

154   Psalm 72:8-11

⁸ From sea to sea will his dominion be,
And from the River to the ends of earth.
⁹ Before him shall the desert dwellers bow,
He'll make his enemies to lick the dust.

¹⁰ The kings of Tarshish, and lands of the sea,
Shall bring their gifts and tribute unto him.
The kings of Sheba and Seba, likewise,
For, with their presents, they too shall draw near.

[Continued →

11 All kings shall bow in reverence to him;
All nations shall unto him homage pay.
Before him every king shall prostrate fall,
And every nation shall his servant be.

155   Psalm 72:12-14

12 He'll save the needy when he calls for help.
And the afflicted, when no one gives aid.
13 He'll have compassion on the one who's weak.
And have compassion on the needy one.

And the souls of the needy ones he'll save,
14 For he will give a ransom for their soul
To free them from deceit and violence,
And their blood will be precious in his eyes.

156   Psalm 72:15-20

15 He shall live, and be given Sheba's gold,
Prayer shall be made for him continually.
And they shall bless him throughout all the day.
16 Corn in abundance shall be in the land;

It shall be even on the mountain top.
Its fruit shall shake like trees of Lebanon.
Those from the city shall flourish as grass.
17 So shall his name endure for evermore.

His name shall prosper while the sun still shines.
And men shall count themselves as blest in him.
All nations shall declare his happiness.
18 Blest be the LORD God: God of Israel.

For he alone is doing wondrous things.
19 Blest be his splendid name for evermore.
His glory shall fill all the earth. Amen!
Amen. 20 The prayers of David are fulfilled.

Book 3

Psalms 73 - 89

157   Psalm 73:1-12

[1] Yes, surely, God is good to Israel -
Even to such as are of a pure heart.
[2] But, as for me, my feet were almost gone.
The steps I took had nearly slipped away.

[3] Because I envied vain and foolish men.
I saw the wicked in prosperity;
[4] For in their death there are not any pains,
And in their body they are fit and strong.

[5] They're not in trouble as are other men;
Nor are they plagued and smitten as mankind.
[6] Therefore is pride a chain about their neck;
And with a robe of violence they dress.

[7] Because of fatness their eye bulges out;
They overflow with all their heart could wish.
[8] They scoff and speak with malice wickedly;
It is as from a high place that they speak.

[9] They set their mouth within the heavens high;
It is as though their tongue struts through the earth.
[10] Therefore his people turn back to this place,
And a full measure shall be poured to them.

[11] And so they say, 'How can it be GOD knows?'
And 'Is there knowledge with the Most High God?'
[12] Take note of them! - these are the wicked ones.
These always prosper and increase in wealth.

158   Psalm 73:13-22

[13] Surely, it is in vain I've cleansed my heart.
And that I washed my hands in innocence.
[14] Because I have been stricken all day long,
And every morning brought my chastisement.

[Continued →

¹⁵ If I had said that I will speak like this,
Truly, I'd be a traitor to your sons.
¹⁶ So, when I pondered how I might know this,
It was a thing of trouble, in my eyes -

¹⁷ Till I went in the Holy Place of GOD;
Till I considered what their end will be.
¹⁸ Yes, surely, you've put them where they will slip!
In utter ruins you then cast them down.

¹⁹ How suddenly they are made desolate!
They are consumed with terrors utterly.
²⁰ As when one wakes up from a dream, My Lord,
When you rise up, their shadow you will scorn.

²¹ For my heart was embittered and was grieved,
My feelings hurt, as pierced right through my side.
²² For I was brutish, and I did not know:
Toward you I was even like a beast.

159   Psalm 73:23-28

²³ In spite of that I am always with you.
You've taken hold of me by my right hand.
²⁴ So by your counsel you will lead me on,
To glory you'll receive me afterward.

²⁵ Who is there in the heavens on my side?
Beside you I have no delight on earth.
²⁶ And, though my flesh and heart should waste away,
God's my heart's strength and portion evermore.

²⁷ Those far from you will surely be destroyed.
You put an end to all who whore from you.
²⁸ It's good that I draw near to God. My Lord -
The LORD's my refuge; All your works I'll tell.

160   Psalm 74:1-4

¹ O why, O God, have you rejected us?
Why have you cast us off continually?
Why does your anger fume and smoke against -
Against the sheep, those in your shepherd care?

² Remember your own gathered company -
Even the people you have bought of old;
The rod to you assigned, which you redeemed;
This mount of Zion in which you did dwell.

³ Unto the utter ruins turn your steps.
The enemy wrecked all the holy place.
⁴ Your foes have roared within your meeting place.
They have replaced the signs by their own signs.

161   Psalm 74:5-11

⁵ Once one was known as he who chopped down trees
As one who raised up axes in the wood.
⁶ And now they break all its carved work at once;
With axes and with hammers break it down.

⁷ And they have set your Holy Place on fire;
Brought to the dirt the place where your name dwells.
⁸ For they have spoken thus within their heart,
'Let us together crush them utterly!'

They have burned all GOD's meetings in the land.
⁹ We see no signs! No prophet anymore!
And there is none of us who knows how long,
¹⁰ O God, for how long shall the foe reproach?

Will those who hate you ever scorn your name?
¹¹ What is the reason you hold back your hand?
Why is it that you hold back your right hand?
O draw your hand forth, and then make an end!

162   Psalm 74:12-17

¹² Yet nonetheless, God is my king of old.
Working deliverances in the earth.
¹³ You - you divided the sea by your might,
Upon the waters broke the monsters' heads.

¹⁴ The heads of the leviathan you crushed:
Gave it as food for people of dry lands.
¹⁵ You did divide both water-spring and brook,
And you dried up the ever-flowing streams

¹⁶ Yours is the day - yours also is the night.
You have established the light and the sun.
¹⁷ You have set all the borders of the earth.
Summer and winter have been formed by you.

163   Psalm 74:18-23

¹⁸ Remember, LORD, the enemy's contempt!
A foolish people have blasphemed your name.
¹⁹ Give not the soul of your dove to the beast:
Your poor one's life do not always forget.

²⁰ Regard your covenant: The land's dark parts
Are habitations full of violence.
²¹ O let not the oppressed return in shame.
The poor and needy – they shall praise your name.

²² Arise, O God! Arise, defend your cause!
Mind how the fool reproaches you all day.
²³ Do not forget your adversaries' voice.
The rebels' tumult goes up constantly.

164   Psalm 75:1-6

¹ We give you thanks, O God. We give you thanks.
Your name is near - your wondrous deeds do tell.
² 'When I shall take the set, appointed, time,
I, even I, will judge with equity'

[Continued →

³ 'The earth and all that dwell therein shall melt
I am the one who made its pillars firm
⁴ I told the boasters, "Do not make your boast".
And told the wicked, "Do not lift the horn"'.

⁵ See that you do not lift your horn on high,
And do not speak with a proud outstretched neck.
⁶ For neither from the east, nor from the west,
Nor from the desert, is the lifting up.

165 Psalm 75:7-10

⁷ For God is judge; so this man he brings down,
And yet another man, he raises up.
⁸ For in the LORD's hand there's a cup of wine,
The wine is foaming and is mixed right up.

And from that cup of wine the LORD pours out -
Surely, the very dregs they shall drain out.
Yes, all the wicked of the earth shall drink;
⁹ And I will tell of it for evermore

Unto the God of Jacob I'll sing psalms.
¹⁰ The horns of all the wicked I'll cut off.
Not so for him who is the righteous one
His horns shall be exalted - lifted high!

166 Psalm 76:1-6

¹ It is in Judah that God is made known:
In Israel his name is very great.
² It is in Salem that his tent is set:
And Zion is the place in which he dwells.

³ There - there he broke the arrows of the bow.
The shield, the sword, and weapons of the war.
⁴ You are resplendent. You are excellent.
As you come from the mountains of the prey.

[Continued →

⁵ The brave have been despoiled. They slept their sleep.
None of the mighty men could use their hands.
⁶ At your rebuke (you who are Jacob's God),
Both chariot and horse fell fast asleep.

167   Psalm 76:7-12

⁷ But you indeed, are the One to be feared;
When you are angry who stands before you?
⁸ You, from the heavens, made the judgment heard;
The earth was then afraid, and it was still.

⁹ When God arises to give judgment out,
All the afflicted of the earth to save.
¹⁰ The wrath of man will yield its praise to you.
All that remains of wrath you will gird on.

¹¹ Make vows - perform them to the LORD your God.
All those around God-to-be-feared bring gifts.
¹² The spirit of the princes he'll cut off.
He is a terror to the kings of earth.

168   Psalm 77:1-6

¹ With my voice I cried out aloud to God;
My voice to God! And he gave ear to me.
² I sought My Lord the day of my distress
My outstretched hand was not weary by night.

My soul would not take comfort from its grief.
³ I would remember God, and I would sigh.
I think on this, and then my spirit faints.
⁴ You have held back the watches of my eyes.

I am so troubled that I cannot speak.
⁵ I thought upon the days that were of old
Upon the years that were of ages past.
⁶ I will recall what I sang in the night!

[Continued →

I will commune and ponder with my heart,
And with my spirit I will search out well.
I will commune and ponder with my heart,
And with my spirit I will search out well.

169   Psalm 77:7-15

7 So will My Lord reject for evermore?
Will he not show his favour anymore?
8 And has his kindness reached a final end?
Has his word failed for ages yet to come?

9 Has GOD forgotten to act graciously?
Has he in anger shut his mercies up?
10 I said that 'This is my infirmity.
The years of the Most High's right hand are these'.

11 I will recall the deeds of JAH - the LORD.
Your wonder I'll remember from of old.
12 I'll meditate on all that you have done,
Speak with myself about your mighty deeds.

13 O God, your pathway is in holiness.
The way of God is in the Holy Place.
Who is a GOD who's great as is the God?
14 You are the GOD who's done this wondrous thing.

Among the peoples you've made your strength known.
15 You have redeemed your people with your arm,
You bought them back by your own mighty power
You brought them back, Jacob and Joseph's sons.

170   Psalm 77:16-20

16 The waters saw you - they saw you, O God -
The waters saw you, and they were in pain.
The very depths did tremble and did quake;
17 The clouds poured water; skies gave out a sound.

[Continued →

Your arrows also went out round about;
[18] Noise of your thunders in the whirling wind.
Lightnings lit up the world - earth shook and quaked.
[19] And your highway, it was within the sea.

In mighty waters were the paths you took,
And yet your footprints were not traceable.
[20] You led your people like a flock of sheep,
Even by Moses' and by Aaron's hand.

171   Psalm 78:1-8

[1] My people, give your ear unto my Law;
Incline your ear unto words of my mouth.
[2] My mouth I'll open in a parable;
I will pour forth dark sayings from of old.

[3] Things we have heard, and things that we have known
Things which our fathers have declared to us,
[4] We'll not conceal nor hide them from their sons:
And tell the generation yet to come.

To tell to them the praises of the LORD;
Tell of his strength, and wonders he has done.
[5] In Jacob he a Testimony raised;
In Israel a Law he did appoint.

These he commanded to our fathers then,
So they should make them known unto their sons.
[6] To let the future generation know,
Even the sons that should be born to them.

They should rise up to tell them to their sons,
[7] So they might put their confidence in God,
That they might not forget the deeds of GOD,
And that they might observe what he commands.

[8] So they might not be as their fathers were:
A stubborn generation that rebelled,
A generation with unsettled heart,
Whose spirit was not faithful unto GOD.

172   Psalm 78:9-16

9 The sons of Ephraim, armed and bearing bows,
Retreated in the day the battle raged.
10 They did not keep the covenant of God;
Refused to walk according to his Law.

11 And they forgot the things that he had done -
His wondrous works that he showed unto them.
12 He did a marvel, in their fathers' sight,
In Egypt's land, even in Zoan's field.

13 He parted sea, and made them to pass through.
He made the waters stand up like a heap.
14 By day he also led them with a cloud,
And, all night long, led with the light of fire.

15 Rocks he split open in the wilderness,
And gave them drink, as if from the great deeps.
16 He brought forth flowing waters from the rock,
And he made waters flow as rivers do.

173   Psalm 78:17-29

17 They still went on to sin against him more -
Provoked the Most High in the arid land.
18 And, in their heart, they put GOD to the test -
Demanding food, the food that their soul craved.

19 They contradicted God, 'Can GOD' they said
'Prepare a table in the wilderness?'
20Behold! He struck the rock and waters gushed;
Streams overflowed. 'Can he give bread also?'

'Can he supply his people yet with meat?'
21 Therefore the Lord heard. He was full of wrath.
A fire was kindled against Jacob then,
Anger ascended against Israel.

[Continued →

22 Because they did not put their faith in God -
On his salvation they did not depend.
23 The clouds he had commanded from above.
Had opened up the doors of heaven then.

24 He had rained manna down on them to eat,
And gave to them of heaven's wheaten grain.
25 Man then did eat the bread of mighty ones.
Food in abundance he sent them to eat.

26 In heaven went the East wind, which he drove,
And the South wind was guided by his power.
27 And he rained flesh upon them, as the dust.
And birds with wings, like to the sand of seas.

28 He made them to fall down within their camp,
Even around the places where they dwelt.
29 So they did eat, and so they were well-filled.
And so he gave to them what they desired.

174   Psalm 78:30-39

30 They were not yet estranged from their desire -
But - when their food was still within their mouth -
31 The anger of God rose against them then.
He slew their finest; smote Israel's young men.

32 And yet, in all this, they sinned even more.
Despite his wonders, they did not believe.
33 He made their days to vanish like a breath;
Their years in sudden terror passed away.

34 But when he slew them, they sought after him.
Turned back again and sought GOD earnestly.
35 And they remembered that God was their rock,
That GOD Most High was their redeemer too.

[Continued →

³⁶ Still they would yet deceive him with their mouth;
And they dissembled to him with their tongue.
³⁷ Their heart was not steadfast and sure with him.
Nor were they faithful in his covenant.

³⁸ But he in tender mercy hid the sin.
Forgave iniquity. Did not destroy.
His anger, many times, he did turn back,
Not stirring up full measure of his wrath.

³⁹ And he remembered that they were but flesh -
A wind that passes and comes not again.
Yes, he remembered that they were but flesh -
A wind that passes and comes not again.

175   Psalm 78:40-51

⁴⁰ How often they rebelled against him there -
In wilderness; grieved him in desert waste.
⁴¹ Repeatedly they turned and tested GOD,
And vexed the Holy One of Israel.

⁴² It was his hand; but they remembered not
The day that he redeemed them from the foe.
⁴³ How he had worked his signs in Egypt's land -
The wonders that he did in Zoan's field.

⁴⁴ He turned their watercourses into blood -
Their flowing waters so they could not drink.
⁴⁵ He sent devouring swarms of flies to them
And sent the frogs that devastated them.

⁴⁶ To caterpillar he gave their increase,
And to the locust the fruit of their toil.
⁴⁷ Their vines he caused to die by sending hail;
Also their sycomores he killed by frost.

[Continued →

⁴⁸ He gave their livestock also to the hail;
He gave their flocks to fiery thunderbolts.
⁴⁹ He let his burning anger loose on them -
Wrath, indignation, and adversity.

They were a band of hurtful messengers
Of evil angels sent to do great harm.
⁵⁰ He prepared a way for his anger to go.
He did not spare or keep their soul from death.

But he gave up their life unto the plague.
⁵¹ All the firstborn in Egypt he struck down.
He struck down the first issue of their strength.
And killed their firstfruits in the tents of Ham.

176　　　　　Psalm 78:52-57

⁵² Then his own people he led out like sheep.
The flock he guided in the wilderness.
⁵³ He led them safely, so they did not fear.
Their enemies were covered by the sea.

⁵⁴ Unto the border of his holy place,
He brought them: even to this mountain here -
The mountain that his right hand had obtained,
⁵⁵ And he drove out the nations from their face.

He portioned out their heritage by line,
And in their tents made Israel's tribes to dwell.
⁵⁶ In spite of this, they tested and provoked -
Tested, provoked against, the Most High God.

His testimonies they did not observe,
⁵⁷ But they turned back and acted faithlessly.
Just like their fathers, turned back faithlessly:
Changing direction like a faulty bow.

177   Psalm 78:58-64

58 With their high places they moved him to wrath.
They made him jealous with their images -
Moved him to jealousy with their carved stones.
59 God heard this, and then he was full of wrath.

He forcibly rejected Israel,
Concerning Israel he felt disgust.
60 The tabernacle of Shiloh he left -
The tent that he had pitched to dwell with men.

61 His strength he gave up to captivity.
He gave his glory into the foe's hand.
62 He gave his people over to the sword,
And he was angry with his heritage.

63 Their choice young men were then consumed by fire
And so their virgins had no marriage song.
64 Their priests fell by the sword, and were laid low.
Their widows shed no tears - did not lament.

178   Psalm 78:65-72

65 My Lord then woke as one who wakes from sleep
Just like a mighty man, shouting from wine.
66 He smote his foes, and so he drove them back.
And he gave to them everlasting shame.

67 The tent of Joseph he rejected then,
And did not choose the tribe of Eph-ra-im.
68 It was the tribe of Judah that he chose -
even the mount of Zion which he loved.

69 He built his Holy Place like heights sublime,
And as the earth, established evermore.
70 His servant David he also did choose,
And from the sheepfolds he then took him out.

[Continued →

⁷¹ From following the ewes that nursed their young,
He brought him out to shepherd and to rule:
To shepherd Jacob - people who are his:
To shepherd Israel - his heritage.

⁷² And so he shepherded, and pastured them,
According to his heart's integrity.
He led them out, just as a shepherd does,
And guided with his skilful, prudent, hands.

179   Psalm 79:1-4

¹ O God, the Gentile nations have come in.
They have invaded your inheritance.
Your Holy Temple is by them defiled.
They made Jerusalem just ruined heaps.

² Your servants' corpses they have given up
As food for birds of heaven to devour.
The flesh of your beloved they gave up
Unto the wild beasts of the earth to eat.

³ Around Jerusalem they poured their blood -
Poured out like water - with none burying!
⁴ We are unto our neighbours a reproach;
Scorn and derision to those round about.

180   Psalm 79:5-9

⁵ How long, LORD? Will your anger always last?
And will your jealousy burn just like fire?
⁶ O let your burning anger be poured out
On nations that do not acknowledge you.

O let your burning anger be poured out
On kingdoms that do not call on your name.
⁷ Jacob's devoured; His pasture they laid waste.
⁸ Do not recall against us our past faults!

[Continued →

Let your kind mercies meet us speedily,
For we have been brought down so very low.
[9] Help us, our Saving God, for your name's praise;
For your name, rescue, cover our sins up.

181   Psalm 79:10-13

[10] Why should the nations say, 'Where is their God?'
Make known before the nations in our sight
The vengeance for your servants' outpoured blood!
[11] The captive's sighs - let them come unto you.

According to the greatness of your power
Spare those who are appointed unto death.
[12] Return unto our neighbours sevenfold
The taunts with which they taunted you, My Lord.

[13] So we, who are your people and your flock,
And are the object of your shepherd care -
We will give thanks to you for evermore -
To endless ages we'll recount your praise.

182   Psalm 80:1-3

[1] O Israel's Shepherd, do incline your ear,
You who have guided Joseph like a flock.
The One enthroned upon the cherubim -
Dwelling between the cherubim - Shine forth!

[2] In Ephraim's sight stir up your mighty strength -
In sight of Benjamin, Manasseh too.
And come and save us! [3] O God, turn us back!
Make your face shine, and then we will be saved.

183   Psalm 80:4-7

[4] How long, O LORD the God of Hosts? Till when?
Your anger fumes against your people's prayer.
[5] For you have fed them with the bread of tears,
And in full measure gave them tears to drink.

[Continued →

⁶ Unto our neighbours you make us a strife;
Our enemies just laugh among themselves.
⁷ O God of hosts, restore us, turn us back.
Shine with your face, and then we will be saved.

184   Psalm 80:8-14

⁸ From out of Egypt you have brought a vine.
You drove out nations, and you planted it.
⁹ You cleared the ground to make a space for it.
You made it take deep root. It filled the land.

¹⁰ By it the mountains were cast in the shade,
And, by its branches, the cedars of GOD.
¹¹ It sent its branches even to the Sea,
And to the River it sent out its shoots.

¹² Why have you broken her enclosures down?
So, all the passers-by do pick her fruit.
¹³ The boar out of the wood tears it apart.
The wild beast of the field devours it up.

¹⁴ O God of hosts return again, we pray.
Oh, turn again, from heaven look and see!
Oh, come and visit, take care of this vine.
Oh, come and visit, take care of this vine.

185   Psalm 80:15-19

¹⁵ Prepare what your right hand has set in place
Also the son you made strong for yourself.
¹⁶ See, it is burned with fire. It is cut down.
You look in anger and they are destroyed.

¹⁷ Your hand be on the man of your right hand,
The son of man you made strong for yourself.
¹⁸ Then we shall not backslide away from you.
Revive us and we shall call on your name.

[Continued →

¹⁹ LORD God of hosts, restore us, turn us back.
Make your face shine, and then we shall be saved.
LORD God of hosts, restore us, turn us back.
Make your face shine, and then we shall be saved.

186   Psalm 81:1-5

¹ Sing out with joy to God who is our strength;
Unto the God of Jacob raise a shout.
² Take up the psalm! Bring here the tambourine!
Sweet harp with lyre! ³ Blow shofar at new moon.

At the full moon, for the day of our Feast.
⁴ For this decree was made for Israel.
It is an ordinance that should be kept -
A right arrangement made by Jacob's God

⁵ To be a witness, he appointed this.
A Testimony he in Joseph set.
When against Egypt he was going forth;
When I heard speech that was unknown to me.

187   Psalm 81:6-10

⁶ 'I took his shoulder from the burden then.
Likewise, his hands were from the basket freed.
⁷ You called in trouble, and I rescued you.
I gave you answer from the thunder cloud'.

'I proved you at waters of Meribah.
⁸ My people, Hear. I'll testify to you.
O Israel, if you'll listen to me,
⁹ There will not be among you a strange GOD'.

'You won't bow down to any foreign GOD,
¹⁰ For it is I, the LORD, who is your God -
The One who brought you up from Egypt's land.
'Open your mouth wide and I'll fill it up'.

113

188   Psalm 81:11-16

11 'My people would not listen to my voice,
And Israel would not submit to me.
12 I gave them up to their own stubborn heart,
That they might walk in counsels they devised.

13 O that my people would listen to me,
That Israel would walk within my ways.
14 Then I would soon subdue their enemies,
And I would turn my hand against their foes.

15 The haters of the LORD would yield to him.
Their time should then endure for evermore.
16 He'd feed them with the finest of the wheat
'I'd fill you with the honey from the rock'

189   Psalm 82:1-4

1 God stands up in the Gathering of GOD,
And he holds judgment in the midst of gods.
2 'How long will you give judgment that is wrong?'
'How long show favour to the wicked ones?'

3 'Give judgment to the weak and fatherless;
Maintain the right of the oppressed and poor;
4 Rescue the weak, the one who is in need;
Deliver from the hand of wicked men'.

190   Psalm 82:5-8

5 'They neither know, nor do they understand,
And they in darkness wander round about.
All the foundations of the earth do shake.
6 I said, 'You're gods. All sons of the Most High'.

7 'But you will die just like all other men,
And as one of the princes you will fall.
8Arise, O God, give justice to the earth,
For all the nations are your heritage.

191   Psalm 83:1-8

[1] O GOD, please do not stay in silence now.
Hold not your peace, and be not still, O God!
[2] For - See! - the uproar of your enemies;
Those who hate you have lifted up the head.

[3] Against your people they plot craftily,
And they conspire against your hidden ones.
[4] And they say, 'Come, the nation we'll wipe out;
No more remembered will be Israel's name'

[5] For they consulted as with one accord;
Against you they have made a covenant.
[6] The tents of Edom and the Ishmaelites,
The tents of Moab and the Hagarenes.

[7] The tents of Gebal, Ammon, Amalek,
Philistia, and those who dwell at Tyre.
[8] Assyria has also joined with them.
They give support unto the sons of Lot.

192   Psalm 83:9-12

[9] Do unto them as unto Midian,
As unto Sisera and to Jabin
(When they were at the Kishon torrent stream),
[10] At Endor they were cut off and destroyed.

For they became as dung upon the ground.
[11] Their nobles make like Oreb and Ze'eb;
Their princes as Zeba and Zalmunna,
[12] Who said 'Let's take God's pastures for ourselves!'

193   Psalm 83:13-18

[13] My God, make them just like the whirling dust,
And as the stubble blown before the wind;
[14] Just as the fire that burns the forest up;
And as a flame that sets mountains on fire.

[Continued →

¹⁵ Just so, pursue them with your storm of wind,
And terrify them with your hurricane.
¹⁶ And make their faces to be full of shame,
So they may come to seek your name, O LORD.

¹⁷ Make them ashamed and troubled evermore.
Yes, let them be confounded and destroyed.
¹⁸ And let them know that you, your name - the LORD.
Alone are over all the earth, Most High.

194   Psalm 84:1-7

¹ How lovely are your dwellings, LORD of hosts.
² My soul both longs – even faints - for the LORD's courts
My heart and flesh cry to the living GOD,
³ Just as the sparrow has secured a home,

The swallow has secured itself a nest -
A nest in which it may lay down its young -
A place that's near your altars, LORD of hosts -
Your altars, LORD of hosts, my King, my God.

⁴ Blesséd are those who dwell within your house.
They shall continually give praise to you.
⁵ Blesséd the man who has his strength in you,
Who has your highways set within his heart.

⁶ When through the valley of Baca they pass,
They turn it to a place of water springs.
The autumn rain thus covers it with pools;
Clothes it with blessings of the early rain.

⁷ Onward they go, increasing strength to strength,
Each shall be seen in Zion before God.
Onward they go, increasing strength to strength,
Each shall be seen in Zion before God.

195   Psalm 84:8-12

8 O LORD, the God of hosts, do hear my prayer!
O God of Jacob, Do give ear to me!
9 O God, behold our shield, and do regard -
Regard the face of your anointed one.

10 Because a day spent in your courts is good,
Far better than a thousand spent elsewhere.
I'd rather keep the door in my God's house,
Than dwell among the tents of wickedness.

11 Because the LORD God is both sun and shield.
The LORD gives grace and glory - Won't withhold -
A good thing from those who walk blamelessly.
12 The man who trusts you, LORD of hosts, is blest!

196   Psalm 85:1-7

1 You have shown favour to your land, O LORD;
You have turned back Jacob's captivity.
2 You've covered over all your people's faults,
And you have lifted, pardoned, all their sin.

3 You have entirely set aside your wrath;
From your hot anger you have turned away.
4 O God of our salvation turn us back;
And end the grief that you have over us.

5 Will you be angry with us evermore?
And will your anger ever be prolonged -
To every generation yet to come?
6 Will you not give new life to us again?

Will you not give new life to us again -
So that your people may rejoice in you?
7 Your loving-kindness show to us, O LORD,
And grant us the salvation that you give.

117

197   Psalm 85:8-13

8 I'll listen to what GOD the LORD will speak,
Because unto his people he speaks peace.
Yes, he speaks peace unto those whom he loves,
But let them not turn back to foolishness.

9 His saving help is near those who fear him,
So that the glory may dwell in our land.
10 Mercy and truth have now together met;
Yes, righteousness and peace together kissed.

11 Truth, faithfulness, have sprung up from the earth,
And out of heaven righteousness looks down.
12 the LORD will truly give that which is good,
And so our land will yield its harvest home.

14 Before his face shall righteousness go forth,
And will establish his steps in the way.
Before his face shall righteousness go forth,
And will establish his steps in the way.

198   Psalm 86:1-5

1 Incline your ear, O LORD, and answer me;
Because I am afflicted and in need.
2 Preserve my soul, for I am loved by you.
Your servant save, who trusts in you, my God!

3 O please, My Lord, be gracious unto me;
For unto you I cry out all the day
4 Make the soul of your servant to be glad;
For unto you, My Lord, I lift my soul.

5 For you, My Lord, are good and pardoning.
Yes, you are good, and ready to forgive.
You are abounding in your steadfast love
Unto all those who call on you for help.

199   Psalm 86:6-13

6 LORD, hear my prayer. My supplications heed.
7 I'll call on you in my day of distress;
Because you will then hear and answer me.
8 There's none like you among the gods, My Lord.

There are not any works like unto yours.
9 All of the nations - made by you - shall come,
And they shall worship before you, My Lord,
And they shall greatly glorify your name.

10 For you are great, and you do wondrous things.
You're God alone! 11 LORD, teach your way to me;
And I will walk in your sure, faithful, truth.
Make my heart one, that I may fear your name.

12 I'll thank you Lord, my God, with my whole heart.
I'll glorify your name for evermore;
13 Because your steadfast love is great to me.
From depths of Sheol you've rescued my soul.

200   Psalm 86:14-17

14 O God, the proud have risen against me.
A band of ruthless men have sought my soul,
And they have not kept you before their eyes -
15 My Lord, the merciful and gracious GOD.

You're slow to anger, very kind and true.
16 O turn to me, be gracious unto me.
Grant to your servant your strength and your power.
Give your salvation to your handmaid's son.

17 O make a sign, a sign with me for good
That those who hate me may see and be shamed.
For LORD you helped, and gave comfort to me.
For LORD you helped, and gave comfort to me.

201 Psalm 87

¹ His place is founded on the holy hills.
² The LORD has greater love for Zion's gates -
Than all the places in which Jacob dwells.
³ City of God your glories are foretold!

⁴ Unto remembrance to those who know me
Rahab and Babylon I'll call to mind
Note this - Philistia and Tyre, with Cush.
This is the one, the one who was born there.

⁵ But unto Zion it will be declared
That every one of them is born therein.
The Most High will establish it himself.
The Most High will establish it himself.

⁶ The Lord shall count - the peoples he'll write down
He will record that 'This one was born there',
⁷ And they will sing, and they will dance for joy
'The fountain-head of all my springs is you!'

202 Psalm 88:1-8

¹ O LORD, the God of my deliverance,
Both day and night I've cried out in your sight.
² O let my prayer come in before your face;
To my entreaty do incline your ear.

³ My soul is full of troubles to excess;
Unto Sheol my life is drawing near.
⁴ I'm counted with those sinking to the Pit.
I have become a man who has no strength.

⁵ I am a castaway among the dead.
I'm like the slain ones lying in the grave -
Those who you don't remember any more -
Like those who have been cut off from your hand.

[Continued →

⁶ You put me down into the deepest pit,
And in dark places, regions dark and deep.
⁷ Your burning anger presses hard on me.
You have afflicted me with all your waves.

⁸ You have removed my best friends far from me;
You made me as a loathsome thing to them.
I am shut up and I have no way out.
I am shut up and I have no way out.

203   Psalm 88:9-12

⁹ Through my affliction my eye wastes away.
LORD, I have called upon you every day;
LORD, I have called on you all through the day,
And unto you I have stretched out my hands.

¹⁰ Will you show wonders to those left for dead?
The mighty ones - shall they rise and praise you?
¹¹ And shall your mercy be told in the grave?
Your faithfulness told where Destruction is?

¹² Or will your wonders be known in the dark?
Your righteousness, shall it indeed be known?
Shall it be known in the forgotten land?
Shall it be known in the forgotten land?

204   Psalm 88:13-18

¹³ But as for me - I've cried to you, O LORD,
And in the morning my prayer meets with you.
¹⁴ Why is it, LORD, that you reject my soul?
Why do you turn your face away from me?

¹⁵ Afflicted, close to death from my youth up,
I bear your terrors, everywhere I turn.
¹⁶ Fires of your wrath have gone right over me;
Your dreadful terrors, they have cut me off.

[Continued →

17 Like waters, they've come round me all day long;
Together they enclosed me round about.
18 Lover and friend you've put far off from me,
And my best friends are put in a dark place.

205   Psalm 89:1-5

1 I'll ever sing the mercies of the LORD,
And with my mouth I'll tell your faithfulness,
Unto all generations I'll make known
2 Mercy, I said, 'shall be built evermore!'

In heaven you will set your faithfulness.
3 'I've covenanted with my chosen one;
And to my servant, David, sworn an oath
4 Your offspring I'll establish evermore'.

'I'll build your throne through generations long'.
5 So shall the heavens praise your wonder, LORD!
Indeed, your faithfulness shall be praised too,
In the assembly of your holy ones.

206   Psalm 89:6-14

6 Who in the sky compares unto the LORD?
Who of the sons of might are like the LORD?
7 GOD to be held in awe, and to be feared,
Even in session with the holy ones.

Above all those about him to be feared
8 LORD, God of hosts, who is like you - strong LORD!
Your faithfulness encircles you around.
9 You are the one who rules the raging sea.

When waves rise up, it's you who makes them still.
10 You have crushed Rahab, as one that is slain;
With your strong arm, scattered your enemies.
11 Yours are the heavens. Yes, the earth as well.

[Continued →

The world, and all its fullness, you set up.
12 You have created both the north and south.
Tabor and Hermon shall joy in your name.
13 Your arm is mighty and your hand is strong.

Your right hand is exalted up on high
14 Founded on judgment and on righteousness.
Your throne's established, and is fixed and firm -
Mercy and truth shall be before your face.

207   Psalm 89:15-18

15 Blest be the people who know the glad sound!
They walk, LORD, in the brightness of your face.
16 They will rejoice in your name all day long.
And through your righteousness they're lifted up.

17 Because you are the glory of their strength,
And through your favour you exalt our horn.
18 Because, our shield belongs unto the LORD -
The Holy One of Israel - our King.

208   Psalm 89:19-29

19 You spoke in vision to the One you love:
And said 'I gave help to a mighty man',
One chosen from the people I've raised up
20 'David my servant has been found by me';

Him I've anointed with my holy oil'.
21 My hand will be enduringly with him;
My arm shall also give strength unto him.
22 The enemy shall have no claim on him,

The son of wickedness shall not afflict.
23 I will beat down his foes before his face;
Those hating him I'll strike down, and will plague!
24 My faithfulness and love shall be with him,

[Continued →

In my name shall his horn be lifted up.
²⁵ And I will set his hand upon the sea,
And on the rivers will set his right hand.
²⁶ 'You are my Father', he will call to me.

'The Rock of my salvation and my GOD'
²⁷ I will appoint him as the firstborn one,
And make him Most High of the kings the earth.
²⁸ I'll keep my mercy for him evermore;

My covenant shall stand fast unto him.
²⁹ His offspring I'll establish evermore;
As long as heaven's days shall his throne be.
As long as heaven's days shall his throne be.

209   Psalm 89:30-37

³⁰ If my instruction his sons should forsake:
If in my judgments they decline to go:
³¹ Or my decrees, if they make them profane:
If my commandments they should fail to keep -

³² Their sin will I then visit with the rod;
With scourging, visit their iniquity.
³³ Yet I'll not take my steadfast love from him;
Nor will I let my faithfulness to fail.

³⁴ My covenant I will not violate
Nor alter what has gone out from my lips.
³⁵ For I have once sworn by my holiness;
Surely to David I will not be false!

³⁶ His offspring shall endure for evermore.
Before me, as the sun, his throne shall be.
³⁷ It shall be fixed for ever, as the moon;
As steadfast as the witness in the sky

210   Psalm 89:38-45

38 But it is you who cast off and reject;
You've been enraged with your anointed one!
39 Your servant's covenant you have made void;
You have defiled his crown unto the ground.

40 All his defensive walls you've broken down;
You've made a ruin of his fortresses.
41 All who pass by the road have plundered him,
And to his neighbours he's been a reproach.

42 You've lifted up the right hand of his foes;
And all his enemies you have made glad.
43 And his sword's sharpened edge you've turned away;
And in the battle have not let him stand.

44 You've made the splendour that he had to cease,
And you have hurled his throne down to the ground.
45 The days he was a young man you've cut short,
And (as a garment) covered him with shame.

211   Psalm 89:46-52

46 How long, O LORD? Will you forever hide?
For how long will your wrath burn just like fire?
47 Recall how short a time I have to live -
Are all sons of man made all in vain?

48 What man is he who lives, and won't see death?
Can he set his soul free from Sheol's hand?
49 My Lord, where are your mercies as of old?
You swore to David in your faithfulness.

50 Take note, My Lord, the taunt your servants bear,
For, in my bosom, I bear the reproach.
That all the great and many peoples make -
51 With which your enemies reproach, O LORD

[Continued →

For they discredit your anointed thus,
Reproach the footsteps your anointed takes.
52 Blest be the LORD for ever, evermore.
Amen, and yet again, Amen. Amen.

Book 4

Psalms 90 - 106

212   Psalm 90:1-6

[1] My Lord, you've been a dwelling place for us,
In every age, [2] before mountains were born
Before you brought the earth and world to birth.
Yes, you are GOD for ever, evermore.

[3] O, how you turn frail man back to the dust!
You say 'Go back again, you sons of man!'
[4] Even a thousand years are, in your eyes,
A day that's past, and a watch in the night.

[5] They're swept away by you. They are as sleep!
At morning, they sprout up like fresh green grass;
[6] It flourishes at morning, and sprouts up;
When evening comes it's cut and withered dry.

213   Psalm 90:7-11

[7] For by your anger we have been consumed;
By your hot anger we are terrified.
[8] You've set before you our iniquities;
Our secret sins in the light of your face.

[9] For all our days decline under your wrath;
We've spent our years just as a passing thought.
[10] Our days, in years, are only seventy;
Perhaps, because we're strong, it's eighty years.

But their pride is just toil and vanity,
For it soon passes, and we fly away,
[11] The power of your anger who can know?
As your wrath is, so ought we thus to fear.

214   Psalm 90:12-17

[12] Teach us to count the number of our days -
So that a heart of wisdom we may gain.
[13] Turn back, O LORD, for how long will it be?
Show your compassion on your servants now.

[Continued →

14 At morning satisfy us with your love;
So all our days we'll joy, and we'll be glad.
15 For days that you've afflicted, make us glad -
The years that we have seen adversity.

16 Show to your servants the thing you have done;
And show your majesty upon their sons.
17 The beauty of the LORD our God give us;
The work our hands have done establish sure.

215   Psalm 91:1-7

1 The dweller in the Most High's secret place
In the Almighty's shadow will abide.
2 'He is my refuge', I'll say of the LORD,
'My fortress and my God - in whom I trust'.

3 He, from the fowler's snare, will rescue you,
and from the devastating pestilence.
4 For with his feathers he will cover you;
You'll flee for refuge underneath his wings.

His truth's a great shield; armour round about.
5 You will not fear the terror of the night;
Nor fear the arrow that flies in the day;
6 Neither the pestilence that stalks at dark;

Nor yet destruction that lays waste at noon.
7 For, though a thousand may fall at your side,
And though ten thousand fall at your right hand,
It won't approach or come near unto you.

216   Psalm 91:8-16

8 For you will only look on with your eyes,
And you will see the wicked's recompense.
9 Because you've made the LORD (who's my Refuge)
Even the Most High for your dwelling place.

[Continued →

[10] So shall no harm or evil come to you;
Neither shall any plague come near your tent.
[11] He will command his angels about you,
So that they'll keep and guard in all your ways.

[12] For they will carry you upon their hands,
Lest you should strike your foot against a stone.
[13] On lion and on adder you will tread;
The lion's young and serpent you'll tread down.

[14] 'Because his love to me is very great,
I will give unto him deliverance.
I will exalt him, for he knows my name.
[15] He'll call on me and I will answer him'.

'I'll be the one who's with him in distress.
I will deliver, and I'll honour him.
[16] I'll give to him a long fulfilling life,
And my salvation I will show to him'.

217   Psalm 92:1-4

[1] It's a good thing to give thanks to the LORD,
And to sing psalms to your name, O Most High.
[2] By morning to proclaim your steadfast love,
And then your faithfulness with every night.

[3] With ten-stringed-instrument, and with the lyre,
Even with meditation on the harp.
[4] By what you've done, LORD, you have made me glad.
For what your hands have wrought I'll sing for joy.

218   Psalm 92:5-9

[5] How great, LORD, are the things that you have done!
The things that you devise are very deep.
[6] The carnal, brutish man just cannot know,
And he who is a fool can't understand.

[Continued →

⁷ When wicked flourish, and spring up as grass,
And when all evil doers are in flower;
It is so that they they'll ever be destroyed.
⁸ But you are God Most High, LORD, evermore.

⁹ For - See! - Behold! - your enemies, O LORD;
For - See! - your enemies shall be wiped out.
So likewise those who do iniquity
Scattered and separated they shall be.

219   Psalm 92:10-15

¹⁰ You've lifted up my horn as a wild ox.
With fresh green oil you have anointed me
¹¹ My eye has viewed my watchful enemies.
My ears have heard the wicked who assailed.

¹² The righteous one shall flourish like the palm,
And as a cedar grows in Lebanon.
¹³ Those who are planted into the LORD's house
Shall flourish well in the courts of our God.

¹⁴ And, in old age, they shall still bring forth fruit;
They will be full of sap, and verdant green.
¹⁵ This is to show the LORD is just and right.
My rock, in whom is no unrighteousness.

220   Psalm 93

¹ The LORD now reigns! He's robed in majesty!
The LORD is robed with strength, which he's put on.
The world's established so it won't be moved.
² Your throne's established, even from that time.

You are the one from all eternity.
³ The floods of waters are raised up, O LORD;
The floods of waters have raised up their voice;
The floods of waters raise their pounding waves.

[Continued →

4 More than the sounds that many waters make -
Yes, than the mighty breakers of the sea -
The LORD on high is mighty, excellent!
The LORD on high is mighty, excellent!

5 Your testimonies are extremely sure.
The beauty of your house is holiness
And holiness is fitting for your house,
O LORD, for length of days, for evermore.

221   Psalm 94:1-7

1 Avenging GOD, O LORD, avenging GOD!
Shine forth! 2 Be lifted up, Judge of the earth!
Return a recompense upon the proud.
3 Till what time shall the wicked be, O LORD?

Till what time shall the wicked ones rejoice?
4 They bluster and in arrogance they speak;
The evildoers all act boastfully.
5 They crush and break your people down, O LORD!

They humble and afflict your heritage;
6 The widow and the sojourner they slay;
They kill the orphan, 7 say, 'the LORD won't see',
'Nor will the God of Jacob come to know'.

222   Psalm 94:8-15

8 You stupid of the people, think on this;
You fools, when will you come to understand?
9 He who has planted ears, shall he not hear?
He, who formed eyes, shall he not look and see?

10 The nations' Tutor, shall he not chastise?
- The One who teaches knowledge to mankind.
11 The thoughts of man are known unto the LORD.
They are just vanity, only a breath.

[Continued →

¹² Blest is the worthy man you chasten, LORD,
Even the one you teach out of your Law,
¹³ It is to give him rest in adverse days,
Till for the wicked one the pit is dug.

¹⁴ Surely, the LORD won't give his people up;
Neither will he forsake his heritage.
¹⁵ For unto righteousness judgment shall come,
All those of upright heart shall follow on.

223   Psalm 94:16-23

¹⁶ Who rises for me against wicked men?
Who stands for me against those that do wrong?
¹⁷ Unless the LORD had been a help to me,
My soul would soon have dwelt in silent death.

¹⁸ When I had said, 'My foot falters and slips',
Your loving-kindness, O LORD, held me up.
¹⁹ When I have many anxious thoughts and doubts,
Your consolations then delight my soul.

²⁰ Will evil's throne have fellowship with you?
Which frames and causes trouble by decree.
²¹ Against the righteous one they join in league,
The guiltless one they wickedly condemn.

²² Yet nonetheless the LORD is my high tower;
My rock of refuge is my God to me.
²³ He's turned their evil back upon themselves.
The LORD our God will cut them down in sin!

224   Psalm 95:1-5

¹ O come, let's sing unto the LORD with joy!
The rock of our salvation give loud praise!
² Let's come before his face in giving thanks!
Let's make a joyful noise to him with psalms!

[Continued →

134

Let's come before his face in giving thanks!
Let's make a joyful noise to him with psalms!
3 Because the LORD's a great and mighty GOD,
He's a great king, who is above all gods.

4 The very depths of earth are in his hand;
The summits of the mountains are his too.
5 The sea belongs to him - it is his work -
The dry land he then fashioned with his hands.

225　　　Psalm 95:6-11

6 O come and let us worship and bow down.
Before the LORD, our Maker, let us kneel.
7 For he's our God. We're in his shepherd care,
A people who are sheep under his hand.

Today - today! - if you would hear his voice,
8 Be not hard-hearted, as at Meribah.
As in the desert - the day of Massah -
9 Your fathers tried me. Proved me. Saw my work.

10 That generation grieved me forty years;
Said 'It's a people who err in their heart'.
They do not know my ways, 11 I therefore vowed -
Swore in my wrath - 'They shall not have my rest'.

226　　　Psalm 96:1-6

1 O sing unto the LORD a brand-new song;
O let the whole earth sing unto the LORD.
2 O sing unto the LORD, and bless his name.
From day to day make his salvation known.

3 Among the nations tell his glory forth;
Among all peoples tell his wondrous works.
4 The LORD is great. He should be greatly praised.
He should be held in fear above all gods.

[Continued →

⁵ For, all the peoples' gods are empty things.
The one who made the heavens is the LORD.
⁶ Before him majesty and honour dwell;
Beauty and strength are in his holy place.

227   Psalm 96:7-13

⁷ Let peoples' families give to the LORD -
Give to the LORD the glory and the strength
⁸ Give to the LORD the glory of his name,
And with an offering, enter his courts.

⁹ In lovely holiness bow to the LORD.
Before him shake with trembling all the earth!
¹⁰ Among the nations say, 'The LORD is king!'
The world is fixed that it shall not be moved.

In uprightness he shall the peoples judge.
¹¹ The heavens shall be glad - the earth rejoice.
The sea and all its plenitude shall roar;
¹² The field, and all that's in it, shall rejoice.

Then all the forest trees shall shout for joy
¹³ Before the LORD. He comes, he comes!
To judge the earth; The world with righteousness,
And comes to judge the peoples with his truth.

228   Psalm 97:1-6

¹ The LORD is king! The earth shouts out for joy!
The many islands and the coasts are glad!
² Cloud and thick darkness circle him about.
His throne's by righteousness and judgment fixed!

³ Before his face is going out a fire;
And it burns up his foes on every side.
⁴ His lightnings flash, and bathe the world in light;
The earth looks on, and trembling is afraid.

[Continued →

⁵ Like wax, the mountains melt before the LORD -
Before him who is Lord of all the earth.
⁶ The heavens do declare his righteousness,
And all the peoples do his glory see.

229   Psalm 97:7-12

⁷ Carved-image worshippers will all be shamed;
All those who serve such will be put to shame -
Those who take pride in idols (worthless things)!
You gods, bow down and worship before him!

⁸ Zion, with joy, heard. Judah's daughters danced
At the just judgments that you made, O LORD.
⁹ Above all earth you are the LORD Most High;
You are exalted far above all gods.

¹⁰ O you who love the LORD, hate wickedness!
He guards and keeps the souls of those he loves.
He from the wicked one delivers them -
Recovers them out of wicked's hand.

¹¹ He, for the righteous, sows the light as seed,
And he sows joy for the upright in heart.
¹² You who are righteous, be glad in the LORD,
With thanks commemorate his holiness.

230   Psalm 98:1-3

¹ O sing unto the LORD a brand-new song!
For wondrous are the things that he has done.
He has procured salvation to himself,
By his right hand, and by his holy arm.

² The LORD caused his salvation to be known;
Before the eyes of nations he has shown -
He has revealed to them his righteousness;
He has revealed to them his righteousness.

[Continued →

³ His loving-kindness and his faithfulness
He's called to mind concerning Israel's house.
And the salvation that our God has wrought
All the remotest ends of earth have seen.

231   Psalm 98:4-9

⁴ The whole earth, shout with joy unto the LORD!
Break out, and shout for joy, yes, and sing psalms!
⁵ Sing psalms unto the LORD, sing with the harp
With harp and with the sound of psalmody

⁶ With trumpets and the sound of the shofar -
Shout in the presence of the LORD, the King!
⁷ Let the sea roar, and all its plenitude;
The world as well, and those who dwell therein.

⁸ Let floods applaud - Let mountains shout as one -
⁹ Before the LORD: He comes to judge the earth!
For he will judge the world with righteousness,
And he will judge the peoples uprightly.

232   Psalm 99:1-5

¹,² The LORD is King! The peoples tremble now!
He sits enthroned upon the cherubim.
Great is the LORD in Zion. The earth quakes.
Above all peoples he's exalted high.

³ Praise your great, fearful name! Holy is he
⁴ Justice is loved by the strength of the king
And now you have established equity;
In Jacob you've made justice, righteousness.

⁵ Exalt and lift the LORD our God on high
And worship at the footstool of his throne.
Holy is he. He is the Holy One!
Holy is he. He is the Holy One!

233   Psalm 99:6-9

⁶ Moses and Aaron were among his priests;
Samuel with those who call on his name.
They called upon the LORD. He answered them.
⁷ In the cloud-column he spoke unto them.

They kept the testimonies that he gave -
Kept the decree that he gave unto them.
⁸ O LORD, our God, you heard and answered them;
For GOD Propitious you were then to them.

Yet you took vengeance upon their misdeeds.
⁹ Exalt and lift the LORD our God on high!
Bow down in worship at his holy hill.
Holy, yes, holy is the LORD our God.

234   Psalm 100

¹ All earth, shout joyfully unto the LORD!
² With glad delight give service to the LORD.
Come, with a joyful song, before his face.
³ Know and acknowledge that the LORD is God.

He made us, for we did not make ourselves;
We are his people; the sheep in his care.
⁴ With a thanksgiving come into his gates;
O enter, go into his courts with praise.

O give your thanks to him, and bless his name.
⁵ Because the LORD is good. The LORD is good!
His loving-kindness is for evermore;
All generations-long his faithfulness.

235   Psalm 101:1-4

¹ Of mercy, and of judgment, I will sing.
Yes, unto you, O LORD, I will sing psalms.
² I will act wisely in a blameless way.
When is the time when you will come to me?

[Continued →

I will walk with integrity of heart
The times when I'm indoors within my house.
3 I will not put, or set, before my eyes
A thing of uselessness and wickedness.

I hate the work of those who turn aside,
And it will not attach itself to me.
4 A crooked heart will thus depart from me;
A wicked person I'll refuse to know.

236   Psalm 101:5-8

5 He who, in secret, slanders with his tongue
against his neighbour. I will cut him off!
The one with haughty eyes, and a proud heart;
I will not suffer and I cannot bear.

6 My eyes are on the faithful of the land,
So they may stay and they may dwell with me.
The one who's walking in an upright way.
He is the one who'll minister to me.

7 The one who acts in order to deceive;
He shall not dwell or stay within my house.
The one who speaks with falsehoods, and tells lies;
He shall not be established in my sight.

8 When every morning comes I will destroy,
And silence all the wicked of the land.
So that all evildoers are cut off,
And severed from the city of the LORD.

237   Psalm 102:1-5

1 LORD, hear my prayer. Let my cry come to you.
2 And in the day when my distress shall come,
Do not then hide your face away from me.
Incline your ear and listen unto me.

[Continued →

Answer me quickly in the day I call,
³ For all my days have disappeared like smoke.
My bones have burned as hot as in a hearth,
⁴ My heart is smitten, and withered like grass.

I have forgotten I should eat my bread,
⁵ Because of the loud groans my voice lets out,
It is as though my bone sticks to my flesh.
It is as though my bone sticks to my flesh.

238   Psalm 102:6-11

⁶ I'm like a pelican of the wild land;
And I am as an owl of desert wastes.
⁷ Sleepless, I watch, and so I have become
Just like a lonely sparrow on the roof.

⁸ My enemies reproach me all the day;
Those raging at me use me as a curse.
⁹ For I have eaten ashes, just like bread;
My tears are also mingled with my drink.

¹⁰ Your wrath and indignation was the cause.
You took me up, and then cast me away.
¹¹ My days are like a shadow that declines,
And I am withered - withered like the grass.

239   Psalm 102:12-17

¹² But you, LORD, are enthroned for evermore;
For ever you will dwell, and will remain.
Throughout all generations it shall be
That your memorial shall still abide.

¹³ You will arise, and will share Zion's grief,
The time for pity on her now has come
For now the set, appointed, time has come.
For now the set, appointed, time has come

[Continued →

¹⁴ For in its stones your servants take delight,
And they have pity, even on its dust.
¹⁵ And the LORD's name the nations then will fear.
Your glory will make all earth's kings afraid.

¹⁶ For now the LORD has built Zion again.
He now appears in glory, and is seen!
¹⁷ He turns unto the destitute one's prayer -
Does not despise or disregard their prayer.

240　　　　Psalm 102:18-22

¹⁸ This shall be written for a future time;
Yes, for a generation yet to come.
A new-created people shall bring praise;
A people yet unborn will praise the LORD.

¹⁹ Because he looked down from his holy height;
And, from the heavens, looked upon the earth
²⁰ To hear the sighing of the prisoner:
To let the very sons of death go free.

²¹ That the LORD's name they may in Zion tell,
And in Jerusalem declare his praise -
²² When peoples come and meet with one accord,
The kingdoms too, that they may serve the LORD.

241　　　　Psalm 102:23-28

²³ My strength he weakened and broke in the way.
'My days have been cut short by him', ²⁴I said,
'My GOD, don't take me halfway through my days,
Throughout all generations are your years'.

²⁵ In the beginning, you founded the earth;
The heavens also are your handiwork.
²⁶ Though they will perish, you yourself remain.
All, as a garment, will wear out with age.

[Continued →

Like clothing you will change them. They'll be changed!
27 You are the same. Your years will never end.
28 Your servants' children will securely dwell.
Their offspring in your presence fixed and sure.

242   Psalm 103:1-5

1 O my soul, give your blessing to the LORD,
And all within me bless his holy name.
2 O my soul, give your blessing to the LORD;
And all his benefits do not forget.

3 He who forgives all your iniquities;
The one who heals all your infirmities.
4 He who redeems your life out of the Pit,
From going down to the destroying Pit.

He is the one who puts a crown on you -
Yes, loving-kindness - tender mercies too!
5 He gives your mouth its fill of what is good,
So, like an eagle, you renew your youth.

243   Psalm 103:6-13

6 The LORD works out his deeds of righteousness,
And judgments for all those who are oppressed.
7 To Moses he gave knowledge of his ways;
To Israel's children made his actions known.

8 The LORD shows pity, and is gracious too;
He's slow to anger and is very kind.
9 He will not endlessly contend, or chide;
Nor will he store his anger up always.

10 He's not repaid us as our sins deserve;
Nor dealt in line with our iniquities.
11 As heavens' height is stretched above the earth
His mercy's strong above those fearing him.

[Continued →

¹² As far apart as East is from the West
He has removed our wilful sins from us.
¹³ Just as a father is toward his sons,
The LORD shows pity on those who fear him.

244 Psalm 103:14-18

¹⁴ Because he knows how we are formed and made,
And he is mindful that we are but dust.
¹⁵ As for frail man, his days are as the grass.
He blossoms as a flower of the field.

¹⁶ The wind blows over it, and it is gone.
And where it was is then no longer known.
¹⁷ But the LORD's mercy is from ages past
To endless ages - on those who fear him.

To children's children is his righteousness;
¹⁸ This is to those who keep his covenant.
Who, so that they may do what he commands,
Recall his precepts, and keep them in mind.

245 Psalm 103:19-22

¹⁹ The LORD, in heaven has set up his throne;
His kingdom's government is over all.
²⁰ O bless the LORD, his angels of great strength,
Who do his bidding, heeding his word's call.

²¹ O bless the LORD, all you his army hosts -
You ministers who do what pleases him!
²² All his works, Bless the LORD! In every place
Of his dominions! My soul, bless the LORD!

246 Psalm 104:1-5

¹ O my soul, give your blessing to the LORD
O LORD my God, for you are very great.
You're clothed with honour, and with majesty.
² Wrapping yourself in light as with a robe.

[Continued →

Like a tent curtain spreading heaven out,
3 Who, on the waters, frames his upper rooms.
Making the clouds to be his chariot.
And who goes forth upon the wings of wind.

4 Who makes his angels spirits, like the wind.
Who makes his ministers a blazing fire.
5 Who sets the earth in its established place.
So that it never ever shall be moved.

247   Psalm 104:6-9

6 You clothed the earth with sea, as with a robe.
Over the mountain tops the waters stood.
7 Because of your rebuke they took to flight.
Your thunder sounded. They hasted away!

8 The mountains rose, and valleys did subside
Unto the place which you had set for them.
9 You've set a limit that they cannot cross,
So that they shall not cover earth again.

248   Psalm 104:10-15

10 He sends out springs into the torrent beds,
Between the mountains they go on their way.
11 To all the wildlife of the field give drink,
And the wild donkeys there do quench their thirst.

12 Near them the birds of heaven have their home;
Among the branches they give out their song.
13 He waters mountains from his upper rooms
Your fruitful work thus satisfies the earth.

14 To feed the livestock, he makes grass to grow.
He makes the green herb grow to serve man's needs;
So that he may bring bread out of the earth.
15 And he gives wine so it may cheer the heart.

[Continued →

The wine to cheer the heart of mortal man;
Also, the oil to cause his face to shine;
And then the bread to make a man's heart strong;
Even the heart of a frail mortal man.

249   Psalm 104:16-19

[16] The LORD's trees have a bountiful supply -
Cedars of Lebanon - planted by him;
[17] And there the little birds prepare their nests;
As for the stork, the fir trees are its home.

[18] The lofty mountains are for the wild goats;
The rocky cliffs give conies a refuge.
[19] He made the moon for the appointed times;
He made the sun, which knows where it should set.

250   Psalm 104:20-24

[20] You make the darkness, and then it is night,
In which the forest beasts all prowl around.
[21] Then the young lions roar after their prey,
Seeking that they may get their food from GOD.

[22] The sun comes up, and then they get away,
And in their dwelling places they crouch down.
[23] To his employment, man goes out to work,
and to his labour, until evening comes.

[24] How many are the things you've done, O LORD!
With skill and wisdom you achieved them all.
The earth is full of riches you possess.
The earth is full of riches you possess.

251   Psalm 104:25-30

[25] There is the sea - that great and wide expanse!
And countless moving creatures are in it;
In it are living things both small and great;
[26] And there the vessels go upon their way.

[Continued →

Leviathan, you formed to play in it!
²⁷ All these in hope wait on you anxiously.
That you may give them food when it is due;
²⁸ You give it to them, and they gather it.

Your hand you open. They're well satisfied.
²⁹ You hide your face, and then they are dismayed:
You take away their spirit and they die:
They then go back again unto their dust.

³⁰ You send your Spirit out and they are made.
So you renew the face of earth again.
You send your Spirit out and they are made.
So you renew the face of earth again.

252   Psalm 104:31-35

³¹ The glory of the LORD forever lasts.
The LORD will joy in things that he has done.
³² He looks upon the earth, and then it quakes;
He touches mountains, causing them to smoke.

³³ I'll sing unto the LORD while I yet live;
Sing psalms unto my God while I shall be.
³⁴ O Let my inmost thoughts be sweet to him,
And, as for me, I'll be glad in the LORD.

³⁵ Let sinners be consumed out of the earth,
And let the wicked people be no more.
O my soul, give your blessing to the LORD.
O Hallelujah, give praise to the LORD

253   Psalm 105:1-7

¹ Give thanks unto the LORD! Proclaim his name!
Make known among the peoples what he's done!
² Sing unto him! O, yes, sing psalms to him!
And meditate on all his wondrous works.

[Continued →

³ O let your boast be in his holy name.
The heart of those that seek the LORD be glad!
⁴ O seek the LORD, and seek after his strength;
His face seek constantly for evermore

⁵ Recall his wondrous works, which he has done;
His wonders, and the judgments of his mouth.
⁶ O offspring of his servant Abraham -
Children of Jacob - You his chosen ones!

⁷ He is the LORD our God. The LORD our God!
In all the earth his judgments are set forth.
He is the LORD our God. The LORD our God!
In all the earth his judgments are set forth.

254   Psalm 105:8-15

⁸ He ever keeps his covenant in mind -
The word that he commanded and confirmed
Yes, to a thousand generations on -
⁹ The covenant he made with Abraham.

To Isaac gave it as his solemn oath -
¹⁰ To Jacob made it stand as a decree,
And for an everlasting covenant -
the covenant he gave to Israel.

¹¹ He said, 'To you I will give Canaan's land,
The measured lot of your inheritance'.
¹² In number they were only a few men -
Yes, very few, and sojourners in it.

¹³ From nation unto nation they walked on,
From kingdom to another people went.
¹⁴ He let no man oppress, or do them wrong,
And for their sakes brought punishment on kings.

¹⁵ He said, 'Do not touch my anointed ones,
And to my prophets see you do no harm'.
He said, 'Do not touch my anointed ones,
And to my prophets see you do no harm'.

255   Psalm 105:16-23

16 And then he called a famine on the land:
He broke all staff of their support - their bread.
17 He sent ahead of them a certain man:
Joseph it was, who was sold for a slave.

18 His feet were put in chains so that they hurt;
His very soul went into iron bands.
19 Until the time that his word came to pass,
The thing the LORD spoke tried and tested him.

20 The king then sent to set at liberty:
The ruler of the peoples set him free.
21 He set him up as master of his house,
And ruler over all that he possessed.

22 To bind his princes as he chose to do,
And to teach wisdom unto his old men.
23 Then Israel came into Egypt too:
And Jacob sojourned in the land of Ham.

256   Psalm 105:24-36

24 He gave his people great fertility,
And made them stronger - stronger than their foes.
25 He turned their heart to hate his people then -
To act against his people cunningly.

26 Moses and Aaron were the ones he sent -
Moses his servant, Aaron whom he chose.
27 They set among them the words of his signs -
His stunning wonders in the land of Ham.

28 He sent the darkness: Caused it to be dark
(And they did not rebel against his words).
29 To blood he turned their waters: Killed their fish.
30 With frogs their land swarmed, even their king's rooms

[Continued →

³¹ He spoke the word, and there came swarms of flies.
In all the margins of their land were gnats.
³² He made their heavy showers to be hail,
Along with flaming fire within their land.

³³ Their vines and fig trees he also did smite:
In all the margins of their land broke trees.
³⁴ He spoke the word, and then the locusts came,
And caterpillars, more than one can count.

³⁵ They ate up all the green plants in their land,
And ate up all the produce of their ground.
³⁶ He struck down all the firstborn in their land.
The firstfruits of all their virility.

257   Psalm 105:37-45

³⁷ He brought them out, with silver and with gold.
No one among his tribes was faltering.
³⁸ Egypt was glad as they were going out,
Because their fear had fallen upon them.

³⁹ He spread a cloud out for a covering,
Along with fire to lighten up the night.
⁴⁰ They made request, and he brought quail to them:
Gave them the bread of heaven to the full

⁴¹ He opened up the rock: Waters gushed out,
Which, in dry places, as a river flowed.
⁴² For he was mindful of his holy word,
And mindful of his servant Abraham.

⁴³ He brought his people out with joyfulness -
His chosen ones with song and shout for joy.
⁴⁴ The nations' homelands he gave unto them.
What peoples toiled for, they inherited.

⁴⁵ That they might keep the things that he decrees,
And might observe the things that he directs.
O Hallelujah, give praise to the LORD.
O Hallelujah, give praise to the LORD.

258   Psalm 106:1-5

¹ O Hallelujah, give praise to the LORD!
Give thanks unto the LORD, for he is good!
His loving-kindness is for evermore.
² Who can express the LORD's great mighty works?

And who shall cause all his praise to be heard?
³ Those who keep judgment, they are truly blest
He who, at all times, acts in righteousness.
⁴ Your people's favour, LORD, recall for me.

With your salvation help and visit me
⁵ So I may see the good your chosen have:
So I may share your nation's joyfulness:
So I may glory with your heritage.

259   Psalm 106:6-12

⁶ Together with our fathers we have sinned;
We've been perverse, and acted wickedly.
⁷ Our fathers did, in Egypt, not discern;
Your wondrous works they did not understand.

Your many mercies they did not recall
But at the sea - the Red Sea - they rebelled.
⁸ Yet, nonetheless he saved, for his name's sake,
That he might make his mighty power known.

⁹ The Red Sea he rebuked, and it dried up:
He led them through the depths as a dry land.
¹⁰ Saved from the hand of him who hated them;
And ransomed them from out of the foe's hand.

¹¹ The waters overspread their enemies,
And not a single one of them was left.
¹² In his words they believed, and sang his praise.
In his words they believed and sang his praise.

13 They very soon forgot the things he did;
They did not wait until he gave advice.
14 They craved intensely in the wilderness;
And in the desert waste they tested GOD.

15 He gave to them what they requested him,
Yet, with it, he sent leanness to their soul.
16 They envied Moses where they were encamped,
And envied Aaron, the LORD's holy one.

17 The earth then opened; swallowed Dathan up;
Abiram covered, and his company.
18 A fire was kindled in their company!
And so the flame burned up the wicked ones.

19 In Horeb they then fashioned a bull-calf:
Before a metal image bowed themselves.
20 So they exchanged the glory of their God,
For likeness of an ox that eats the grass.

21 So they forgot GOD, who delivered them -
He, who in Egypt had done mighty things;
22 The things of wonder in the land of Ham;
Even, the fearful things by the Red Sea.

23 Therefore he said that they should be destroyed,
Had not his chosen, Moses, then stood up:
He stood up in the breach, before his face,
To turn his deadly wrath away from them.

261   **Psalm 106:24-31**

24 Then they despised the pleasant, longed-for land,
And in his word they did not place their trust;
25 But, in their tents, they murmured and repined,
They did not listen unto the LORD's voice.

[Continued →

²⁶ He raised his hand and swore an oath to them -
To make them fall down in the wilderness,
²⁷ Among the nations to make their seed fall,
And in the countries, he would scatter them.

²⁸ They put themselves in yoke with Baal Pe-or,
And sacrifices of the dead did eat;
²⁹ Stirred up his anger with the things they did,
And then the plague broke in upon them there.

³⁰ In righteous vengeance Phineas stood up.
Because of this, the plague was then held back.
³¹ It was accounted to him righteousness
Unto all generations, evermore.

262   Psalm 106:32-40

³² At waters of Meribah they caused wrath
Moses fared badly on account of them.
³³ Because, against his Spirit they rebelled,
And he in haste spoke rashly with his lips.

³⁴ The peoples they did not wipe fully out,
Which was the word the LORD had said to them.
³⁵ They mixed themselves up with the peoples then,
And also learned to do the things they did.

³⁶ They served their idols, and they were a snare;
³⁷ To demons sacrificed daughters and sons.
³⁸ The blood of innocents they then poured out! -
Blood of their sons, and of their daughters, shed.

To Canaan's idols they were sacrificed;
The land was thus polluted with the blood.
³⁹ And by their works they made themselves defiled,
And played the harlot by the things they did.

⁴⁰ And so the anger of the LORD blazed up -
His anger then against his people burned.
His heritage became a thing he loathed,
And he abhorred his own inheritance.

41 He then gave them into the nations' hand,
And those who hated them ruled over them.
42 Their enemies oppressed them - They were crushed
Under their hand they were brought to their knees.

43 Many a time he did deliver them,
Yet nonetheless, they purposed to rebel.
They were brought low for their iniquity.
44 He saw them in distress. He heard their cry.

45 He brought to mind for them his covenant.
In his great mercy he relented then.
46 He caused compassion to be shown to them
By all who held them in captivity.

47 Salvation give to us, O LORD our God!
And from the nations truly gather us!
So to your holy name we shall give thanks,
And so our glory shall be in your praise.

48 Blest be the LORD, the God of Israel,
From everlasting and for evermore
Let all the people say 'Amen', 'Amen'.
O Hallelujah, give praise to the LORD!

Book 5

Psalms 107 - 150

264   Psalm 107:1-9

1 'Give thanks unto the LORD, for he is good;
His loving-kindness is for evermore!'
2 Let them say this, those ransomed by the LORD,
Those he has ransomed out of the foe's hand.

3 For he has gathered them out of the lands -
From East and West, from North, and from the sea.
4 Some roamed in wilderness - a desert way.
They found no settled town in which to dwell.

5 Hungry and thirsty, their soul failed within,
6 Then in their trouble they cried to the LORD.
From their afflictions he delivered them,
7 He led them straight unto a settled town.

8 For loving-kindness let them thank the LORD,
And for his wonders to the sons of men.
9 He satisfies the longing soul's desire,
And fills the hungry soul with what is good.

265   Psalm 107:10-16

10 Some sat in darkness and in deathly shade,
Bound in affliction and by iron bands.
11 For they rebelled against the words of GOD;
They spurned the counsel of the Most High God.

12 Therefore, with labour he brought their heart down.
They stumbled, and there was no-one to help.
13 Then, in their trouble, they cried to the LORD,
From their distresses he delivered them

14 He brought from darkness and from deathly shade;
The chains that bound them he asunder broke.
15 For loving-kindness, let them thank the LORD,
And for his wonders to the sons of men.

[Continued →

For loving-kindness, let them thank the LORD,
And for his wonders to the sons of men.
[16] The doors of brass he utterly broke down;
The bars of iron he has hacked apart.

266 Psalm 107:17-22

[17] Because the foolish went their sinful way -
Their empty things - they brought themselves down low
[18] And so their soul loathed any kind of food,
And they drew near unto the gates of death.

[19] Then, in their trouble, they cried to the LORD;
From their distresses he delivered them.
[20] He sent his word. He healed them and restored.
He rescued them out of their pits of death.

[21] For loving-kindness, let them thank the LORD.
And for his wonders to the sons of men.
[22] Offer the sacrifice of grateful thanks;
Declare what he has done with shouts of joy.

267 Psalm 107:23-32

[23] Some others go in ships down to the sea,
And in great waters are engaged in trade.
[24] They too have seen the works the LORD has done
And saw his works of wonder in the deep.

[25] He spoke, and made the stormy wind to rise.
It made the swelling waves to surge up high.
[26] Which soared to heaven, and dropped to the deeps.
Their soul was melted in their troubled state.

[27] They reeled and staggered, like a drunken man,
At their wits end - their wisdom swallowed up.
[28] Then, in their trouble, they cried to the LORD,
From their anxieties he rescued them.

[Continued →

29 He stilled the tempest to a quiet hush,
So that its waves were silently at rest;
30 Because the waves calmed down, they were then glad:
He led them to the haven they desired.

31 For loving-kindness, let them thank the LORD,
And for his wonders to the sons of men,
32 Exalt him in the people's gathering,
And let them praise him in the elders' seat.

268   Psalm 107:33-43

33 He caused the rivers to be desert land
And springs of waters to be thirsty ground.
34 A fruitful land became a salty waste -
Because the people living there were bad.

35 He turned the barren land into a pool;
And a dry land he turned to water springs;
36 Those who were hungry he caused to dwell there,
And there they made themselves a settled town.

37 They sowed the fields; the vineyards they did plant;
A fruitful increase they did therefore yield.
38 He blest them, so they greatly multiplied;
He didn't let their cattle to decrease.

39 And yet they were decreased. They were bowed down
Under oppression, evil times, and grief.
40 Upon the princes he poured out contempt.
He made them wander in the trackless waste.

41 Out of affliction he exalts the poor,
And makes his families just like a flock.
42 The upright ones shall see, and will be glad,
And all unrighteousness shall shut its mouth.

43 He who is wise, and will observe these things,
They will discern the mercies of the LORD.
He who is wise, and will observe these things,
They will discern the mercies of the LORD.

269   Psalm 108:1-6

1 My heart is fixed, O God, and I will sing!
I will sing psalms, yes, with my glory too.
2 Awake the lyre! Awake the harp as well!
Yes, I would even wake the morning dawn!

3 Among the peoples, I will thank you LORD;
Among the nations, I'll sing psalms to you.
4 Your loving-kindness is so very great,
Over above the heavens it extends.

Likewise, your truth extends up to the clouds.
5 High over heaven be exalted, God!
Above the whole earth may your glory be.
6 For your beloved give deliverance.

For those who are so very dear to you,
O give salvation, with your own right hand.
And please do hear, give answer unto me;
And please do hear, give answer unto me.

270   Psalm 108:7-13

7 God has declared this in his holiness,
'I will rejoice, and Shechem I'll divide;
The valley of Succoth I'll measure out;
8 Gilead and Manasseh are both mine'.

'Ephraim's the strong defence unto my head;
Judah's my sceptre, 9Moab's my wash-pot;
And over Edom I will throw my shoe;
Over Philistia I'll shout for joy'.

10 O who will bring me to the fortress-town?
And who will guide me unto Edom's land?
11 Have you not spurned and cast us off, O God?
For with our armies you no longer go.

[Continued →

¹² From out of tribulation give us help:
For man's deliverance is all in vain.
¹³ Through God we shall contend courageously,
For he himself will trample on our foes.

271   Psalm 109:1-5

¹ Do not be silent, O God of my praise.
² Against me they have opened up their mouth -
A wicked mouth and a deceitful mouth.
Against me with a lying tongue they spoke.

³ With words of hatred they surrounded me,
And they have fought against me without cause.
⁴ They are my adversaries for my love.
They stand against me - but I pray, I pray!

⁵ They have repaid me evil for the good;
And recompensed me hatred for my love'
They have repaid me evil for the good;
And recompensed me hatred for my love.

272   Psalm 109:6-15

⁶ The Wicked One shall be set over him;
And so, shall Satan stand at his right hand.
⁷ When he is judged he shall go out condemned.
Even his prayer, it shall be reckoned sin!

⁸ His days shall be in number but a few;
Another take the charge given to him.
⁹ Orphaned and fatherless shall be his sons,
And she who was his wife a widow too.

¹⁰ His sons shall ever wander round and beg;
Out of their ruins they shall go and seek
¹¹ The moneylender seize all that he has,
And all he laboured for shall strangers spoil.

[Continued →

¹² No-one shall keep up kindness unto him.
No one show pity on his orphaned sons.
¹³ And his posterity shall be cut off:
Within a generation their name gone.

¹⁴ His fathers' folly shall the LORD recall;
His mother's sin shall not be blotted out;
¹⁵ They shall remain before the LORD always;
And his remembrance cut off from the earth.

273　　Psalm 109:16-21

¹⁶ For he did not remember to be kind,
He persecuted the poor, needy man;
The broken-hearted he set out to kill.
¹⁷ As he loved cursing, it shall come to him.

He disliked blessing; it shall be far off.
¹⁸ He clothed himself with cursing as his coat,
As water it went to his inner parts,
And just like oil it went into his bones,

¹⁹ Just like a garment he wraps round himself;
And like a belt that he always puts on.
²⁰ To my accusers this - the LORD's reward!
To those who speak bad things against my soul.

²¹ But you, LORD - My Lord, work on my behalf;
On my behalf do work, for your name's sake.
Because your loving-kindness is so good.
Your steadfast love is good. Deliver me.

274　　Psalm 109:22-31

²² For I'm afflicted, and I am in need.
Also, my heart is wounded within me.
²³ Like a declining shadow I depart,
And as a locust I am shaken off.

[Continued →

²⁴ Because of fasting, my knees are now weak;
My flesh is failing and is lank and lean.
²⁵ I've been to them an object of reproach,
And, when they look on me, they shake their head.

²⁶ Give help to me, O LORD. You are my God;
Save me according to your steadfast love;
²⁷ And they shall then know that this is your hand;
That you yourself, O LORD, have done this thing.

²⁸ They'll curse, but you will bless. Though they rise up`
They'll be ashamed: Your servant shall rejoice.
²⁹ So my accusers will put on disgrace;
Array themselves with shame as with a robe.

³⁰ My mouth shall give great thanks unto the LORD.
 Among the many, I will give him praise.
³¹ For at the poor one's right hand he shall stand
To save him from the judges of his soul.

275　　　　Psalm 110:1-3

¹ The word the LORD declared unto my Lord -
'Sit down at my right hand until the time -
Until I shall have set your enemies -
Till they've been set a footstool for your feet'.

² The LORD shall send the sceptre of your power,
from Zion. 'Rule among your enemies!
³ Your people shall be freewill offerings,
When in your day of strength you shall make war.

When in your day of strength you shall make war,
They shall be beautiful in holiness,
As issuing out of the morning's womb.
Your offspring shall be as the morning dew.

276   Psalm 110:4-7

4 The LORD has sworn, and he will not repent:
'You are a priest - a priest for evermore,
After the order of Melchizedek'
5 My Lord at your right hand; he'll shatter kings.

He'll shatter kings in the day of his wrath.
6 He'll sit in judgment on the nations then;
He'll fill them with the bodies of the dead;
He'll crush the head of an extensive land;

7 He shall drink from the wayside rushing stream,
Because of this he will lift up his head.
He shall drink from the wayside rushing stream,
Because of this he will lift up his head.

277   Psalm 111:1-6

1 O Hallelujah, give praise to the LORD!
I'll give thanks to the LORD with the whole heart,
In fellowship of just and upright men,
Even among the gathered company.

2 Great are the works and doings of the LORD,
Sought out by all who have delight in them.
3 His work has splendour and has majesty.
His righteousness stands fast for evermore.

His work has splendour and has majesty.
His righteousness stands fast for evermore.
4 He's made his wonders a memorial;
The LORD is gracious and compassionate.

5 To those who fear him he's supplied their food;
Forever keeps his covenant in mind.
6 His works of power to his people showed,
In giving them the nations' heritage.

278   Psalm 111:7-10

7 Judgment and truth are the works of his hands
All things that he appoints are fixed and sure;
8 They are established ever, evermore;
They're done in faithfulness and uprightness.

9 He sent a ransom for his people's sake.
For ever is his covenant ordained.
His name is holy, and is to be feared -
10 The start of wisdom is to fear the LORD.

His name is holy and is to be feared -
The start of wisdom is to fear the LORD.
Good understanding have all who do this.
Established is his praise for evermore.

279   Psalm 112:1-4

1 Hallelujah! Blest man who fears the LORD!
In his commandments he takes great delight;
2 His offspring shall be mighty upon earth.
The issue of the upright shall be blest;

3 And wealth and riches shall be in his house.
His righteousness stands fast for evermore.
4 For upright men light rises when it's dark.
He's gracious, merciful, and righteous too.

280   Psalm 112:5-10

5 It's well for that man who acts graciously
Who lends and justly deals with his affairs;
6 Because he'll never stagger or be moved;
The righteous is remembered evermore.

7 He will not be afraid to hear bad news;
His heart is steadfast, trusting in the LORD.
8 His heart's upheld. He will not be afraid.
Until the time he looks upon his foes.

[Continued →

⁹ He's open-handed - He gives to the poor;
His righteousness will stand for evermore.
With glory will his horn be lifted up;
¹⁰ The wicked one will see and will be grieved.

The wicked one will gnash and grind his teeth,
And then he will just melt and pine away;
What wicked men desire will all be lost.
What wicked men desire will all be lost.

281   Psalm 113

¹ O Praise the LORD! Praise, servants of the LORD!
Praise the LORD's name! ² The LORD's name will be blest
from now, for ever. ³ From the rising sun
to where it sets. The LORD's name will be praised!

⁴ High over all the nations is the LORD;
His glory is above the heavens too!
⁵ Who's like the LORD our God, who dwells on high;
⁶ Who stoops to view the heavens and the earth.

⁷ He raises up the poor one from the dust;
He lifts the needy from the rubbish heap,
⁸ That he among the princes may be sat,
Among his people's princes he will be.

⁹ He sets the barren woman in a home,
And as a joyful mother of her sons.
O, Hallelujah, give praise to the LORD!
O, Hallelujah, give praise to the LORD!

282   Psalm 114

¹ When out of Egypt Israel came forth,
From foreign people Jacob's house went out.
² Judah became a holy place for him,
And Israel the place where he did rule.

[Continued →

³ The sea beheld, and then it fled away;
The Jordan turned around, and it went back.
⁴ The mountains skipped about like they were rams;
The hills as though they were just little sheep.

⁵ What's wrong with you, O sea, to flee away?
You Jordan, that you turned and you went back?
⁶ You mountains, why did you skip round like rams?
You hills, that you should act like little sheep?

⁷ Tremble, and shake before the LORD, O earth
Yes, tremble from the face of Jacob's God!
⁸ Who changed the rock into a water pool;
The stone of flint into a water spring.

283   Psalm 115:1-8

¹ Not unto us, O LORD, not unto us;
But no, instead, give glory to your name.
Both for your mercy, and for your truth's sake
² Why should the nations say, 'Where is their God?'

³ Our God's in heaven. He does what he will,
⁴ Their grievous idols are silver and gold,
No more than workmanship of human hands:
⁵ They have a mouth, and yet they do not speak;

Yes, they have eyes, and yet they do not see;
⁶ And they have ears, and yet they do not hear;
They have a nose and yet they cannot smell;
⁷ As for their hands, they do not handle things;

As for their feet, with them they do not walk;
And with their throat they cannot make a sound.
⁸ And those who make them are the same as them!
And everyone who puts their trust in them.

284   Psalm 115:9-14

9 Put your trust in the LORD, O Israel
For he's their helper, and he is their shield.
10 Put your trust in the LORD, O Aaron's house
For he's their helper, and he is their shield.

11 You who do fear the LORD, trust in the LORD,
For he's their helper, and he is their shield.
12 The LORD's been mindful of us. He will bless -
Yes, he will bless the house of Israel!

13 He will give blessing unto Aaron's house -
Bless them that fear the LORD, both small and great.
14 The LORD will add to you and give increase -
Increase you more and more - your children too!

285   Psalm 115:15-18

15 You are the ones who are blest of the LORD -
The LORD who made the heavens and the earth.
16 The heavens, yes, the heavens, are the LORD's -
He gave the earth unto the sons of man.

17 The dead do not give praise unto the LORD,
None who sink to the silence of the grave.
18 But we will bless the LORD now, evermore!
O Hallelujah, give praise to the LORD!

286   Psalm 116:1-9

1 I love the LORD because the LORD has heard -
He heard my voice, and my imploring cries;
2 Because he has inclined his ear to me,
Therefore, I, all my days, will call on him.

3 The cords of death encircled me around;
The pains of Sheol had closed in on me.
I found distress, and I found anguish too -
4 I called upon the LORD's name [and I said].

[Continued →

'LORD, I implore you, let my soul escape!'
5 The LORD is gracious, and is righteous too,
Tender compassion is shown by our God.
6 The simple-hearted are kept by the LORD.

I was brought low, and he delivered me.
7 And now, my soul, go back and have your rest;
The LORD will yet complete his work in you.
8 You surely have rescued my soul from death.

You have relieved my eyes from shedding tears;
And you have kept my feet from stumbling too.
9 In the LORD's presence I will go about
And walk around the lands of those who live.

287   Psalm 116:10-15

10 I have believed, and therefore I did speak,
Yet I have been afflicted very much.
11 So I spoke in my haste, and so I said
That 'all mankind are liars, every one'.

12 O how can I repay unto the LORD
For all the ways he has looked after me.
13 The cup of full salvation I will take
And I will call on the name of the LORD.

14 So I'll fulfil my vows unto the LORD -
In sight of all his people, let it be.
15 The death of those on whom he sets his love
Is in the LORD's eyes a most precious thing.

288   Psalm 116:16-19

16 Ah, yes indeed, I am your servant, LORD -
I am your servant and your handmaid's son.
You loosed my shackles, and you set me free!
17 So unto you I'll offer sacrifice.

[Continued →

A sacrifice of thanks I'll give to you!
And I will call on the name of the LORD;
18 My vows I will fulfil unto the LORD -
In sight of all his people let it be!

19 Let it be in the courts of the LORD's house,
And in the midst of you, Jerusalem.
O Hallelujah, give praise to the LORD!
O Hallelujah, give praise to the LORD!

289   Psalm 117

1 All nations give praise to the LORD alone!
And all the peoples celebrate his praise! -
2 Because his mercy has prevailed on us.
The LORD's truth lasts forever. Praise the LORD!

290   Psalm 118:1-6

1 Give thanks unto the LORD for he is good,
'His loving-kindness is for evermore'.
2 Ah, yes indeed: let Israel now say,
'His loving-kindness is for evermore'.

3 Ah, yes indeed: let Aaron's house now say,
'His loving-kindness is for evermore'.
4 Indeed: let those who fear the LORD now say,
'His loving-kindness is for evermore'.

5 I was shut in and I cried to the LORD,
With the wide place the LORD has answered me.
6 The LORD is on my side, I will not fear,
What can my fellow man do unto me?

291   Psalm 118:7-14

7 The LORD is on my side to be my help;
I'll look upon those who are hating me.
8 It's better to take refuge in the LORD,
Than to rely upon your fellow man.

[Continued →

⁹ It's better to take refuge in the LORD
Than to rely upon the great and good.
¹⁰ All of the nations circled me around;
In the LORD's name I'll surely cut them off.

¹¹ They closed me in, yes, closed me round about;
In the LORD's name I'll surely cut them off.
¹² They were around me like a swarm of bees;
They were extinguished, like a fire of thorns.

In the LORD's name I'll surely cut them off.
¹³ You thrust against me hard to make me fall;
The LORD helped me ¹⁴ – JAH is my strength and song,
And he's become salvation unto me.

292   Psalm 118:15-21

¹⁵ The sound of joy and of deliverance
Is now within the tents of righteous men!
The right hand of the LORD works mightily -
¹⁶ The right hand of the LORD is lifted high.

The right hand of the LORD works mightily;
¹⁷ I shall not die, but, rather, I shall live!
I shall declare the works the LORD has done.
I shall declare the works the LORD has done.

¹⁸ The LORD has chastened me so very much,
But he has not delivered me to death.
¹⁹ Open to me the gates of righteousness,
Through them I'll enter in. I'll thank the LORD!

²⁰ This is the gate - the gate that's for the LORD;
The righteous ones will enter in through it.
²¹ Because you answered me, I will give thanks;
You have become salvation unto me.

293   Psalm 118:22-29

22 The stone that was refused by those who built
Has now become the chief head-cornerstone.
23 The LORD did this. In our eyes - Wonderful!
24 This is the day, the day the LORD has worked.

Let us rejoice and in this day be glad.
25 Hosanna! Save! O LORD, for this we plead!
We plead, O LORD. Oh give us good success!
26 Blest is the one who comes in the LORD's name.

'We bless you all, from out of the LORD's house';
27 The LORD is GOD and he has shined on us!
The pilgrim-sacrifice bind up with cords,
Even unto the very altar's horns.

28 You are my GOD, and I will give you thanks;
You are my God, and I will lift you up.
29 Give thanks unto the LORD for he is good,
His loving-kindness is for evermore.

294   Psalm 119:1-8

1 Blest are those who are blameless in the way!
Those who are walking after the LORD's Law.
2 Blest are those who his testimonies keep!
Those who seek after him with all the heart.

3 Truly, they do not act unrighteously,
And they have kept their walk within his ways.
4 You have commanded your precepts for us
That we might keep them very carefully.

5 O that my ways were settled and secure,
So I might keep the things that you decree.
6 For, if I did, I would not be ashamed,
When I look into all that you command.

[Continued →

⁷ I will give thanks to you with upright heart,
And learn the righteous things that you ordain.
⁸ And the decrees that you have made, I'll keep;
O do not utterly abandon me!

295   Psalm 119:9-16

⁹ How can a young man keep his pathway pure?
By guarding it according to your word.
¹⁰ With all my heart I have sought after you;
From your commandments do not let me stray.

¹¹ I've treasured up your word within my heart,
To keep myself from sinning against you
¹² O LORD you only are the blesséd one!
Teach your decrees to me, and make me learn.

¹³ With my lips I have numbered and declared
All of the ordinances of your mouth.
¹⁴ Your Testimonies' way has made me glad,
As much as riches - wealth of every kind.

¹⁵ Upon your precepts I will meditate;
To all your pathways I will have regard;
¹⁶ And your decrees I will make my delight;
I will make sure I don't forget your word.

296   Psalm 119:17-24

¹⁷ I am your servant. Fully deal with me! -
That I may live; so I will keep your word.
¹⁸ Open my eyes and then I will behold
The things of wonder that are in your Law.

¹⁹ I'm just a sojourner upon the earth;
Don't hide from me the things that you command.
²⁰ My soul is crushed and broken with desire,
Constantly longing for what you ordain.

[Continued →

²¹ You have rebuked the proud - those who are cursed;
Those who are straying from what you command.
²² Take insult and contempt away from me,
Because your testimonies I have kept.

²³ Princes have sat and spoken against me;
Your servant meditates on your decrees.
²⁴ Your testimonies - they are my delights;
They are to me as men who give advice.

297 Psalm 119:25-32

²⁵ My soul is fastened to the dust of earth;
O give me life, according to your word!
²⁶ I have declared my ways - You answered me;
Teach your decrees to me, and make me learn.

²⁷ Help me to understand your mapped-out way,
So, on your wonders I will meditate.
²⁸ My soul's poured out because of heaviness;
Establish me, according to your word.

²⁹ Remove from me the false unfaithful way,
And graciously impart your Law to me.
³⁰ The way of faithfulness has been my choice;
Your ordinances I have set for me.

³¹ I hold fast to your Testimonies, LORD
O do not leave me hopeless and ashamed!
³² The way of your commandments I will run;
For you will open and enlarge my heart.

298 Psalm 119:33-40

³³ O teach me, LORD, the way of your decrees,
And I will keep it to the very end.
³⁴ Give understanding and I'll keep your Law;
I will observe your Law wholeheartedly.

[Continued →

³⁵ Cause me to tread the path of your commands;
For I desire this - It is my delight.
³⁶ Unto your Testimonies turn my heart,
And keep it from the selfish love of gain.

³⁷ Divert my eyes from looking at vain things,
Quicken and give me life within your way.
³⁸ Your word unto your servant please confirm,
For it produces reverence for you.

³⁹ Make the reproach I dread to pass from me,
Because your ordinances are so good
⁴⁰ Behold and see! I've for your precepts longed!
Oh, in your righteousness, give life to me.

299 Psalm 119:41-48

⁴¹ LORD, let your loving-kindness come to me,
And your salvation, just as you have said;
⁴² I'll have an answer for him who taunts me,
Because I've set my trust upon your word.

⁴³ Do not remove your true word from my mouth,
For in your ordinances is my hope.
⁴⁴ So I will keep your Law continually -
Even forever and for evermore.

⁴⁵ I will walk freely in an open place,
Because your precepts I have sought with care.
⁴⁶ About your testimonies I would speak,
And before kings I would not be ashamed.

⁴⁷ In your commandments which are loved by me
I will make my delight. ⁴⁸I'll lift my hands
To your commandments, which are loved by me,
And so I'll meditate on your decrees.

300 Psalm 119:49-56

⁴⁹ The word unto your servant keep in mind -
The word that you have made me hope upon.
⁵⁰ In my affliction this is my relief,
Because the word you spoke gave life to me.

⁵¹The arrogant have mocked me, O so much!
But from your Law I have not turned aside.
⁵² Your ancient ordinances I recall,
O LORD, I comforted myself in them.

⁵³ Hot indignation then took hold of me,
Over the wicked who forsake your Law.
⁵⁴ Psalms were to me the things that you decreed,
In this house where I dwell but for a time.

⁵⁵ I've kept in mind your name by night, O LORD.
I have observed - Yes, I've observed your Law.
⁵⁶ This I have had and this happened to me
Because I kept the precepts you appoint.

301 Psalm 119:57-64

⁵⁷ LORD, you are mine, my portion, and my lot;
And I have said that I would keep your words.
⁵⁸ I did entreat your face with all my heart;
Be gracious to me, just as you have said.

⁵⁹ I have considered the ways that I go,
And to your testimonies turned my feet.
⁶⁰ I acted quickly, and did not delay,
So I might keep the things that you command.

⁶¹ The cords of wicked men encircled me;
Despite this, I did not forget your Law.
⁶² At midnight I'll get up and give you thanks
For righteous ordinances that you give.

[Continued →

⁶³ I am a friend of all those who fear you -
To those who keep the precepts you appoint.
⁶⁴ Your loving-kindness, O LORD, fills the earth;
The things that you decree, O teach to me!

302　　　Psalm 119:65-72

⁶⁵ You have done well unto your servant, LORD;
It's been to me according to your word.
⁶⁶ Teach me good judgement; teach me knowledge too,
For I have trusted in what you command.

⁶⁷ Before I was afflicted, I transgressed,
But now I have kept fast the word you spoke.
⁶⁸ For you are good, and you are doing good;
Teach your decrees to me, and make me learn.

⁶⁹ The arrogant spread falsehood about me,
But your precepts I keep with my whole heart.
⁷⁰ Their heart is bloated, and as fat as grease;
But as for me, in your Law I delight.

⁷¹ I was afflicted - it was for my good -
In order that I might learn your decrees.
⁷² The Law of your mouth is good unto me
Better than thousands of silver and gold.

303　　　Psalm 119:73-80

⁷³ Your hands have made me, and have fashioned me.
Give understanding to learn your commands.
⁷⁴ Those who fear you will see me and be glad;
Because in hope I wait upon your word.

⁷⁵ I know what you ordain is righteous, LORD;
And you in faithfulness afflicted me.
⁷⁶ I plead your steadfast love to comfort me;
As, to your servant, you said it would be

[Continued →

⁷⁷ Send tender mercies to me, and I'll live;
Because your Law is my special delight.
⁷⁸ Shamed be the proud! With lies they bent me down,
But, in your precepts, I will meditate.

⁷⁹ Let those who fear you turn again to me,
Even those who your testimonies know.
⁸⁰ Let my heart be perfect in your decrees,
In order that I may not be ashamed.

304   Psalm 119:81-88

⁸¹ For your salvation, my soul is consumed;
Yet, in sure hope, I've waited for your word.
⁸² And, for your word, my eyes too are consumed;
For I have said, 'When will you comfort me?'

⁸³ Though I've become a bottle in the smoke;
Yet I do not forget what you decree.
⁸⁴ How many are the days your servant has?
When will you judge those who so harass me?

⁸⁵ The proud have dug out pits for me to fall -
Those who don't act according to your Law.
⁸⁶ All your commandments are faithful and true;
They harass me with falsehood. O help me!

⁸⁷ They almost made an end of me on earth;
But I your precepts still did not forsake.
⁸⁸ According to your mercy give me life;
The Testimony of your mouth I'll keep.

305   Psalm 119:89-96

⁸⁹ Forever, LORD, your word is firmly set;
Forever in the heavens it is sure.
⁹⁰ To generations is your faithfulness;
The earth was founded by you and stands firm.

[Continued →

91 As you've ordained, they still to this day stand,
Because all things are servants unto you.
92 Unless your Law were my special delight,
In my affliction I'd have been destroyed.

93 Your precepts I will never more forget,
For by them you have given life to me.
94 Yes, I am yours; therefore deliver me,
Because your precepts I have sought with care.

95 The wicked lie in wait to end my life;
Your testimonies I considered well.
96 To all perfection I have seen an end;
But your commandment is immensely wide.

306   Psalm 119:97-104

97 O I do love your Law so very much!
It is my meditation all the day.
98 Through your commands I'm wiser than my foes
For it is with me to eternity.

99 More than my teachers, I have understood,
For on your Testimonies I reflect.
100 I understand more than those who are old,
For I have kept the precepts you appoint.

101 I've kept my feet from every evil path,
In order that I may but keep your word.
102 I've not departed from what you've ordained,
Because you've been a teacher unto me.

103 How sweet to me have been the words you speak
Yes, even more than honey to my mouth.
104 I, from your precepts, come to understand,
And every path of falsehood I do hate.

307   Psalm 119:105 -112

105 Your word is as a lamp unto my foot,
And as a light unto the path I tread.
106 I swore an oath and surely will fulfil:
To keep the righteous things that you ordain.

107 I was afflicted, O so very much!
Give life to me according to your word.
108 My mouth's free offerings, O LORD accept;
Cause me to learn the things that you ordain.

109 My soul is in my hand continually;
Yet, even so, I don't forget your Law.
110 The wicked ones have laid a trap for me;
But from your precepts I've not gone astray.

111 Your Testimonies I took for my lot -
For ever! They're the gladness of my heart!
112 I've turned my heart to do what you decree -
For ever! Even to the very end.

308   Psalm 119:113-120

113 I hate those who are of a double mind,
Because my love is set upon your Law.
114 You are my hiding place. You are my shield;
And I have hoped and waited for your word.

115 Depart from me, you who do wicked things,
Because my God's commandments I will keep.
116 Uphold me, as you said, and I will live;
And in my hope let me not be ashamed.

117 Give strength, support me, then I shall be safe;
On your decrees I'll wonder constantly.
118 All those who turn from them you will reject;
For their deceitfulness is but in vain.

[Continued →

119 As dross, you end the wicked of the earth;
Therefore your testimonies I do love.
120 My flesh shrinks back in trembling fear of you;
And your right judgments, they make me afraid.

309   Psalm 119:121-128

121 I acted justly, and with righteousness;
Do not forsake me to those who oppress;
122 But be the surety for your servant's good;
And do not let the arrogant oppress.

123 For your salvation my eyes are consumed,
And for the word of righteousness you speak.
124 Deal with your servant in your steadfast love;
Teach me what you decree, and make me learn.

125 I am your servant. Make me understand;
So that your testimonies I may know.
126 This is the season for the LORD to work;
Your Law they've broken and they've made it void.

127 Therefore I love the things that you command;
I love them more than gold - than finest gold.
128 I count your precepts on all things as right;
And every path of falsehood I do hate.

310   Psalm 119:129-136

129 Your Testimonies - they are wondrous things;
Therefore, my soul has kept them carefully.
130 When your words open it makes light to shine;
And so, it makes the simple understand.

131 With my mouth open wide I gasp and pant;
Because I thirst and long for your commands.
132 Turn to me and be gracious unto me;
Just as is right for those who love your name

[Continued →

¹³³ My steps keep steady in the word you spoke;
Let no iniquity rule over me.
¹³⁴ Redeem me when oppression comes from man;
And I will keep the precepts you appoint.

¹³⁵ Upon your servant, make your face to shine;
The things that you decree make me to learn.
¹³⁶ Rivers of waters run down from my eyes,
Because of those who have not kept your Law.

311   Psalm 119:137-144

¹³⁷ You are the one who is righteous, O LORD;
The things that you ordain are just and right.
¹³⁸ Your testimonies are, by your command,
in righteousness and in great faithfulness.

¹³⁹ My zeal and grief is so consuming me,
Because my enemies forgot your words.
¹⁴⁰ The word you speak is pure and well-refined,
Because of this your servant loves your word.

¹⁴¹ I'm only little, and I am despised,
And yet your precepts I do not forget.
¹⁴² Your righteousness is endless righteousness;
It's everlasting, and your Law is truth.

¹⁴³ Distress and anguish have took hold on me,
Yet your commandments are still my delights.
¹⁴⁴ Your Testimonies - righteous evermore -
Give understanding to me, and I'll live.

312   Psalm 119:145-152

¹⁴⁵ I'm crying out to you with all my heart;
Give answer, LORD, and I'll keep your decrees.
¹⁴⁶ I've called upon you. O deliver me;
And then, your testimonies I will keep.

[Continued →

147 Ready to meet the dawning I arose;
I cried for help and waited for your word.
148 Ready to meet each night-watch were my eyes;
To meditate upon the word you spoke.

149 After your mercy, listen to my voice;
O LORD, as you've determined, give me life.
150 Those who pursue an evil plan draw near;
But they're far off - a long way from your Law.

151 But you yourself are near at hand, O LORD;
All the commandments that you give are truth.
152 Your testimonies showed me this of old;
That you have founded them for evermore.

313   Psalm 119:153-160

153 See my affliction and deliver me,
For I am not forgetful of your Law.
154 O plead my cause for me; redeem me back;
And give me life according to your word.

155 Salvation is far off from wicked men,
For your decrees they have not sought with care.
156 O LORD, how great your tender mercies are!
According to your judgments, give me life.

157 Many are my pursuers and my foes -
Yet from your Testimonies I've not turned.
158 I saw transgressors, and I felt disgust;
Because they did not keep the word you spoke.

159 Look - see that I have loved your precepts, LORD;
According to your mercy, give me life.
160 The sum and substance of your word is truth;
All your right judgment is for evermore.

314   Psalm 119:161-168

161 Princes, without a cause, have harassed me;
But, at your word, my heart just stands in awe.
162 I am rejoicing at the word you spoke;
Even as one who finds a treasure store

163 Falsehood and lying I hate and I loathe;
But I have set my love upon your Law.
164 Within a day I praise you seven times,
For all the righteous things that you ordain.

165 Great peace belongs to those who love your Law;
And there shall be no stumbling block for them.
166 For your salvation I have waited, LORD;
And I have done what your commandments say.

167 Your testimonies are kept by my soul;
And I do love them very much indeed.
168 Your testimonies and precepts I've kept;
For all my ways are manifest to you.

315   Psalm 119:169-176

169 Let my loud cry come near before you, LORD;
Make me discern according to your word.
170 My prayer for grace will come before your face;
According to your word, deliver me.

171 O let my lips be bursting forth with praise;
For you are teaching your decrees to me.
172 My tongue will witness to what you have said;
For all things you command are righteousness.

173 O let your hand be ready to help me;
Because your precepts are my settled choice
174 For your salvation I have longed, O LORD;
And your Law also is my great delight.

[Continued →

¹⁷⁵ Let my soul live, and it shall give you praise;
Your ordinances - let them be my help!
¹⁷⁶ Like a lost sheep, I've strayed - your servant seek!
For your commandments I do not forget.

316   Psalm 120   Song of Ascents (1)

¹ In my distress I cried unto the LORD,
I cried out, and he heard and answered me;
² My soul deliver, LORD, from lying lip,
From lying lip, and from deceitful tongue.

³ What shall he give you, O deceitful tongue?
And what more shall he reckon up for you? -
⁴ The sharpened arrows of the mighty one,
Even with burning coals of juniper!

⁵ Alas for me, I am a sojourner;
And, as a stranger, I in Meshech dwell;
Among the tents of Kedar I have camped.
⁶ My soul has had its dwelling here too long.

My soul has had its dwelling here too long
Close by him who hates peace; ⁷but I am peace!
Yes, I'm a man of peace, but when I speak -
I speak of peace; but all they want is war.

317   Psalm 121   Song of Ascents (2)

¹ Unto the mountains I'll lift up my eyes,
Asking, 'Where shall the help I need come from?'
² My help is with the LORD and comes from him -
The Maker of the heaven and the earth

³ He'll not allow, nor cause your foot to slip;
The one who keeps you has no slumbering;
⁴ Take note of this: he who keeps Israel,
He does not slumber, and he does not sleep.

[Continued →

⁵ The LORD's the one who watches over you;
The LORD's your shade, and he's at your right hand;
⁶ Therefore the sun won't strike you down by day;
Nor will the moon cause harm to you by night.

⁷ The LORD will keep you from all that is bad;
He'll be a guard and keeper of your soul;
⁸ The LORD will keep your going out and in;
From this time onwards and for evermore.

318 Psalm 122 Song of Ascents (3)

¹ I was made glad by those who said to me,
'O come and let us go to the LORD's house';
² Within your gates, Jerusalem, we stand -
³Jerusalem, the city builded up!

The city built and joined in unity
⁴ To it the tribes, yes, the LORD's tribes - go up;
A Testimony unto Israel;
So that they may give thanks to the LORD's name.

⁵ For there the thrones of judgment are set up -
Even the thrones that are for David's house.
⁶ Pray that Jerusalem may be in peace;
Those who love you will prosper peacefully.

Pray that Jerusalem may be in peace;
Those who love you will prosper peacefully;
⁷ There will be peace within your city walls;
And in your palaces, prosperity.

⁸ For brothers', and for my companions', sake
I will plead this: 'May there be peace in you!'
⁹ And for the house – the house of God the LORD -
The LORD our God - I will seek good for you.

319 Psalm 123. Song of Ascents (4)

¹ It is to you I've lifted up my eyes -
You are the one who in the heavens dwells -
The one who sits in heaven, there enthroned.
² As servants' eyes look to their master's hand,

Like a maid's eyes look to her mistress' hand;
Likewise, our eyes look to the LORD our God,
Until he shall be gracious unto us.
³ Be gracious, LORD, be gracious unto us!

For of contempt we've had more than enough;
⁴ Our soul has had more than enough of this -
The mocking scorn of those who are at ease,
And the contempt heaped on us by the proud.

320 Psalm 124. Song of Ascents (5)

¹ 'Had it not been the LORD who is for us',
Let Israel thus say with certainty,
² 'Had it not been the LORD who is for us
When up against us men were rising up;

³ 'Surely, they would have swallowed us alive,
Such was their anger burning against us;
⁴ The waters would have overwhelmed us then,
The torrent would have gone over our soul';

⁵ 'Rough waters would have covered our soul too'.
⁶ Blest be the LORD who has not given us
Unto their teeth, just as a hunted prey!
⁷ Our soul escaped away, just as a bird -

A bird that's freed out of the trappers' snare;
The snare is broken, so we have escaped.
⁸ On the LORD's name our help and aid depend -
The LORD who made the heavens and the earth.

321   Psalm 125. Song of Ascents (6)

¹ Those who are putting their trust in the LORD
Are like Mount Zion, which cannot be moved;
For it is set, established, evermore
² As mountains are around Jerusalem,

Around about his people is the LORD.
From this time forward, and for evermore.
³ Because of this, the rod of wickedness
Will not rest on the lot of righteous men.

So that the righteous do not stretch their hands
To reach out and to do iniquity.
⁴ O LORD, do good unto those who are good;
And unto those who are upright in heart;

⁵ But as for those who turn themselves aside -
To those who turn unto their crooked ways -
The LORD will, with wrongdoers, lead them off
And upon Israel there will be peace!

322   Psalm 126. Song of Ascents (7)

¹ When the LORD turned Zion's captivity,
Then we were like those who are in a dream;
² And then our mouth was full of laughter too;
Our tongue was taken up with shouts of joy.

Among the nations they then spoke like this:
'The LORD has done such mighty things for them!'
³ The LORD has done such mighty things for us!
So we rejoice, for we have been made glad.

⁴ Turn back again, LORD, our captivity;
Just like the watercourses of the South.
⁵ Those who with tearful crying sow the seed;
Shall reap the harvest with glad shouts of joy.

[Continued →

⁶ He who goes out, and weeping as he goes;
Taking along a measure of the seed;
He'll surely come back, with glad shouts of joy;
Taking along with him his harvest sheaves.

323   Psalm 127. Song of Ascents (8)

¹ Unless the LORD's the builder of the house,
Its builders will have toiled on it in vain;
Unless the LORD should keep a city safe,
Its keeper will watch over it in vain.

² For you to get up early is in vain,
To sit up late - eat bread earned by hard work.
Surely, he gives to his beloved sleep -
Gives to his loved one even as he sleeps

³ Behold! - sons are a gift that the LORD gives;
The issue of the womb is his reward;
⁴ Like arrows in the hand of a strong man;
So are the sons you have when you are young.

⁵ Such blessings rest upon that mighty man -
He who has filled his quiver full of them!
So at the gate they shall not be ashamed,
When they shall speak there with the enemies.

324   Psalm 128. A Song of Ascents (9)

¹ How blest is everyone who fears the LORD!
The person who is walking in his ways;
² The labour of your hands you'll surely eat -
How blest you are! It will go well for you!

³ Your wife will be just like a fruitful vine
Within the inner chambers of your house;
As olives, round your table are your sons
⁴ So shall the man be blest who fears the LORD

[Continued →

⁵ The LORD from out of Zion will bless you
And you will see Jerusalem set fair -
All of your life's days. ⁶And also you'll see -
Your children's' children. Peace on Israel!

325   Psalm 129. Song of Ascents (10)

¹ 'They have oppressed me much, for a long time,
From my youth up' - May Israel please say -
² 'They have oppressed me much from my youth up,
But yet, against me they have not prevailed'.

³ The ploughmen ploughed long furrows on my back.
⁴ The righteous LORD, he cut the wicked's cord;
⁵ They will be shamed, and they will be turned back,
All who are Zion's hate-filled enemies.

⁶ They will be as the grass upon the roofs,
Which withers even before it's plucked up;
⁷ It does not fill the hand of him who reaps,
Nor yet the arms of him who binds the sheaves.

⁸ Nor will the passers-by say unto them,
'The blessing of the LORD be unto you'.
Nor will the passers-by say unto them,
'In the LORD's name we give blessing to you'.

326   Psalm 130. Song of Ascents (11)

¹ Out of the depths, LORD, I've cried unto you;
² My Lord, I pray that you will hear my voice;
And may your ears listen attentively;
Unto the pleas for mercy my voice speaks.

³ If you, O LORD, should mark iniquities,
My Lord, who would be able then to stand?
⁴ But the forgiving pardon is with you,
So that, because of this, you may be feared.

[Continued →

⁵ I've waited for the LORD. My soul awaits;
And for his word I've hoped expectantly;
⁶ My soul waits for My Lord - more than the watch
More than the watchmen who await the dawn!

⁷ Hope in the LORD for mercy, Israel;
It's with the LORD - redemption plenteous!
⁸ And he himself will rescue Israel;
Redeem him from all his iniquities.

327 Psalm 131. Song of Ascents (12)

¹ O LORD, my heart is not raised up in pride,
Nor do my eyes look down as from on high;
I'm not involved in great, important things;
Nor in the things that are too hard for me.

² I've surely calmed and quieted my soul,
Like a weaned child who on his mother rests;
As the weaned child my soul rests upon me;
As the weaned child my soul rests upon me.

³ O Israel, you shall hope in the LORD,
from this time forward, and for evermore;
O Israel, you shall wait on the LORD,
from this time forward, and for evermore.

328 Psalm 132:1-10. Song of Ascents (13)

¹ For David's sake, O LORD, do call to mind
All his afflictions and his weary toils;
² Of how he swore an oath unto the LORD;
He made a vow to Jacob's Mighty One.

³ 'Into the tent of my house I'll not go;
Upon the couch of my bed I'll not go;
⁴ And I will not unto my eyes give sleep;
Nor yet in slumber shall my eyelids close'.

[Continued →

5 'Until I shall find a place for the LORD -
Places to dwell for Jacob's Mighty One.
6 Behold! - We heard of it in Ephrathah;
We found it in the district of Ja'ar.

7 Into his dwelling places we will go;
We'll bow in worship at his footstool there.
8 Arise, O LORD, into your resting place;
You, and the Ark of your strength and your power.

9 O let your priests be clothed with righteousness;
Let your beloved ones shout out for joy;
10 Let this be for your servant David's sake;
And your anointed's face turn not away.

329   Psalm 132:11-18

(Song of Ascents 13 continued)

11 The LORD swore unto David what is true;
He won't retract from it, or turn away:
'Of your descendants, who are born to you,
For you I'll make them sit upon your throne'.

12 'And if your sons will keep my covenant,
And this my testimony that I'll teach;
Their sons shall also sit upon the throne -
They shall sit on your throne for evermore'.

13 For Zion has been chosen by the LORD;
He has desired it for his dwelling place:
14 'This is my resting place for evermore;
Here I will dwell, for this I have desired'.

15 'Zion's provision I will greatly bless;
Its needy ones I'll satisfy with bread;
16 And with deliverance I'll clothe its priests;
And its beloved ones will shout for joy'.

[Continued →

192

¹⁷ There will I make a horn for David grow;
For my anointed I've prepared a lamp;
¹⁸ And I will clothe his enemies with shame;
But his resplendent crown shall be on him.

330   Psalm 133. Song of Ascents (14)

¹ Behold! How good, and what a pleasant thing!
When brothers dwell and are in unity;
² It's like the precious oil, upon the head;
Descending on the beard, yes, Aaron's beard

Descending down unto his garments' edge;
³ Like Hermon-dew descends on Zion's hills,
Because the LORD commands the blessing there -
The blessing - even life for evermore.

331   Psalm 134. Song of Ascents (15)

¹ Take note of this and come and bless the LORD!
All servants of the LORD who stand to serve!
Who stand by night in the house of the LORD;
² Lift up your hands unto the holy place.

Lift up your hands unto the holy place;
So bless the LORD again, and bless the LORD!
The LORD from Zion will bless each of you -
The One who made the heavens and the earth.

332   Psalm 135:1-7

¹ O Hallelujah, give praise to the LORD!
The LORD's name praise! Praise, servants of the LORD!
² Who stand to serve in the house of the LORD -
Yes, in the courts of the house of our God.

³ Praise! Praise the LORD, because the LORD is good;
Sing psalms unto his name for it is sweet;
⁴ For JAH has chosen Jacob for himself:
His treasured property is Israel

[Continued →

⁵ I surely know the LORD is very great,
And that our Lord is greater than all gods.
⁶ The LORD has done whatever pleases him
In heaven, earth, in seas, and in all deeps.

⁷ He brings the clouds up from earth's farthest point,
And he has made the lightnings for the rain.
He sends the wind out from his treasure stores;
He sends the wind out from his treasure stores.

333   Psalm 135:8-14

⁸ Egypt's firstborn he struck down, man and beast;
⁹ He sent out signs and wonders unto you;
O Egypt, even in your very midst!
On Pharaoh and on all his servants too.

¹⁰ He smote great nations and slew mighty kings:
¹¹ He slew Sihon, king of the Amorites;
And then slew Og, the king of the Bashan.
And all of Canaan's kingdoms he smote too.

¹² He gave their land up as a heritage -
For Israel, his people's heritage.
¹³ O LORD your name is evermore the same;
And your renown, LORD, is from age to age.

¹⁴ The LORD will vindicate his people's cause;
And judgment on them he will execute;
Yet for his servants' sake he will relent;
And he will have compassion upon them.

334   Psalm 135:15-21

¹⁵ The nations' idols are silver and gold,
The workmanship that human hands have made;
¹⁶ They have a mouth, and yet they cannot speak;
They have two eyes, and yet they cannot see.

17 They have two ears, but they do not give ear
And in their mouth there is no breath at all;
18 All those who make them will be just like them;
Yes, everyone who puts his trust in them.

19 O bless the LORD, you house of Israel!
O bless the LORD, you who are Aaron's house!
20 O bless the LORD, you who are Levi's house!
And, you who fear the LORD, bless him alone!

21 From out of Zion the LORD shall be blest;
He who is dwelling in Jerusalem.
O Hallelujah, give praise to the LORD!
O Hallelujah, give praise to the LORD!

335   Psalm 136:1-9

1 O give thanks to the LORD for he is good;
His loving-kindness is for evermore.
O give thanks to the LORD for he is good;
Because his loving-kindness has no end.

2 To him who is the God of gods give thanks,
His loving-kindness is for evermore.
3 To him who is Lord of lords give thanks;
Because his loving-kindness has no end.

4 To him who does great wonders all alone;
His loving-kindness is for evermore.
5 To him who made the heavens skilfully;
Because his loving-kindness has no end.

6 To him who on the waters spread the earth;
His loving-kindness is for evermore.
7 To him who made in heaven the great lights;
Because his loving-kindness has no end.

8 Even the sun that it should rule the day;
His loving-kindness is for evermore.
9 The moon and stars that they should rule the night;
Because his loving-kindness has no end.

10 To him who struck Egypt in their firstborn;
His loving-kindness is for evermore.
11 And from among them brought out Israel;
Because his loving-kindness has no end.

12 With a strong hand and with an outstretched arm;
His loving-kindness is for evermore.
13 Who into parts divided the Red Sea;
Because his loving-kindness has no end.

14 And he made Is-ra-el pass through the midst;
His loving-kindness is for evermore.
15 Pharaoh, his army, shook in the Red Sea;
Because his loving-kindness has no end.

16 He led his people through the wilderness;
His loving-kindness is for evermore.
17 To him who struck great kings; 18slew famous kings;
Because his loving-kindness has no end.

19 Sihon who was king of the Amorites;
His loving-kindness is for evermore.
20 And Og who was the king of the Bashan;
Because his loving-kindness has no end.

21 He gave their land up as a heritage;
His loving-kindness is for evermore.
22 For Israel, his people's heritage;
Because his loving-kindness has no end.

23 Who in our lowly state remembered us;
His loving-kindness is for evermore.
24 And broke us free from those who were our foes;
Because his loving-kindness has no end.

[Continued →

25 He who gives food unto all living things;
His loving-kindness is for evermore.
26 Unto the GOD of heaven, O give thanks;
Because his loving-kindness has no end.

338   Psalm 137

1 We sat beside rivers of Babylon;
As we remembered Zion, so we wept;
2 We hung our harps upon the willows there;
3 For there our captors asked of us a song.

For our tormentors urged us to be glad;
'Sing some of Zion's songs to us' they said;
4 Alas, how could we sing the LORD's song there?
When we are in a strange and foreign land.

5 If I forget you, O Jerusalem;
Let my right hand forget, 6and let my tongue
Stick to my jaws, if I do not recall;
If my chief joy is not Jerusalem.

7 Oh, Edom's children do remember, LORD;
Who said in the day of Jerusalem:
'To its foundation, strip it! Strip it bare!'
8 Daughter of Babylon who'll be destroyed

Blest be the one who will pay back to you;
What you brought on us. 9 Yes, and blest he'll be -
The one who grasps upon your little ones -
The one who dashes them against the rock.

339   Psalm 138:1-5

1 I will give thanks to you with my whole heart;
Before the gods I'll sing with psalms to you;
2 Toward your holy Temple I'll bow down;
And I will give my thanks unto your name.

[Continued →

Thanks for your loving-kindness and your truth;
You've made your word great, more than all your name!
³ You answered me in the day when I called,;
You gave me courage - put strength in my soul.

⁴ All kings of earth will give you thanks, O LORD;
For they have heard the words that your mouth spoke;
⁵ And they will sing, of the LORD's ways they'll sing;
Because the glory of the LORD is great.

340   Psalm 138:6-8

⁶ The LORD is high, but sees those who are low;
And from afar he knows those who are proud.
⁷ If, in the midst of trouble, I should walk,
You will revive me, and preserve my life.

Against the anger of my enemies -
Against their anger - you will stretch your hand;
You will deliver me by your right hand;
Yes, you will save me by your own right hand.

⁸ The LORD will finish what he does for me;
He brings to pass his purposes for me.
Your mercy is to everlasting, LORD;
Do not forsake the works of your own hands

341   Psalm 139:1-6

¹ Lord, you have searched me, therefore you have known;
² You know my sitting down and getting up;
And from afar you understand my thought;
³ My walking and my resting you sift through.

You are acquainted well with all my ways,
⁴ For there is not a word upon my tongue,
But, surely, LORD, you know about it all;
⁵ Behind, before me, you've surrounded me.

[Continued →

Your hand you've rested and placed over me.
⁶ Such knowledge is too wonderful for me!
It is so lofty, well beyond my reach;
It is so lofty, well beyond my reach.

342   Psalm 139:7-12

⁷ Wherever shall I from your spirit go?
Wherever from your presence shall I flee?
⁸ If I should climb to heaven - you are there!
If I bed down in Sheol you're there too!

⁹ If I rise up as on the wings of dawn;
If I should dwell on sea's most distant shore;
¹⁰ Yet even there your hand would guide me on;
And your right hand would still hold on to me.

¹¹ If I should say that 'Darkness covers me,
And so, the light around me will be night';
¹² Yet darkness does not darken things from you;
Night shines as day: Darkness and light the same.

343   Psalm 139:13-18

¹³ You are the one who formed my inner parts;
And you did weave me in my mother's womb;
¹⁴ I will be thankful unto you for this -
That such an awesome wonder I've been made.

The things you've made are awesome, wonderful;
And this my soul knows, O so very well!
¹⁵ My body's frame was not hidden from you;
When I was made within the secret place.

I was complexly made in depths of earth!
¹⁶ Your eyes have seen my undeveloped form;
All days were written in your book, as planned;
When there was yet not even one of them.

[Continued →

¹⁷ How precious to me are your thoughts, O GOD!
How vast are they in their entirety!
¹⁸ If I should count them, they outnumber sand;
And when I wake, then I am still with you.

344   Psalm 139:19-24

¹⁹ Will you not slay the wicked one, O God?
You men of bloodshed go away from me!
²⁰ (They speak against you with a scheming plan -
Your enemies who raise themselves in vain).

²¹ Do I not hate those who hate you, O LORD?
Do I not loathe insurgents against you?
²² With utter hatred I have hated them;
And I consider them my enemies.

²³ Examine, search me, know my heart, O GOD;
Refine and try me, know my anxious thoughts;
²⁴ See if there be a hurtful way in me;
And lead me in the everlasting way.

345   Psalm 140:1-7

¹ Deliver me, LORD, from the evil man;
Preserve me from the man of violence;
² Who in their heart have made up evil plans;
Each day they gather and they stir up wars.

³ Their tongue they sharpen, like a serpent's tongue;
The adder's poison is under their lips.
⁴ From the hands of the wicked guard me, LORD;
And keep me from the man of violence.

Those who have schemed to push away my steps;
⁵ The arrogant have hid a trap for me;
With cords they have spread out a net to catch -
Along the road. They have set snares for me.

[Continued →

⁶ I said unto the LORD, 'You are my GOD.
O hear my voice - my pleas for help, O LORD
⁷ O LORD My Lord, you're my salvation's strength;
When battle raged you covered up my head'.

346   Psalm 140:8-13

⁸ 'Don't give the wicked his desires, O LORD.
Aid not his scheme, lest they be set on high'
⁹ As for the chief of those surrounding me -
Their lips make trouble. Lay it upon them!

¹⁰ Let hot and burning coals fall upon them!
Throw them in chasms deep, no more to rise!
¹¹ A slanderer shall not stand in the earth;
The violent man - evil shall hunt down.

¹² I know the LORD will judge the poor man's cause;
He will give judgment to the ones in need.
¹³ Truly, the righteous shall confess your name!
And upright ones will dwell before your face.

347   Psalm 141:1-4

¹ I've called to you, LORD. Quickly come to me!
To my voice listen, when I call on you;
² Let my prayer be as incense before you;
My lifted hands the evening offering.

³ O LORD, please set a watch over my mouth;
And on the door of my lips set a guard;
⁴ O do not let my heart be turned aside;
Let it not turn to any evil thing.

Lest I persist in deeds of wickedness;
With the great men who work iniquity;
Keep me from feeding on what pleases them.
Keep me from feeding on what pleases them.

[Continued →

348   Psalm 141:5-10

5 The righteous will smite me in faithful love;
He will reprove me. It's oil on my head.
My head will not refuse, nor disallow;
(My prayer is still against their wickedness).

6 Their judges have been stumbled at the rock;
And they shall hear my words, that they are sweet.
7 Like ploughing, and like breaking up the earth;
At Sheol's mouth our bones are cast about.

8 My eyes look unto you, O LORD, My Lord;
In you I've taken refuge, put my trust;
Do not pour out my soul or lay it waste;
9 Preserve me from the trap they laid for me.

Preserve me from the snares that they have laid -
Laid by the workers of iniquity.
10 The wicked shall each fall in his own net;
While I myself will pass on safely by.

349   Psalm 142

1 With my voice I'll cry out unto the LORD;
My voice will plead for mercy to the LORD;
2 I will pour out before him my concern;
Before him I will make my trouble known.

3 My spirit was with fainting overwhelmed;
Yet you're the one who knows the path I tread;
But in the path in which I am to walk;
There they have spread a hidden trap for me.

4 Look unto the right hand and you will see
There is no-one who has regard for me
The way I could escape is closed to me
There is no-one who seeks for my soul's good!

[Continued →

5 I cried to you, O LORD, and I have said:
'You are my refuge and my portion too';
A portion in the land of those who live;
6 Attend unto my cry, I'm very low'.

Deliver me from those pursuing me;
They are too strong! 7From prison take my soul!
I'll praise your name, the righteous all around;
Because you will complete your work in me.

350　　Psalm 143:1-6

1 LORD, hear my prayer and to my pleas give ear,
In faithfulness. In righteousness reply;
2 Don't come unto your servant as a judge;
No living thing is righteous before you.

3 Because the enemy pursued my soul;
My life he crushed right down unto the ground;
He made me dwell in places that were dark;
Even as those who are forever dead.

4 Therefore my spirit languishes in me;
My heart within me is filled with dismay.
5 The days that were of old I call to mind;
I meditate on the things that you've done.

I ponder what your hands have brought about.
6 I spread my hands, and I reach out to you;
Like a dry land my soul thirsts after you.
Like a dry land my soul thirsts after you.

351　　Psalm 143:7-12

7 Give answer quickly, LORD, my spirit fails;
Don't hide your face from me - lest I should be
With those who go descending to the Pit.
8 At morning make me hear your steadfast love.

[Continued →

At morning - for on you I've placed my trust -
Cause me to know the way that I should walk;
For unto you I've lifted up my soul;
⁹ Deliver me, LORD, from my enemies.

Deliver, for in you I take refuge;
¹⁰ Teach me to do your will; you are my God.
In a plain land let your good Spirit lead;
¹¹ For your name's sake, O LORD, give life to me.

In righteousness take my soul from distress;
¹² In steadfast love cut off my enemies;
Destroy all those who cause my soul distress;
For I'm a servant, I belong to you.

352　　　　Psalm 144:1- 8

¹ Blest be the LORD for he is my strong rock;
He is the one who trains my hands for war;
And, for the battle, trains my fingers too -
² My Loving-kindness, Fortress of defence.

He's my Deliverer, and my High Tower,
My Shield, and in him I take my refuge;
Who makes my people subject under me.
³ LORD, what is man that you acknowledge him?

LORD, what is man that you acknowledge him? -
Son of frail man - and you consider him!
⁴ And as for man, he's only but a breath;
His days are like a shadow passing by.

⁵ Bow down your heavens and come down, O LORD;
Just touch the mountains, and they then will smoke;
⁶ Flash out your lightnings. Scatter them about;
Send out your arrows. Bring them to defeat;

⁷ Your hands send down; Rescue and snatch me out,
From many waters, from the strangers' hand,
⁸ Whose mouth tells false and empty vanity,
And their right hand is a right hand of lies.

353   Psalm 144:9-15

9 I'll sing a brand-new song to you, O God!
With ten-stringed lyre, I will sing psalms to you;
10 The One who gives deliverance to kings -
His servant David, - from the evil sword

11 Rescue and snatch me from the strangers' hand,
Whose mouth tells false and empty vanity;
And their right hand is a right hand of lies.
And their right hand is a right hand of lies.

12 But our sons are, in youth, as plants full-grown,
Our daughters as carved palace-cornerstones;
13 Our stores are full - provide all kinds of things;
Our flocks bear many thousands in our fields.

14 Our cattle bear without mishap or loss;
There is no cry of sorrow in our streets.
15 Blesséd the people to whom it is so!
Blesséd the people whose God is the LORD!

354   Psalm 145:1-7

1 I will exalt you, My God and the King;
I'll bless your name for ever, evermore;
2 In each and every day I will bless you;
I'll praise your name for ever, evermore.

3 Great is the LORD and greatly to be praised;
His greatness is beyond all searching out.
4 Each generation shall extol your works;
And shall declare your acts of might and power.

5 I'll meditate, and I will speak upon
The splendour of your glory's majesty;
And on your wondrous words I'll meditate;
6 They'll tell the fearful power of your works.

[Continued →

I will recount your acts of might and power;
7 They will speak out, yes, they will pour out words;
Remembering you are so very good;
They'll sing out loud your righteousness with joy.

355   Psalm 145:8-13

8 The LORD is gracious and is merciful,
Forbearing anger, great in steadfast love;
9 The LORD is good to each and every thing;
His tender mercies over all his works.

10 Your works shall all give thanks to you, O LORD;
Those whom-you-love-with-kindness will bless you;
11 The glory of your kingdom they will tell;
And they will speak of all your mighty power.

12 His acts of might they'll make known to mankind
The glory of his kingdom's majesty;
13 Your kingdom is a kingdom without end;
To every generation your domain.

356   Psalm 145:14-21

14 The LORD upholds all those about to fall;
He raises up all those who are bowed down.
15 The eyes of all things wait in hope on you;
You give their food in its appointed time.

16 Your hand you open and, as pleases you,
You fill the need of every living thing.
17 In all his ways the LORD is right and just;
And he is merciful in all his works.

18 The LORD is near to all who call on him -
Unto all those who call on him in truth.
19 For those who fear him, he meets their desire;
He saves them when he hears their cry for help.

[Continued →

²⁰ All those who love the LORD he guards and keeps,
But all the wicked ones he will destroy;
²¹ The praises of the LORD my mouth will speak;
All flesh will ever bless his holy name.

357 Psalm 146

¹ Hallelujah. O praise the LORD my soul!
While I yet live, I'll give praise to the LORD.
² While I have being, I'll sing psalms to God.
While I have being, I'll sing psalms to God.

³ Don't trust in princes, nor a son of man:
For there is no salvation found in him.
⁴ His breath departs; he goes back to his earth;
In that same day his thoughts and plans die too.

⁵ Blest is the one whose help is Jacob's GOD,
Whose hope is resting on the LORD his God;
⁶ He who has made the heavens and the earth,
And the sea too, and all that they contain.

He is the one who keeps truth evermore;
⁷ Judgment he gives to those who are oppressed;
To those who suffer hunger He gives food;
The LORD is freeing those who are bound up.

⁸ The LORD is giving sight unto the blind;
The LORD is raising those who are bowed down;
The LORD has loving care to righteous men;
⁹ The LORD protects the strangers in the land.

The orphan, and the widow, he sustains;
He makes the wicked's way to twist and turn;
¹⁰ Zion, Your God, the LORD, forever reigns!
Your God all generations! Praise the LORD!

358   Psalm 147:1-6

¹ O Hallelujah, give praise to the LORD!
For it is good to sing psalms to our God;
For it is pleasant: praise - a comely thing.
² The LORD is building up Jerusalem!

And Israel's outcasts he will gather up;
³ The broken-hearted heals, and binds their wounds;
⁴ Yet he appoints the number of the stars!
And every one of them he calls by name.

⁵ Great is our Lord, and of abundant power;
His understanding is just measureless;
⁶ The poor, afflicted ones the LORD sustains;
But brings the wicked down unto the ground.

359   Psalm 147:7-11

⁷ Respond unto the LORD by giving thanks;
Sing psalms unto our God upon the harp.
⁸ He covers up the heavens with the clouds;
And he appoints the rain upon the earth.

Upon the mountains he makes grass to grow;
⁹ And for the cattle he provides their food;
And he does likewise for the ravens' young;
Even for ravens' young when they do cry.

¹⁰ The horse's strength does not give him delight;
He takes no pleasure in the legs of man:
¹¹ The LORD takes pleasure in those who fear him -
Those who in hope wait for his steadfast love.

360   Psalm 147:12-20

¹² Jerusalem, commend the LORD with praise!
And Zion bring your praise unto your God!
¹³ For he's made strong the bars upon your gates;
He's blest your children who are in your midst.

[Continued →

¹⁴ He is the one who makes your border peace;
He satisfies you with the finest wheat.
¹⁵ He sends out his command upon the earth;
And then his word runs very speedily.

¹⁶ He is the giver of the wool-like snow;
The frozen dew like ash he scatters round;
¹⁷ He casts about the fragments of his hail;
And who is able to withstand his cold?

¹⁸ He sends his word, and he makes them to melt;
He makes his wind to blow; the waters flow.
¹⁹ It is to Jacob he declares his word -
Decrees and judgments unto Israel.

²⁰ He has not dealt with any nation thus;
As for his judgments, they're to them unknown.
O Hallelujah, give praise to the LORD!
O Hallelujah, give praise to the LORD!

361   Psalm 148:1-6

¹ O Hallelujah, give praise to the LORD!
And from the heavens praise the LORD alone!
Praise in the heights! ²All you his angels, Praise!
Praise all his host! ³Praise him both sun and moon!

Praise him all stars - praise all you stars of light!
⁴ Heavens of heavens, give your praise to him!
You waters, that are over heaven too!
⁵ O let them praise - give praise to the LORD's name!

For he created them at his command;
⁶ He has established them for evermore;
And he has given to them a decree;
Which none can break. It will not pass away.

7 From earth give praise unto the LORD alone!
You great sea creatures, praise; and all you deeps.
8 Both fire and hail; together, snow, and smoke,
With stormy wind, fulfilling his command.

9 Give praise to him, you mountains, and all hills;
Trees that bear fruit, and all the cedar trees;
10 Wild beasts, and all domestic cattle, Praise!
The things that creep, and birds upon the wing.

11 Praise, kings of earth, and all the peoples too,
Princes, and all you judges of the earth!
12 Praise him young men! Praise him young women too!
Praise him you old men, with the children, Praise!

13 O let them praise - give praise to the LORD'S name,
For his name only is the name most high;
His splendour is above that of the earth,
His splendour is above the heavens too.

14 And for his people he's raised up a horn.
He is the praise of all those whom he loves;
A people near him - sons of Israel.
O Hallelujah, give praise to the LORD!

363   **Psalm 149:1-4**

1 Praise the LORD! Sing a new song to the LORD -
Praise in the company of those he loves.
2 Rejoice in him who made you, Israel!
Let Zion's children be glad in their king -

3 With dancing, praise his name, with tambourine;
With harp, sing psalms to him. 4 The LORD is pleased-
Pleased with his people; and he beautifies -
Gives beauty with salvation to the meek.

364   Psalm 149:5-9

5 Those the LORD loves in glory shall rejoice.
And they shall sing for joy upon their beds,
6 With GOD's exalted praises in their mouth,
And in their hand a sword, a two-edged sword.

7 Vengeance upon the nations to requite,
And punishments upon the peoples too;
8 To bind their kings as prisoners in chains,
With iron fetters bind their honoured ones.

9 To execute the judgment upon them,
Even the judgment that's been written down.
This honour is for all of those he loves.
O Hallelujah, give praise to the LORD!

365   Psalm 150

1 O Hallelujah, give praise to the LORD!
Give praise to GOD within his holy place!
Praise him within his firmament of power!
2 Give praise unto him for his acts of power!

Give praise to him as he is very great!
3 Give praise to him with sound of the shofar!
Give praise to him with lyre, and with the harp!
4 Give praise to him with tambourine and dance!

Give praise to him with strings, and with the flute!
5 Give praise to him with cymbals sounding loud!
Give praise to him with cymbals sounding high!
6 All breath shall praise the LORD. Hallelujah!

APPENDIX 1
How to sing this book

In some ways, Psalm-singing will never be 'easy'. As praise and worship of our most holy God, it requires effort. As an expression of love to the Lord, it should be done with all our heart, all our soul and all our mind. Singing may be 'easy' in a large gathering, singing a well-known song, to loud accompaniment, in congenial surroundings. Such a description would fit a beach party where alcohol has been flowing freely, but personal and family worship is something different.

Psalm-singing requires singing with understanding, often singing unfamiliar words (at least unfamiliar at first). James 5:13 indicates that our singing of Psalms should be when we are by ourselves, as well as when we are in Church. In family terms there may be challenges in terms of the age of our children, learning disability, or dyslexia.

The task could be made easier for the singer in various ways. The number of Psalms sung could be reduced to a limited number of favourites; but personal choice exercised in relation to God's Word is a very dangerous thing. It can be easier to sing with accompaniment, but one should always remember that the essence of Christian worship is 'the fruit of our lips' (Hebrews 13:15), not skill at a keyboard. The one providing accompaniment is often impeded or prevented from singing God's praise by their role. Well-formed rhyming verse is no doubt easier to sing, but as we have noted elsewhere rhyming verse severely limits the available vocabulary to accurately translate and express words given by the Holy Spirit.

Psalm singing should give sufficient time for the singer to think on the words, and gain blessing from them. Unless this psalter is used many times, the wording will remain unfamiliar. It has to be sung slowly enough for the singer to profit from it.

By using only one metre, it is hoped that the added complication of new words + new music will be avoided, so that the singer's focus will be on the words. This was the principle adopted by Edmwnd Prys for his Welsh language Psalter (1621) and by the Scottish Metrical Psalter (1650).

All the Psalms in this book are set to the 10.10.10.10. metre. This means that they can all be sung to the tune 'Eventide' (the usual tune for the hymn 'Abide with me') or, perhaps even more simply, to the two line tune 'Pax Tecum' (the usual tune to the hymn 'Peace, perfect peace in this dark world of sin').

We suggest the following tunes, several of which we have simplified. They are available as pdfs and as playable audio files on the Pearl Publications website. The character of the passage should determine the tune type chosen

A. Prayerful, Restful and Didactic
- Eventide.
- St Agnes (aka Langram, or Hoyland).
- Pax Tecum.

B. Cheerful and Rejoicing
- Waldo.
- Ffigysbren (aka Clod).
- Speranza.

C. Confident and Strong
- Toulon (Old 124th shortened, aka Navarre).
- Huntingdon.
- Bontnewydd.

D. Sorrowful and Plaintive
- Georgetown.
- Ellers.
- Griddfaniad.

The tunes follow in alphabetical order

Bontnewydd (C)

John Roberts [Ieuan Gwyllt] (1822-1877)

Ellers (D)

(aka Benediction)

Edward J. Hopkins (1818-1901)

Eventide (A)

Dr W.H. Monk (1883-1929)

Ffigysbren (B)

(aka Clod)

(from 'Caniadau Seion', 1840)

Georgetown (D)

From *Hymns of Consecration and Faith*, 1902

Griddfaniad (D)

Morris Davies (1796-1876)

Huntingdon (C)

S. Wellens

Pax Tecum (A)

George T. Caldbeck (1852-1918)
and Charles Vincent (1852-1934)

Speranza (B)

C. Leflaive (1864-1938)

St Agnes (A)

aka Langram, or Hoyland)

James Langram (1835-1909)

Toulon (C)

(aka Navarre)
Adapted from Genevan Psalm 124)
Claude Goudimel (1510-1572)

Waldo (B)

Anonymous 1855

APPENDIX 2

Resources used in preparing this Psalter

The renderings of a large number of Bible versions have been considered in preparing this psalter, as we sought a helpful and accurate turn of phrase that would fit the metre. However, in translation, we have primarily sought help from Reformation and post-Reformation versions. These have included the translation which accompanies Calvin's commentary (1557); the Geneva Bible (1560); the Latin translation of Tremellius and Junius (1575); the Welsh Bible (1620); the Statenvertaling Dutch Bible commissioned by the Synod of Dort (1637); and, of course, the Authorised Version (1611). The Segond French translation (revised 1910) has also been helpful, as has Young's Literal Translation (revised 1907).

The Dutch Annotations (1657), a translation of the Statenvertaling with its marginal notes by Theodore Haak, reportedly commissioned by the Westminster Assembly, has proved invaluable.

We have used a several key commentaries to clarify the meaning of the Hebrew. As well as Calvin's commentary we have particularly used the commentaries Dr Gill, J.J. Stewart Perowne, Keil and Delitzsch, and Alec Motyer.

The exegetical comments of a select group of expositors have been carefully considered. These have included: Bishop Samuel Horsley, William De Burgh, Andrew A. Bonar, Benjamin Wills Newton, Adolph Saphir, and David Baron.

The Hebrew lexicons of Gesenius, Davies (Student's Hebrew Lexicon), Brown-Driver-Briggs, Koehler-Baumgartner, and the Theological Wordbook of the Old Testament have been used to clarify the meaning and usage of Hebrew words. Girdlestone's Synonyms of the Old Testament has been helpful throughout. The Interlineary Hebrew and English Psalter (probably by Tregelles) has been invaluable, and some of its translations of difficult words have been adopted (e.g. on Ps. 68:13).

Constant reference has been made (particularly in the latter part of this work) to Gesenius Hebrew Grammar and the Hebrew Syntaxes of A.B. Davidson, and of Heinrich Ewald.

ADVERTISMENT
Other books by Pearl Publications

Every Psalm for Easy Singing: expanded study edition

This expanded edition in larger format has extensive footnotes and appendices. The extra materials explain translation issues and show the basis of the decisions made in translating, as well giving exegetical comments. For example, it shows how we have carefully distinguished Hebrew words in the translation, such as the different words used for man and for God.

It shows how, in the preparation of this translation for singing, constant reference was made to Reformation and post-Reformation translations such as the Geneva Bible, the Authorised Version, the Welsh Bible, the Dutch States Bible (*Statenvertaling*), and Calvin's translation.

It uses the same 365 portions as *A Help for using the Psalms in Personal and Family Worship*. It is an aid to serious Bible Study, and will assist anyone who leads group or family worship working through the Psalms.

409 pages.

Every Psalm for Easy Singing: A translation for singing arranged in daily portions. Expanded Study Edition

Paperback:	ISBN 978-1-901397-09-3
Hardback:	ISBN 978-1-901397-10-9
E Book:	ISBN 978-1-901397-11-6

A Help for using the Psalms in Personal and Family Worship

Many Christians today do not know where to start in singing the Psalms, They are unaware of the resources that are available.

The *Help* meets that need. The *Help* provides 365 one-page devotional and expository notes for the whole book of the Psalms. It includes eleven appendices and a supplement of 'Talking Points' for each portion.

It can be used simply for devotional Bible study, but we believe that if it enables Christians and their families to sing the Psalms God's blessing will surely follow.

Its sister book *Every Psalm for Easy Singing* uses the same 365 portions

455 pages

A Help for using The Psalms in Personal and Family Worship

Paperback: ISBN 978-1-901397-03-1
Hardback: ISBN 978-1-901397-04-8
E Book: ISBN 978-1-901397-05-5

Chosen – Called – Kept.
The Conclusions of the Synod of Dort translated and arranged for prayerful reflection and study

In 1619 all the Reformed Churches of Europe met to discuss the great subject of 'How God saves'. That gathering was the Synod of Dort. Its decisions were unanimous. Chosen-Called-Kept is a new and very accessible translation of its conclusions. Its imaginative typesetting is designed to encourage regular and prayerful reflection on these great truths. It is not an edited version or a paraphrase. It is particularly useful for the catechising of children and young people.

First published in September 2022.

100 pages

Chosen – Called – Kept. The Conclusions of the Synod of Dort translated and arranged for prayerful reflection and study

ISBN: 978-1-901397-01-7 (Paperback).
ISBN: 978-1-901397-02-4 (Hardback).

PEARL PUBLICATIONS BOOKS are available online on Amazon (and takealot in South Africa) and from bookshops via wholesale distributors.   Ebooks are available from a range of outlets.   Enquiries are invited for direct bulk sales to Bookshops, Churches and Colleges.

Pearl Publications is working on a not for profit basis and any proposals to make our books available more widely and at a cheaper price would be very welcome.

Printed in Great Britain
by Amazon